He said
BEER
She said
wine

Marnie Old
Sam Calagione

Photography by Kellie Walsh

LONDON, NEW YORK, MELBOURNE, MUNICH, AND DELHI

EDITOR Shannon Beatty
DESIGNER Tia Romano
MANAGING ART EDITOR Michelle Baxter
ART DIRECTOR Dirk Kaufman
DTP COORDINATOR Kathy Farias
PRODUCTION MANAGER Ivor Parker
EXECUTIVE MANAGING EDITOR Sharon Lucas

FOOD STYLIST Victoria Escalle
PHOTOGRAPHY Kellie Walsh

First American Edition, 2008   5/08 B&T 25

Published in the United States by
DK Publishing
375 Hudson Street
New York, New York 10014

08 09 10 11 10 9 8 7 6 5 4 3 2 1

BD536 April 2008

Copyright © 2008 Dorling Kindersley Limited
Text copyright © Marnie Old and Sam Calagione
All rights reserved

A catalog record for this book is available from the Library of Congress.
ISBN 978–0–7566–3359–2

DK books are available at special discounts when purchased in bulk for sales
promotions, premiums, fund-raising, or educational use. For details, contact:
DK Publishing Special Markets, 375 Hudson Street, New York, New York 10014
or SpecialSales@dk.com.

Color reproduction by Colourscan (Singapore)
Printed and bound in China by Sheck Wah Tong

Discover more at
www.dk.com

CONTENTS

about
this book

Sam and I have known each other for a long time, but from the beginning it was clear that we disagreed strongly about whether beer or wine was the better beverage for pairing with food. And, being opinionated experts in our respective fields, myself a sommelier, and Sam a brewer, we were each determined to prove ourselves right and the other wrong.

How it all began
About five years ago, we began holding informal dinners and gatherings where we would pit beer against wine for pairing with food. But, the opinions were skewed by whose friends, family, or colleagues were in the group. Predictably, my friends preferred the wine, while Sam's chose beer across the board. So, it was inevitable that we'd have to ask the public to settle the score.

Going public
In 2003, we hosted our first "competitive dinner" for the public at Sam's brewpub, Dogfish Brewings & Eats, in Rehoboth Beach, Delaware. We dubbed it "Beer is from Mars, Wine is from Venus", and it involved providing a five-course menu, where, for each course, Sam would select a beer pairing and I would choose a wine. Diners were asked to vote for the superior pairing when combined with the dish in question, not the beverage they might prefer alone, or on its own merits. We had the guests cast anonymous ballots for each course—to prevent peer pressure from interfering with democracy.

Democracy in action
Sam and I went into this with some preconceived notions, each expecting to win hands down—but we were both wrong. Beer won that first night, but only by a hair. The second time wine won, but just barely. So we tried again and again. Dinner after dinner, vote tallies were closer than we could have imagined. Whether we were at a beer bar, a wine festival, or a "neutral" restaurant, no victory was unanimous. Many years and many sold-out dinners later, Sam and I are still neck and neck.

Expanding horizons
Diners responded passionately to our wine and beer "pair-off" dinners, which triggered remarkable conversations and good-natured debates at nearly every table. However, the most fascinating aspect of this experience has been discovering that beer and wine actually have a lot more in common than either of us had expected. It has been rare to find a wine lover who hasn't felt compelled to vote for at least one epic beer pairing, or a hop-head who hasn't grudgingly admired at least one graceful wine pairing.

❝Beer can be more complex than just light lager, and wine is not as complicated as people might think.❞

6

A drinking revolution

We discovered that there's a larger message here: that there's room for everyone to re-evaluate their favorite drinks, and what "goes" with what. Why not challenge the status quo, and ask the wine afficionado to consider trying beer with their meal, or the die-hard beer fan to choose wine for a change? Or, even better, why not show the "undecided" drinker that it's okay to think outside the box about food and drink pairing?

A level playing field

What this book aims to show is that many of our preconceptions about beer and wine are out of date, and some are just plain wrong. Beer can be more complex than just light lager, and wine is not as complicated and elitist as people might think. Of course, this means that the food pairing potential for both beer and wine is extraordinary. In this book, we'll give you the essential tools to understand wine and beer: what they are, how to taste them, and what to look out for. Then we'll talk you through the principles of how to pair wine and beer with a wide variety of foods, and give specific pairing examples, with explanations for each. Once you've got the basics on how to pair, you can use the recipes and pairing recommendations in the last chapter to host your own beer versus wine dinner at home. Have fun, and may the best beverage win. (And remember, the loser does the dishes!)

the
great

divide

meet *Marnie:* the *wine* woman

I'm pretty sure I've got the coolest job in the world. I'm a sommelier and a wine educator—I drink wine for a living. I got my first taste of introducing people to the world of wine as a young and aimless waitress at a luxury hotel. But I knew immediately that I'd found my niche—not only was wine transcendently delicious, but it was also fascinating on every level.

Geek love

I've always been the consummate geek, with wide-ranging interests from ancient history to science fiction. In the study and tasting of wine, I found a complex, multi-faceted subject that incorporated equal parts science and art, botany and gastronomy, chemistry and anthropology, and even geology and linguistics. Not only that, but tasting wines from around the world provided different flavor experiences, even from within the same grape variety. It was like I'd stumbled on an intoxicating form of vicarious travel.

The tipping point

Learning more about wine quickly became a passion for me, and one that certainly paid off in my work as a fine-dining server. Giving good wine advice translated into better tips, of course.

By the time I turned 24 years old, my wine knowledge belied my years, and I landed the responsibility of managing the wine program and selling wine on the floor of a tiny, but top-ranked, French restaurant in Philadelphia. As luck would have it, I was a natural as a wine steward. I spoke fluent French, thanks to the French immersion schools in Canada, where I grew up. Of course, being an extrovert and a chatterbox didn't hurt either! Even better, though, my mother and father were both educators and had passed on to me their knack for teaching.

Wine as life lesson

In 1996 I was hired by Striped Bass, one of Philadelphia's most luxurious destination restaurants, and certainly its most popular. I found working as a sommelier tremendously rewarding. Guiding people when they need wine advice delivers instant gratification. I could revel in making people happy for a living, watching them enjoy terrific wines with great

> **"In wine, I found a complex, multi-faceted subject that incorporated equal parts SCIENCE AND ART."**

food. I also felt I was doing good work on a grander scale, helping guests learn to stop and smell the roses. Drinking great wine is one of those sensual experiences that forces you to inhabit the "here and now" and appreciate life—something that doesn't come easily to many of us.

Onward and upward

Of course, when you love your job, you tend to get better at it. During my time working at Striped Bass, I grew more experienced and more confident in the spotlight. As the region's highest profile sommelier, who happened to be unusually young, and female to boot, I got a lot of attention, landing awards, articles, and TV appearances. By the time I left the company, we had five restaurants and I was a full-blown beverage director, managing a team of wine professionals and an annual wine budget of over a million dollars.

Simplifying wine

Along the way, I had to train a lot of servers, bartenders, and managers to feel comfortable and confident talking to customers. I developed my own unique teaching approach, designed to overcome the common barriers to comprehension. Distilling traditional wine lore into everyday language made wine far easier to understand, and motivated my students to want to learn more. In an idealistic crusade to bring much-needed wine knowledge to a thirsty public, I helped to found, first a local sommeliers group, and later, a national one, serving as founding education chair for the fledgling American Sommelier Association (ASA) in 1999.

Passing it on

The decision to spend my scarce time off developing and teaching wine courses, no doubt, convinced my friends and family that I'd lost my last few marbles. However, it turned out to be an excellent, if unintentional, long-term strategy. I refined my teaching skills, deepened my wine knowledge, and broadened my circle of contacts, both nationally and internationally. When I left both Striped Bass and the ASA in 2001, I was well-placed to start my own company, Old Wines, providing wine education, sommelier services, and restaurant consulting.

Today, I speak to groups around the country, write for magazines, teach both consumers and culinary students, and design restaurant wine programs. And in this book, I hope to reach an even wider audience, demystifying the wonders of wine for everyone. I wouldn't trade being a sommelier for anything, and thank my lucky stars each day that I've had such terrific support every step of the way.

meet **Sam:** the **beer** guy

I decided to make brewing my calling after tasting my first batch of homebrew in 1993, while living in a cramped apartment in New York City. My second batch wasn't nearly as good, but by then I had already made up my mind. I had also told everyone I knew about my big plans, so I couldn't turn back.

Beer in the Big Apple
Fresh out of college, I was living in New York City and paying my way with a job as a waiter at one of the city's first beer-centric restaurants: Nacho Mama's Burritos. Admittedly, the name doesn't connote images of fine dining, but we carried the world's best and hardest-to-find beers. And we worked hard, tasting and discussing which beers paired best with which of our dishes. While working there, I discovered that I had a talent for tasting and describing all kinds of beer.

One of the restaurant's owners, Joshua, and I began home-brewing beer in our apartment. Soon my hobby spun out of control and into a full-fledged obsession. I decided to fly my freak-flag from the get-go by adding weird stuff like grapefruit peels, sour cherries, and licorice root to my stovetop batches of beer. Joshua used to joke that I would make beer with anything I could out-run, kill, and throw into my brewpot—and that wasn't far from the truth.

The birth of Dogfish Head
My penchant for brewing unusual beers would eventually translate into the philosophy behind my own brewery: "Off-centered ales for off-centered people." After reading about the craft brewing renaissance (and a few batches of homebrew), I decided to transform my hobby into my career and wrote the business plan for my brewery, Dogfish Head. We would produce exotic beers that were stronger in alcohol and flavor-profile than those being made by the multi-national brewing conglomerates. And there's obviously a growing minority that appreciates good craft beer, since today, we are one of the fastest-growing breweries in the country.

The glass ceiling
As I tried to convince restaurants and liquor store owners to carry Dogfish Head, I encountered a snobbery against high-end beers. At that time in the 1990's, most "white-tablecloth" restaurants prided themselves on their elaborate, expansive wine lists, yet their beer selection was usually anemic and unoriginal. So, over the last ten years I've been traveling to spread the message that beer afficionados already know: beer can be every bit as complex, flavorful, and diverse as wine—and just as worthy of a place at the dinner table.

Challenging perceptions
At the same time I was on the road, beating down doors on my "beer and benevolence" campaign, Marnie Old was on a similar mission to demystify the world of wine. It was in the late 1990's when our evangelical paths crossed and we found ourselves doing a beer and wine TV segment together. We hit it off when we discovered that we had a lot of similar goals. She wanted to dispel the myth that wine was elitist and overly complicated,

and I wanted to disseminate the message that there was a lot more to beer than generic, industrially produced light lagers.

The good fight
Soon after that, Marnie and I joined forces to host our wine versus beer tasting dinners, where restaurant diners would vote on their preferred pairing—wine or beer—for each dish. What we quickly realized was that the people who were initially excited to learn more about better beer became equally excited to learn more about better wine—and vice-versa.

Marnie and I have hosted these beer and wine dinners around the country in every kind of venue—from small, casual bistros to large formal restaurants. Amazingly, though, at

"I would MAKE BEER WITH ANYTHING I could out-run, kill, and throw into my brewpot."

every single dinner, wine and beer are neck and neck for most of the way, and sometimes one beats the other by a single vote. It's always a close race.

You can take it with you
The idea for this book came about when we realized that anyone, if given the right information, could experience the excitement and competitive spirit of our beer versus wine dinners at home. And, of course, Marnie and I might win a few converts to the other side: wine-drinkers might reconsider their preferences and choose a high-quality beer now and then, and vice-versa for the die-hard beer fans. Whether you're a drinks novice or an expert, we hope this book will spark a thirst for great beer, wine, and food—and, of course, a little healthy debate.

wine: a symbol of culture

Wine is one of the cornerstones of civilization. Museums around the world contain countless artifacts, frescoes, and paintings that prove this point. In fact, Thucydides, one of ancient Greece's greatest historians, went so far as to say his society "began to emerge from barbarism when they learned to cultivate the vine."

Water to wine

The history of alcoholic beverages, and wine in particular, is no less than the history of civilization itself. Until very recently, it wasn't considered safe to drink water, so people turned to more sanitary fermented beverages, such as wine (and beer, I guess). In the modern day, we may view wine as an indulgence for relaxing after work or celebrating an occasion, but this loses sight of its original role in society.

Elixir of life

For much of history, wine was one of life's essentials—a staple of the everyday diet. Winemaking was a means of preserving the perishable fruits of the harvest for consumption at a later date. This is because wine converts the nutrients and precious calories of grapes into a remarkably healthy form that can keep for a very long time. And today, modern medicine's research on antioxidants corroborates what our ancestors already knew about wine: that it's good for us, as part of a healthy, moderate lifestyle. But wine is also a natural disinfectant. Prior to the pharmaceutical age, wine was used as a treatment for everything from flesh-wounds to disease. Wine's combination of acids and alcohol kills microbes that cause illness. Drinking wine significantly combats food poisoning by neutralizing ingested bacteria, such as salmonella and E. coli.

The ancients' love of the vine

The ancient Greeks planted vines for their delicious, nourishing crop, of course, but wine's stimulating effect was a big draw (and source of wonderment), too. The Greeks are well-known for having created and worshipped Dionysus, their god of wine. Modern philosophy and science also owe a great debt to the Greek symposium, a forum for ideas, which was, of course, lubricated by wine.

Wine was also central to ancient Roman culture. It was a dietary staple for the Romans, and they preferred to drink wine over all other beverages. It was also central to Roman medicine, and was used in making poultices and other remedies. Wine was such an integral part of Roman life that it was even used as a form of currency.

"For much of history, wine was one of life's essentials—a staple of the everyday diet."

Their wine parties may have been less cerebral and more risqué than ours, but we can thank the Romans for their territorial ambition. They spread wine grapes beyond the shores of the balmy Mediterranean into the cooler valleys of Western Europe where our modern winemaking traditions have since taken root.

A holy pursuit

Wine is such a revelation of flavor and so strong in healing powers, it's no wonder it was seen as divine in so many religions. While beer could compete in drowning sorrows, wine's ability to age without spoiling must have seemed positively supernatural. Wine was considered the "nectar of the gods" and was thought to have the power to resurrect the Pharaohs in ancient Egypt.

In Christianity, wine holds an extraordinary place of honor, playing the symbolic role of the blood of Christ. In fact, this inspired medieval monastic orders to painstakingly perfect winemaking, beginning in the French region of Burgundy. Prior to this, winemaking had been a purely agricultural enterprise, like any other, where bumper crops defined success. However, making truly fine wine requires the sacrificing of quantity in favor of quality. Under the powerful aegis of the Catholic Church, the traditional economic motivations of farming were rendered irrelevant. The rewards of patience, discipline, and low yields were flavorful and long-lived wines—success was seen as divine favor, well worth the extra effort.

> **Wine has played an integral role in history. It was was valued as more precious than beer by ancient cultures with access to both. The Egyptians, Persians, Greeks, and Romans all preferred wine to beer.**

An easy choice

Historically, winemaking and beer brewing are among the benchmarks that define civilization as we know it. Brewing beer may predate winemaking, but beer has been increasingly marginalized as man has progressed, while wine has been accorded greater status. In regions where grapes can grow, wine has overwhelmingly been the beverage of choice. Elsewhere, wine has been sought out despite easy access to beer, and imported at great effort and expense. Every culture that has had access to both has judged wine to be superior—from the ancient Mesopotamians straight through to the modern day.

brewing
up a civilization

Beer might not be as complicated as wine, but it's certainly more compelling—and it has a longer history, too! While the earliest evidence of wine dates from the 5000 BCE, the oldest evidence of beer dates from the 7000 BCE. Folks were very happily drinking beer for a very long time before they even thought of giving wine a try!

From nomad to brewer

Mankind's love of beer is much more deeply embedded in human DNA than wine is. In fact, many anthropologists and historians believe that, upon discovering the mysterious wonder that is beer, early man shifted from being a nomadic hunter-gatherer to becoming a settled farmer. Research suggests that our ancestors formed primitive villages around their barley crops so that they could make more beer at harvest time. Yes folks, that's right, beer was the catalyst for civilization as we know it!

The ancients' love of the grain

While I'll concede to Marnie that the ancient Egyptians did drink wine, they also made and drank beer. But the Egyptians weren't alone in their love of the magical alchemy of beer—the Assyrians, Babylonians, and Hebrews were beer drinkers, too. And guess what people drank in Sumer, the oldest known civilization of the ancient Near East? They drank beer, and it was so important to their society that they worshipped Ninkasi, the goddess of beer. (In Sumer, the well-respected role of brewer went to women, not men.)

Monastic (last) orders

The medieval monks are well-known for their high-minded love of culture and learning. They have been credited with transcribing and preserving some of the world's greatest classical texts in philosophy and literature. But, do you know what else certain monastic orders are credited with? Crafting excellent beer, which, during medieval times, was considered a nutritious beverage. Proof positive that beer is an evolved, carefully crafted, and cultured beverage.

Beer: a populist beverage

Throughout history, it wasn't just monks who enjoyed a good pint of beer. During the medieval period, beer was infinitely safer to drink than water (thanks to the "boil" stage of the brewing process), so people drank beer as a primary, healthful, life-sustaining beverage. Unlike wine, though, beer has always been the drink of the common man. Relatively easy and inexpensive to produce, and, of course, delicious to boot, most people drank home-brewed or locally produced beer up until the dawn of the industrial revolution in the late

"Yes folks, that's right, BEER WAS THE CATALYST FOR CIVILIZATION as we know it!"

18th century. Beer was, and still is, the great socio-economic leveller. Anyone, regardless of income, could (and would) stop into a tavern and purchase an affordable pint of beer.

The buck stops here

Up until fairly recently, wine and beer have both been relatively provincial beverages. That is to say, people drank beverages that were produced near where they lived because that's all they had easy access to. Thankfully, due to technological advances in transportation and refrigeration, the world is now a lot smaller in terms of our drinking options.

The world's best beers and wines are now available in nearly every corner of the globe. One would think, then, that we should be in an equally strong position to enjoy the world's most cherished wines and the world's most well-regarded beers. But that just isn't true.

In order to buy the finest wines in the world you would need to be a globe-trotting millionaire. The best bottles of wine regularly command thousands of dollars per bottle at auction. If you are looking for the world's best beers, just go to the liquor store in your town that is known to have a great selection, throw a couple of stellar six-packs down on the checkout counter, hand the cashier a twenty and burp in delight as he actually gives you back some change. There is a price ceiling that prohibits people from enjoying the world's most renowned wines. That ceiling simply doesn't exist in the world of beer.

Primal urge

So, is beer a more civilized drink than wine? I would argue, yes, it is. This is because, when it comes down to it, drinking beer, and the culture that surrounds it, is more primal than sipping wine. There's no pomp and no circumstance. Enjoying a beer is as casual and natural as drinking wine is stuffy and staid.

It's true that beer drinkers may burp more often than wine drinkers, which could seem "uncivilized". However, I've always thought that this is because wine drinkers don't stop yakking about pretentious things like "notes" and "bouquets" for long enough to build up the required internal pressure.

Since its early history, the MAGICAL ALCHEMY of making beer has largely been the domain of women. After all, Ninkasi is the goddess—not the god—of beer. And, in Ethiopia, a man has married well not if his wife is the prettiest or richest, but if she makes the best Tej—which is African honey beer.

Marnie says:
wine is finer

I'm not sure what planet Sam and his beer geeks inhabit, but in the real world, wine is the superior beverage. I mean, picture yourself at a buffet where you have a choice between fresh, luscious grapes or a mash of malted barley, hop flowers, and water. Which would you choose to eat? In my mind, there's no contest.

Why wine rocks

Grapes have it all going on—intense flavor, refreshing acidity, and enough fermentable sugar to create one heck of an alcoholic beverage. Fresh fruit is proof Mother Nature loves us: can any other natural food rival fresh-picked fruit for sheer hedonism?

Grains are pretty boring in comparison. After all, Eve didn't tempt Adam with a cracker, did she? Beer's need for multiple ingredients is a clear signal that none of them are good enough alone. Being made from sweet-tart fruit juice, wine is tangy enough to quench, and is packed with richness and flavor. Unlike weak, watery beer, wine is strong enough that we can savor small sips, each one being deeply satisfying. We don't guzzle pints of wine, so we aren't full before the main course arrives. Since it has the refreshment of fruit juice, wine piques the appetite, rather than sating it, and keeps us coming back for more.

Wine is tailor-made for food

Wine is specifically made to be a food partner, capable of making virtually any food taste better than it does alone. To sweeten the deal, the reverse is often true as well: food makes most wines taste better, too. It's a win-win situation—wine and food can heighten the pleasure of one another, as considerate partners should.

It's not a coincidence that the world's top restaurants have wine lists and sommeliers, and not beer lists and brew-stewards. Chefs know wine is capable of flattering their cuisine—be it French or Japanese—better than beer. That's what wine was designed to do, and that's why its food pairing possibilities are superior to beer's.

Value for money

I do admit that wine has a snooty image. But, it isn't wine that is uptight—in fact, wine is naturally relaxing. It's a small but noisy group of people who use wine as a social yardstick. Wine's exclusive image isn't a reflection of its nature, but rather an unfortunate symptom of its success. There are delicious wines in the same per serving budget as Sam's ales, including many featured in this book. It is true that the prices of top wines do go far higher than those of top beers. But, the laws of

"It's a win-win situation—wine and food can heighten the pleasure of one another, as considerate partners should."

supply and demand would suggest that this is because people are willing to pay a lot for the finest wines. If there were a similar demand for the world's finest beers, wouldn't the same be true for brews?

Summing it up

Wine can certainly seem more intimidating than beer, but then Shakespeare looks scarier than Dr. Seuss, too. If all wines tasted the same, or if they didn't have tremendous quality potential, their labels would be as "simple"

> **❝If all wines tasted the same, or if they didn't have tremendous quality potential, their labels would be as "simple" (ahem, simplistic) as beer labels.❞**

(ahem, simplistic) as beer labels. Beer clearly wasn't worthy of historical ranking systems, like cru classifications. Beer recipes can be replicated anywhere, so regional provenance isn't important. In wine, a vineyard's vine variety and location largely determines its wine's flavor and quality potential. Therefore label statements are tightly regulated.

So, yes, buying wine may require doing a little more "homework" than buying beer, but that merely proves my point. We can only conclude that the world has determined wine to be more desirable than beer. Wine is complicated because it is good enough to need ranks and regulated appellations. Wine is expensive because more people want to drink the good stuff and prices reflect what the market will bear. So, the choice between wine and beer seems an easy one to me.

Sam says:
beer is better

Beer is the better beverage, hands-down. In terms of the variety of quality styles available, and the accessibility of those styles, beer is second to none. Beer is superior to wine because a drink doesn't have to be complicated for it to be complex. And this complexity makes beer the better choice for food pairing.

Beer: stable superiority

It grieves me to hear Marnie say that beer is simple. On the contrary—beer is made from recipes that include a range of ingredients, whereas wine, one-dimensional to the last drop, is made with only one.

Wine kind of hops around on one leg: the sad little grape. Meanwhile, beer smoothly struts by on two legs: the grain and the hop. Grains, most often barley, give a particular beer both its sweetness and its body. Hops, on the other hand, give this amazing drink a spiciness and bitter-kiss. Together, the hops perfectly off-set the sweetness of the barley (or other grain).

Beer has great style

Since beer is carbonated, the effervescence of the bubbles actually allows it to disperse more aromas. (The same cannot be said of wine, which is, more often than not, a still beverage.) Go ahead, swish a great India Pale Ale around in your pint glass. You'll be impressed with the coffee-toffee sweet smells of barley, the piney-quinine scent of hops, and the fruity spice of yeast: there is a lot going on there, to be sure.

But there is an amazing array of beer styles beyond India Pale Ale. And, while there are a lot of wine styles out there too, the important thing to remember is that the beverage made with more ingredients is, by definition, bound to be more complex, and thus, better.

Beer is down-to-earth

It's not just that beer itself is a superior beverage. The culture of beer is infinitely more approachable, forgiving, and understanding than that of wine. How many times have you encountered a snooty waiter or sommelier at some restaurant who tells you what you will want to drink with your meal? It happens all the time with wine, but it rarely happens with beer. It just goes to show that wine culture is daunting and exclusive, while beer culture is enticing and inclusive.

Pedigree or quality?

Wine's snootiness is evident even in the labels on the bottles. They always seem to be referencing *terroir*—the land where the grapes were grown—exclusive chateaux, and all that business. Looking at those cryptic wine labels

❝Wine hops around on one leg: the grape. Meanwhile, beer smoothly struts by on two legs: the grain and the hop.❞

20

is enough to make you think the past is more important than the present—the moment when you are actually deciding what to drink with your meal.

Who cares about which chateau a wine came from, and why does a big, fancy name matter anyway? In life, do you choose your friends based on where they grew up and what school they went to? Hopefully not! You choose your friends based on whether or not they are quality people. And the same logic holds true for beer: in choosing a beer the question is about quality over pedigree every time.

Beer goes with everything

As you are considering what to eat, you will also, of course, be considering what to drink. Choose wisely and don't rush. A great meal is meant to be enjoyed with good friends—a social engagement to relish. And beer is certainly the best choice for a multi-course repast. On average, beer has half the alcohol content of wine. So, you can enjoy more beer styles with more courses and a broader range of foods, without getting drunk in the process.

Beer is far more versatile at mealtime than wine could ever hope to be. Are you having fajitas? The bracing hoppiness of an English Pale Ale will cut right through the dish's spiciness. Are you having spinach salad?

A nice tangy wheat beer will counterbalance the acidity of the dressing. If you're having chocolate cake, then a bold, roasty Imperial Stout will balance the richness of your dessert. Beer works across all these categories—and then some.

Think outside the box

As you read this book, hopefully you will become more inclined to try different beer styles. There are so many superior beers to choose from that it's hard to go wrong. While Marnie and I will agree to disagree as to whether beer or wine is the superior food partner, at the end of the day our main goal is to get everyone to try new and exciting food and drink combinations—and that is the best possible outcome for everyone.

primer

what is wine?

Wine is an alcoholic beverage made from one single, phenomenal ingredient: grapes. Fermentation is the process that elevates simple grape juice to a higher plane. Technically speaking, other fruits could be used, but thanks to their exceptional sweetness, none can rival grapes when it comes to winemaking potential.

Desirable spoilage

All "real" wines are made of grapes, most often those of the European wine grape species known as *Vitis vinifera*. Just like apples or pears, vinifera grapes come in a rainbow of varieties that differ in color and flavor. What they all share, from Chardonnay to Shiraz, is the sweet-tart balance essential for making fine wine.

You might be surprised to learn that wine and beer are actually produced in much the same way. Both undergo a process known as fermentation in which live yeasts convert sugar into alcohol. Wine and beer start from different raw materials—sweet ripe grapes for wine, sweet barley malt for beer.

Fermentation is a fascinating process. It is a form of natural spoilage that man has learned to manipulate. As human beings, we have harnessed the transformative power of fermentation for thousands of years, using it to turn milk into cheese and to help bread dough rise. By taming the wild yeasts, we also learned how to convert highly perishable foods, such as fresh grapes, into a nutritious beverage with a long shelf life—wine.

Sugar and sun

Understanding the role that sugar plays in turning fresh grapes into wine is the key that unlocks all the secrets of the wine kingdom. Everything about wine revolves around sugar, since it is the raw material for making alcohol.

Wines are made from grapes because they have more sugar than other juicy fruits. The most prized grape varieties are those that combine high sugar content with desirable flavors to produce the richest, tastiest wines possible. Since it's the sun's energy that fuels sugar production during ripening, the world's finest wine regions are those with ample sunshine and vine-friendly climates. Grape growers decide when it's time to harvest by measuring the fruit's sugar level, or potential alcohol. Winemaking techniques manipulate the fermentation of sugar into alcohol in order to achieve the results they desire.

Body and sweetness

The most important sensory aspects of wine depend on sugar, too. Wines made from grapes that are low in sugar will have low alcohol, known as "light body" because they feel thin in the mouth. Those made from sweeter grapes will be more "full-bodied", feeling thicker in the mouth due to higher alcohol content. In fresh grapes there is an inverse relationship between sugar and acidity and a direct relationship between sugar and flavor that together define wine's "spectrum of style". Last, but not least, most wines are "dry", which simply means not sweet. Dry wines may smell like sweet things without actually tasting sugary, since all their grape sugar has been transformed into alcohol during the fermentation process.

The metamorphosis

Yeasts are microscopic organisms—the most primitive members of the fungus kingdom. They occur naturally in any environment where life is possible. Yeasts live on sugar, which provides them with the energy they need to reproduce. When yeasts consume sugar (in foods like grapes), they break it down, converting it into alcohol and carbon dioxide, releasing energy and heat in the process.

Fermentation is what adds new "winey" flavors to the original flavors of the grape, as happy, hungry yeasts doing their thing trigger intricate chains of chemical reactions. It is this additional layer of flavors and aromas that gives wine its complexity. Just as the flavors of cheeses range far beyond those of neutral milk, wines rarely taste just like grapes. Instead, they offer a diverse array of aromatics—from spicy to floral, from herbal to earthy.

How red and white wines are made

When decoding wine, understanding the differences between how red and white wines are made is half the battle. With wine grapes, it's important to note that color is only "skin-deep". Regardless of skin color, the pulp and juice of grapes are clear. The color in wine comes only from the grape skins. So, in most instances, red grapes make red wine, and green grapes make white wine. (However, it is possible, though uncommon, to make white wine from red grapes.)

A grape's strongest flavors are in the skin, so "skinless" white wines are more delicate by definition. Winemakers strive to preserve their fresh flavor through refrigeration with long, slow, cold fermentations. Since extracting color and flavor from grape skins requires heat, red wine fermentations are just the opposite: hot and fast (see *illustration, right*).

The resulting flavor difference is much like that found between a cold dish and a cooked one made from the same ingredients. For example, in making gazpacho, you retain the vibrant taste of fresh tomatoes and onions through refrigeration. But, if you simmer the same ingredients overnight, the flavors of your hot tomato soup will not reflect the raw vegetable taste, offering instead a deeper, richer flavor.

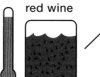

how red and white *wines* are made

red wine

Red wines are fermented hot and fast from whole grapes, clear juice, and dark skins together to extract color and flavor.

White wines are fermented cold and slow from grape juice only; skins are removed before fermentation to retain freshness and delicate aromatics.

white wine

Styles refined over time

Both red and white wines may be fermented grape juice, but they differ in more than just color, thanks to variations on the winemaking process. Red wines acquire compounds from grape skins, like phenolic tannins, that seem harsh in their youth. But over the centuries, winemakers discovered that reds would mellow with time spent in wooden casks. To this day, we continue to mature most red wines in oak before bottling, sometimes choosing "new" barrels for the toasty, spicy flavor they impart along the way. Since white wines vividly retain fresh grape qualities, most were bottled and drunk young and pristine. But, others were found to benefit from a "red wine style" touch of oak, which eventually led to the barrel-fermentation we see in modern Chardonnays.

Beyond red and white

There have been as many innovations in the way we make wine as there are distinct wine styles. Denizens of red wine regions have long known how to change gears during fermentation to make a more refreshing wine for hot weather—shortening the period of skin contact to make a pink rosé. In recent centuries, we've mastered the art of making "sparkling wine" by retaining some of the natural carbon dioxide in bubble form, as pioneered in Champagne, France. We've also figured out dozens of ways to make sweet "dessert wine". For example, when making Asti, we can retain grape sugars by stopping fermentation early. When making Ice Wine, winemakers exclude as much water as possible in order to make the grape juice more

concentrated. There are even wines doctored with additional ingredients. "Fortified wines" such as Port and Sherry are strengthened by adding brandy into the mix, while Vermouth gets its characteristic flavor through the addition of herbs and spices.

Man versus nature

The diversity of wine does not, however, depend on winemaking decisions alone. It is, instead, a complex interplay between nurture and nature. Wine reflects the characteristics and qualities of its single ingredient, grapes, quite clearly. The type of grape used, or "grape variety", has a tremendous influence on wine flavor, as does the geographic conditions in which the grapes have been grown. In fact, grape and region have such a dramatic impact on wine flavor that they are the two most important indicators of style—and because of this they are the two factors named on wine labels (*see pp32–33*).

"There have been as many innovations in the way we make wine as there are distinct wine styles."

wine flavor factors

There is a tremendous range of style and flavor available within the world of wine: from sharp, herbal Sancerre to lush, chocolatey Cabernet Sauvignon. All differences between one wine and another can be traced to one of three flavor factors: the grape factor, the region factor, or the human factor.

The grape factor

Wine is made from 100 percent grape juice, so it's no surprise that using a different type of grape changes a wine's flavor dramatically. As we know, all fine wines are made from a single species, called *Vitis vinifera*, within which there are hundreds of grape varieties. Also known as "varietals", these grapes differ from one another in physical characteristics, such as color, shape, and flavor, in addition to their ability to adapt to vineyard conditions, such as climate and soil.

Grape variety is the main influence on what a wine will taste like. That's why so many modern wines list the name of the grape on the label. The finest wines rely on a short list of only a few dozen grape varieties—those with a track record for making quality wines. Within this group there are seven "noble grapes" that are international icons, benchmarks of style: Chardonnay, Sauvignon Blanc, and Riesling among white grapes, and Cabernet Sauvignon, Merlot, Pinot Noir, and Syrah (aka Shiraz) among reds. The vast majority of the world's top wines are made from this handful of varieties.

Adaptability of the grape

Mankind has cultivated the wine grape species *Vitis vinifera* for millennia. In the same way that we have bred some cattle for meat and others for dairy, we have refined grapevines to suit our winemaking needs. Historically, the goal was to select vines that would grow easily in your region's climate, and would produce the tastiest, most desirable wine possible. Over the centuries, native grape varieties developed in all of Europe's classic wine zones, with each adapting to local conditions. For example, Riesling emerged from Germany's cold

> **Wine's critical flavor factors:**
>
> • The Grape Factor:
> which variety or varieties are used
>
> • The Region Factor:
> the vineyard's geography and climate
>
> • The Human Factor:
> grape growing techniques and winemaking methods

Rheinland, and still performs best in other cold regions of the world, such as Canada. Syrah hails from France's sunny Rhône region, and thrives in other warm places, such as South Australia, where it goes by the alias Shiraz. The premium grape varieties we recognize may share a species, but their fruit differs significantly in color, shape, and size, as well as in aromatics and balance of sweetness to sourness. So, in the same way that Red Delicious apples taste different than Granny Smith apples, golden Chardonnay grapes taste recognizably different than red Merlot grapes. And, of course, if the fruit tastes different, so will the wine.

The grape is so central to wine style that it can be a useful organizing principle when trying to make sense of wine. Wines made from the same grape share a family resemblance, even when produced in different styles (such as French Chablis and California Chardonnay, both made from the same grape). We'll return to these "icon grapes" in the section on major wine styles (*see pp34–39*).

The region factor

Where grapes are grown has a huge impact on wine style—almost as dramatic as the choice of grape variety. Geography has such a tremendous effect on wine's taste, through factors such as climate and soil type, that many wines are named for their region, not their grape. Climate has an especially profound influence, as it controls the vine's life cycle and the fruit ripening process. But regional variation doesn't stop there.

What exactly is *terroir*?

The place where the grapes were grown leaves a "flavor imprint" on the fruit—one that is amplified by the fermentation process. The French sum this concept up neatly in one word: *terroir*. This term is used widely in the wine industry and is simply lingo for the "taste of the place", a region's distinctive fingerprint of flavor.

A vineyard's unique effect on wine flavor arises from all sorts of factors, geographically speaking. Some are "macro", like latitude and altitude, others are "micro", like soil types and the orientation of slopes. However, climate remains most important, since it has the strongest effect on flavor.

Like all plants, vines live on sunshine. And, the connection between climate and a wine region's wine style becomes clear once we understand the ripening process.

wine flavor spectrum

Light white wines
Typically:
- from cooler climates
- juice only flavors; fermented in stainless steel
- made with delicate grapes like Riesling and Sauvignon Blanc

Rich white wines
Typically:
- from warmer climates
- juice and oak flavors; fermented in barrels
- made with lush grapes like Chardonnay and Viognier

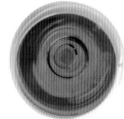

Pink rosé wines
Typically:
- from warmer climates
- delicate skin flavors; brief skin contact
- made with spicy grapes like Grenache and Zinfandel

Pale red wines
Typically:
- from cooler climates
- moderate skin flavors; low skin to juice ratio
- made from earthy grapes like Pinot Noir and Sangiovese

Dark red wines
Typically:
- from warmer climates
- strong skin flavors; high skin to juice ratio
- made from inky grapes like Cabernet Sauvignon and Syrah

Sunshine increases sweetness

Before ripening kicks in, wine grapes are bright green, rock hard, and extremely sour. Only sunlight can turn these sour grapes into sweet, ripe fruit. The more sunshine the vines get, the sweeter and more intensely flavored the grapes become. While sugar and ripe, grapey flavor increase with sunshine, acidity and under-ripe, herbal flavors decrease.

It is exactly the same process for all fruits and vegetables: sour, leafy-tasting green tomatoes get sweeter and more "tomato-ey" as they ripen and turn red. So, in a growing region with a cool, cloudy climate, fruit ripens more slowly and will likely be a little under-ripe at harvest. On the flipside, in a warm, sunny corner of the world,

the ripening process will happen more quickly and the fruit is more likely to taste over-ripe and sweeter. These flavor profiles carry over into the wine, and this can provide useful insight for wine shopping. With some practice, you can learn to accurately predict a wine's style if you know whether its region is relatively warm, like South Australia, or relatively cool, like Germany.

The human factor

Many flavor variations can be traced to man, and the choices we make. Our grape growing decisions can alter the flavor of the fruit before harvest, and our winemaking decisions can alter the flavor of the wine. Do we choose to make bulk wine or fine wine? Are we making red or white wine? Should the wine be sweet or dry? Should we blend multiple grapes, or only use one grape variety? Will the wine taste better if it is aged in barrels, and if so, for how long? The human touch is the third factor that influences a wine's flavor.

Every choice we make in growing grapes and in winemaking has significant effects on a wine's style and flavor. Grape growing, or viticulture, influences the flavor and potential quality of the fruit through actions in the vineyard. Winemaking, or vinification, influences flavor and style through actions taken in the winery.

Grape growing

To make wine, we need only one ingredient: grapes. The quality and flavor of those grapes will control the potential quality and flavor possibilities of the wine. To produce a balanced wine, we must harvest our fruit with just the right balance of sugar, flavor, and acidity. Man has cultivated winegrapes for millennia, and we've found ways to farm them in order to achieve the results we desire. From choosing the best "clone" of Pinot Noir to controlling the ratio of leaves to clusters, a grape grower's decisions govern the flavor potential of winegrapes. The choices made in planting and cultivating a vineyard will determine much about a wine's style and flavor.

Grape growing decisions include:

- Which grapes do we plant and where?
- Do we produce intensely flavored, full-bodied wines by waiting for exceptional ripeness, or harvest earlier for a more refreshing, medium-bodied style?
- Do we shoot for bumper crops and make modest wine, or prune back vines to limit volume in pursuit of higher quality?
- Do we farm organically or use modern methods of pest and disease control?

Winemaking

Techniques for making wine evolved through trial and error over centuries before fermentation was fully understood. Now, modern science gives us a better grasp of the biochemical processes involved. Advances in technology have vastly improved winemaking equipment and options. From selecting a strain of yeast to controlling fermentation temperature, winemakers make lots of decisions that influence wine flavor and style. Many choices facing winemakers are simply a matter of fine tuning, but others are critical in determining a wine's style and flavor.

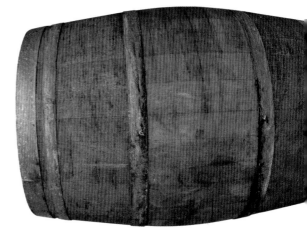

Winemaking decisions include:

- Do we halt fermentation early and retain a little sweetness, or allow the wine to become fully dry?
- Do we ferment white wine in stainless steel (*see left*) to retain freshness, or develop richness through oak barrel fermentation?
- Do we age red wine in old "neutral" barrels to enrich and mellow wine, or in "new" barrels (*see right*) for the toasty flavor of new oak?
- Do we ferment in a sealed container to make a "sparkling" wine, or allow carbonation to escape to make a still wine?

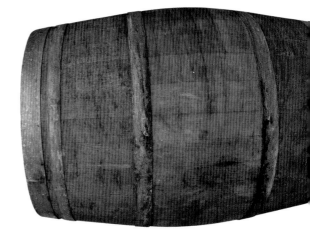

old & new world *winemaking*

There exists a difference in flavor and style found between the wines of Europe and those of every other continent. To account for this, the wine trade draws a distinction between what they call "old" and "new" world wine styles. While this may sound a bit old-fashioned, it is very useful for predicting a wine's style.

Differing flavor profiles

Even when the same grape varieties are used and the wine is made in roughly the same manner, old world and new world wines tend to differ in several ways: in body, acidity, flavor intensity, and level of oak flavor.

In general, old world wines tend to be lower in alcohol than new world wines, which translates into lighter-bodied wines. They are also usually higher in acidity, and favor the lean, earthy (less-ripe) end of the flavor spectrum. They typically display a moderate flavor intensity, with a subtle use of oak flavor.

New world wines, on the other hand, are most often fuller-bodied than old world wines, since they tend to be higher in alcohol. They generally have a high flavor intensity, are lower in acidity, and are brimming with flavors from the lush, fruity (ripe) end of the flavor spectrum. New world wines aged in barrels tend to make bolder use of oak flavor as well.

Why is this?

If we look to our three wine flavor factors, old world and new world variation is a result of regional and cultural differences. It is not a matter of grape variety, as all vineyards grow European grapes and fine wines are made almost exclusively from the "short list" of top varieties.

Instead, the flavor shift is due to the other two factors: region of origin and human choices. Climate is the root source of the distinction, as most new world wine regions were deliberately chosen to be warmer and more arid than their old world counterparts. So, because of the warmer, sunnier climate, fruit simply gets riper in most new world wine zones than in their old world counterparts.

However, social values play a strong role as well. Cultural sensibilities and market priorities guide vintners in their style choices. A little history goes a long way in grasping the old world/new world concept, and understanding how fine wine culture has developed and spread explains the stylistic divide between classic European wines and the innovative styles that have emerged elsewhere.

Old world tradition

Wine was once an exclusively European product, and its successful migration to the new world is relatively recent. Within old world Europe, wine was once an everyday staple of Mediterranean zones—like bread or olive oil. However, when grapes were planted further north, something interesting happened. Vines were forced to struggle for survival outside their balmy natural habitat and produced much smaller crops of more intensely flavored fruit. Cooler regions, such as northern France, weren't ideal for growing grapes on the "wine as food staple" model. But, the tiny amounts of wines produced were something special—luxurious, fine wines worthy of aging, reverence, and higher prices.

Over the centuries, certain wines earned recognition for quality, and came to be known by the names of their regions, like Burgundy and Bordeaux. Each region grew its own native grapes and developed special techniques to best express their potential quality. So, for example, the legendary white wines of cool climate Burgundy were made from local Chardonnay grapes. Their depth and richness were found to be enhanced by fermentation in small oak barrels.

Within Burgundy, towns like Meursault made superior wines. Like most classic European wines, these are still sold under their place-name, or appellation, not as Chardonnay—a traditional system known as "regional labelling" (*see right, top*). Such a new world wine would, however, be labelled very differently from its progenitor. The grape variety Chardonnay would be overtly stated and brand name would be emphasized over region, a system known as "varietal labelling" (*see right, bottom*).

New world innovation

The more desirable a wine, the more it inspires imitation. Once new continents were colonized, European winemaking techniques were spread around the globe. At first, most new world wine zones focused on making simple wines, as staples. But, once viticulture became established, wineries began a push toward improving quality.

It was only natural that an ambitious vintner looking to make the finest possible white wine would follow the Meursault "recipe", by seeking land where Chardonnay vines could thrive and applying Burgundian practices, such as barrel-fermentation.

New world wine regions in the Americas and the Southern Hemisphere grow European grapes and use European techniques. Almost all their wine styles are modeled on the understated old world classics. However, warmer climates, modern science, and a pioneering spirit combine to create bolder wines in these regions of the world. Like a Hollywood remake of a European art film, a California Chardonnay will generally be stronger, riper, and more fruit-driven in flavor than Meursault, its inspiration.

anatomy of a *wine* label

old world regional labelling

Traditional European wines organize their labels around a prominent "appellation", or named region of origin to suggest the style. European appellations are tightly regulated and govern not just origin, but permitted grape varieties and minimum quality standards. Grape varieties are rarely named, especially for the most well-regarded wines.

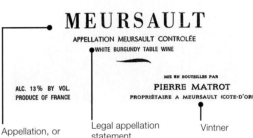

Appellation, or region of origin

Legal appellation statement

Vintner

new world varietal labelling

New world wines organize their labels around grape variety to suggest the style. Typically, the largest typeface is used for branding. Region of origin must appear, but is often less prominent.

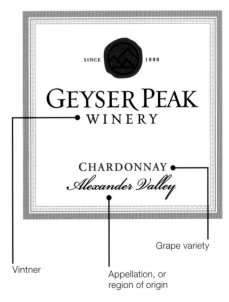

Grape variety

Vintner

Appellation, or region of origin

major
white wine styles

White wines are cool in every way: cool climate grapes fermented cold and served chilled. Made from juice pressed off the skins, clear white wines can be made from grapes of any color, though most often green or yellow. Crisp, clean whites rank among the most versatile and food-flattering wines on earth.

The icon whites

Exceptionally popular Chardonnay hails from Burgundy, France. White Burgundies are made with 100 percent Chardonnay grapes, from modest Macon-Villages to swanky Meursault. International Chardonnays take their cues from these icons. Most, however, come from warmer regions, where riper Chardonnay fruit makes lusher, fruitier wines.

Versatile Sauvignon Blanc comes from Bordeaux, France, where it dominates dry white Bordeaux, like Graves. Further north in the Loire Valley, it makes timeless beauties like Sancerre and Pouilly-Fumé. Vintners elsewhere take after one of the two. Warm regions, like California, favor plumper, lightly oaked Bordeaux styles. Cool zones like New Zealand reflect the sharp zing of the Loire.

Riesling emerged from Germany—a cool climate variety with poignant aromatics. Rieslings range in sweetness from bone dry to dessert. Traditional German styles are generally low-alcohol and off-dry, an approach often followed in North America. Alsace makes stronger, drier Rieslings—a style more commonly adopted in Australia and Austria.

CHARDONNAY

STYLE PROFILE	**Dry, full-bodied white wines with rich texture** Often barrel-fermented and aged on the "lees" to impart spicy, toasty flavors
FLAVOR SPECTRUM	Cool climate flavors: crabapple, apple, pear, lemon Warm climate flavors: pineapple, mango, baked apple
NATIVE OLD WORLD REGIONS	**Burgundy, France** eg: Bourgogne Blanc, Macon-Villages, Chablis, Meursault, Chassagne-Montrachet, Puligny-Montrachet, Pouilly-Fuissé
NEW WORLD REGIONS	**United States** eg: California (Sonoma, Central Coast, Santa Barbara, Napa), Washington, Oregon **Australia** eg: Victoria (Yarra), New South Wales (Hunter), South Australia, Western Australia

34

SAUVIGNON BLANC

STYLE PROFILE	Dry, medium-bodied white wines with high acidity and herbal aromas Usually young, fresh, and unoaked, especially in cool regions
FLAVOR SPECTRUM	Cool climate flavors: lemon peel, grapefruit, green herbs Warm climate flavors: honeydew melon, pear, lemon custard
NATIVE OLD WORLD REGIONS	Bordeaux, France eg: Bordeaux Blanc, Graves Loire Valley, France eg: Sancerre, Pouilly-Fumé
NEW WORLD REGIONS	New Zealand eg: South Island (Marlborough) South Africa eg: Coastal Region (Stellenbosch, Paarl) United States eg: California (Napa, Sonoma, Central Coast), Washington

RIESLING

STYLE PROFILE	Aromatic light-bodied white wines with high acidity Range widely in sweetness, from very dry to very sweet; never barrel fermented
FLAVOR SPECTRUM	Cool climate flavors: green apple, lemon-lime, green tea Warm climate flavors: peach, tangerine, honeysuckle
NATIVE OLD WORLD REGIONS	Germany eg: Mosel-Saar-Ruwer, Rheingau, Pfalz, Nahe, Rheinhessen France eg: Alsace
NEW WORLD REGIONS	United States eg: Washington, New York (Finger Lakes), California Australia eg: South Australia (Clare Valley, Eden Valley) Canada eg: Ontario (Niagara), British Columbia (Okanagan)

major
red wine styles

Red wines are a specialty of warm, sunny climates. Purple skins and clear juice must "stew" together during winemaking to extract red wine's dark colors and flavors, gaining significant richness and complexity. Red wines are concentrated, multi-faceted flavor experiences and dominate the ranks of collectible wines.

The icon reds

Cabernet Sauvignon and Merlot are native to Bordeaux, where they are traditionally blended together. Modest Bordeaux is Merlot-driven, while ambitious wines revolve around Cabernet Sauvignon. Merlot's fruity flavor softens aggressive Cabernet Sauvignon's woodsy grip, while inky Cabernet adds structure to fleshy Merlot. Blending is common worldwide, though labels usually name only the dominant grape.

Pinot Noir, the red grape of Burgundy, is known for silky-textured soft reds like Gevrey-Chambertin and Vosne-Romanée. Pale in color thanks to thin fragile skins, Pinot Noir delivers stunning complexity—layers of earth tones and red fruit aromatics. Low-yielding and difficult to grow, this variety prefers cool climates. Internationally, it excels in cool zones, like Oregon and New Zealand.

Spicy Syrah (also called Shiraz) is native to France's Rhône Valley and known for its fiery flavor and blue-black color. Found in French blends like Chateauneuf-du-Pape, it is more popular overseas. Australia has championed Syrah's alter ego, brash, jammy Shiraz, while most American versions go by Syrah.

CABERNET SAUVIGNON, MERLOT & BLENDS

STYLE PROFILE	Dry, full-bodied red wines with dark color and herbal aromas Cabernet provides more color, tannin, and structure; Merlot provides more fruitiness and softness; the two grapes are commonly blended
FLAVOR SPECTRUM	Cool climate flavors: blackberry, bell pepper, cedar, cassis Warm climate flavors: black cherry, chocolate, cigar tobacco, black olive
NATIVE OLD WORLD REGIONS	Bordeaux, France Cabernet Sauvignon-based, eg: Médoc, Graves, Margaux, Pauillac Merlot-based, eg: Bordeaux, St. Emilion, Pomerol
NEW WORLD REGIONS	United States eg: California (Napa, Sonoma, Central Coast), Washington Chile eg: Valle Centrale (Maipo, Rapel, Colchagua), Aconcagua Australia eg: South Australia (Coonawarra), Western Australia

PINOT NOIR

STYLE PROFILE	Dry, medium-bodied red wines with pale color and earthy aromas Thin skins yield pale color, subtle flavors, and soft tannins
FLAVOR SPECTRUM	Cool climate flavors: cranberry, sour red cherry, black tea Warm climate flavors: raspberry, black cherry, clove
NATIVE OLD WORLD REGIONS	Burgundy, France eg: Bourgogne Rouge, Mercurey, Marsannay, Gevrey-Chambertin, Vosne-Romanée, Nuits-St.-Georges, Beaune, Volnay
NEW WORLD REGIONS	United States eg: Oregon (Willamette Valley), California (Sonoma, Carneros, Santa Barbara) New Zealand eg: South island (Marlborough, Central Otago) Australia eg: Victoria (Yarra Valley)

SYRAH/SHIRAZ

STYLE PROFILE	Dry, full-bodied, red wines with dark color and smoky, spicy aromas Thick skins give deep color and bold fruit-driven flavor
FLAVOR SPECTRUM	Cool climate flavors: wild blackberry, black pepper, smoke Warm climate flavors: blueberry jam, cola bean, smoked meat
NATIVE OLD WORLD REGIONS	Rhône Valley, France eg: Hermitage, Crozes-Hermitage, St. Joseph, Côte Rôtie, Cornas
NEW WORLD REGIONS	Australia eg: South Australia (Barossa, McLaren Vale), Western Australia (Margaret River), Victoria, New South Wales (Hunter) United States eg: California (Santa Barbara, Central Coast, Napa, Sonoma), Washington

specialty *wine styles*

Man has tinkered with fermentation for millennia, but it seems nothing but better grapes can improve on wine's perfection. Unlike brewers, winemakers alter only the process, not the raw materials. Some stop fermentation early, others ferment twice. Some dry their grapes to near raisinhood, others spike with grape spirit.

Special wine styles

Rosé wines have literally been "pinked". In sunny red wine regions, the craving for brisk chillable wines led to the innovation of rosé. These wines begin fermentation as for red (with the dark grape skins on) but are quickly drained off and finished as for white. Brief skin contact gives a blush and a boost of flavor, while cold fermentation retains the snappy tang of fresh fruit; some are not fully dry.

Sparkling wines are a cool climate specialty whose bubbles are a natural product of fermentation. The process, where still white wines undergo a second sealed fermentation to trap carbonation, was first perfected in Champagne, France, but is now practiced worldwide. Aging gives Champagne its luxe, toasty flavor and richness. Modest sparkling wines tend to be younger and fresher.

Fortified wines are a warm climate specialty. With over 15 percent alcohol, these are intense, full-bodied wines. Some styles are fermented dry first, then fortified later, as with Sherry, which may be sweet or dry. Other styles, such as Port, are kept sweet by fortifying mid-fermentation.

ROSÉ WINE

STYLE PROFILE	Light- to medium-bodied pink wines with intense fruit flavor and refreshing acidity Warm climate specialty—range in sweetness, from very dry to moderately sweet, and in color, from pale blush to nearly red
FLAVOR SPECTRUM	Light and sweet styles: strawberry, watermelon, cantaloupe Deep and dry styles: raspberry, cherry, tomato
NATIVE OLD WORLD REGIONS	Southern France eg: Rhône Valley (Tavel, Côtes-du-Rhône), Provence Spain eg: Rioja, Navarra
NEW WORLD REGIONS	United States eg: California (Central Coast, Sonoma, Napa) Australia eg: South Australia, Victoria South Africa eg: Coastal Region

SPARKLING WINE

STYLE PROFILE	Bubbly, light-bodied white wines with refreshing acidity Cool climate specialty—second fermentation in closed container traps carbonation, often aged on "lees" to add yeasty flavor
FLAVOR SPECTRUM	"Lees-aged" style: lemon, green apple, brioche toast Young, fresh style: golden apple, pear, white grape
NATIVE OLD WORLD REGIONS	Champagne, France Champagne ("lees-aging" method) Italy Prosecco (no aging), Asti (no aging; fully sweet) Spain Cava ("lees-aging" method)
NEW WORLD REGIONS	United States eg: California (Napa, Sonoma, Central Coast), New York Australia eg: Victoria, South Australia, Tasmania

FORTIFIED WINE

STYLE PROFILE	Strong, extra-full-bodied wines with pungent aromas and high alcohol Warm climate specialty—standard wine is spiked with brandy to boost flavor, texture, and improve stability
FLAVOR SPECTRUM	Dry styles (white): crabapples, toasted almonds, cider Dessert styles: berry pie, brandied cherry (red), fruitcake, molasses (white)
NATIVE OLD WORLD REGIONS	Portugal Porto (red/dessert), Madeira (red and white/dessert and dry) Spain Sherry (white/dessert and dry)
NEW WORLD REGIONS	Australia eg: New South Wales, South Australia United States eg: California (Central Valley, Napa, Sonoma) South Africa eg: Breede River, Klein Karoo

wine styles
by region

Grape variety and region influence wine flavor, so both factors are used to classify wine styles. The chart below gives a general sketch of which countries and regions are best known for producing wines from which popular grapes and in which specialty styles. (Note: this is not intended to be a comprehensive list.)

COUNTRIES & REGIONS	SPARKLING STYLES (Champagne, Cava, etc.)		WHITE WINES — Chardonnay	Sauvignon Blanc	Pinot Grigio/Pinot Gris	Riesling
FRANCE						
BURGUNDY/CHAMPAGNE	●		●			
BORDEAUX				●		
RHÔNE/MIDI						
ALSACE/LOIRE				●	●	●
ITALY	●				●	
SPAIN/PORTUGAL	●					
GERMANY/AUSTRIA						●
CANADA			●			●
UNITED STATES	●		●	●	●	●
AUSTRALIA	●		●	●		●
NEW ZEALAND			●	●	●	●
CHILE			●	●		
ARGENTINA						
SOUTH AFRICA			●	●		

Wine primer Wine styles by region

40

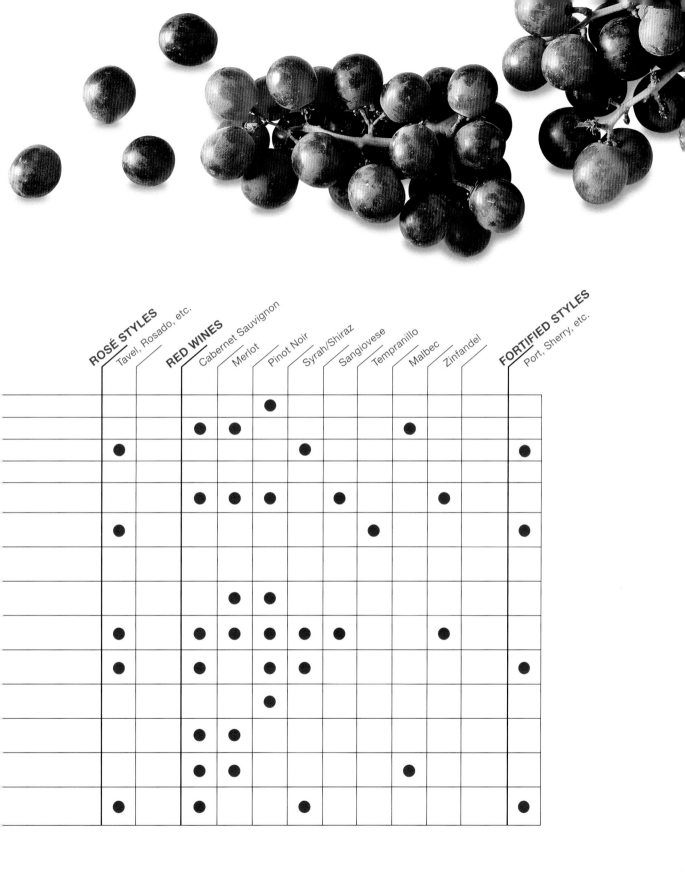

how to taste wine
like a pro

Tasting and evaluating wine is an acquired skill just like any other. But it's not as tricky or complicated as some would have you believe. It simply involves knowing what sensations to look out for, how to describe them, and a bit of highly enjoyable practice.

The sensual world of wine

We use five senses to collect information about the world. Of these, only hearing is completely irrelevant in tasting wine. Sight is obviously important. Every wine list and wine store in the world is organized around color, as in white, red, and rosé (meaning "pinked"). The remaining important characteristics in wine are perceived by the other three senses: taste, smell, and touch. Professionals use the "tastes" of sweetness and acidity, the "smells" of fruit and oak and the "feelings" of body and tannin to frame distinctions between wine styles. Learning to separate which perceptions come from which sense, and which words mean what, gives any wine drinker critical tools for navigating the world of wine.

Objective and subjective descriptions

Evaluating wine becomes a lot easier when you understand that wine can be described in both subjective and objective ways. Subjective characteristics are things that are perceived differently by everyone. So, when people say that a wine has notes of "honey" or hints of "tobacco", they are making loose analogies about the wine's aroma based on their personal experiences. While subjective descriptors can be engaging metaphors for wine flavor, their meanings are very fluid.

Objective characteristics, on the other hand, are more concrete qualities that are roughly measurable, and experienced in the same way by almost everyone. In wine, the presence of qualities such as sweetness and tannin are either there or they're not. They can be assessed more easily than, say "peachiness". As with most things measured on a scale

"Since we ferment grape sugar away into alcohol, a wine's sweetness is expressed in terms of its absence."

from low to high, medium is the norm. When describing a wine, the unusual attributes are what distinguish it from the crowd. For example, since most wines are "dry" we don't really need to mention sweetness unless it is unusually high or unusually low. So, when a particular characteristic doesn't jump out as being uncommon, it's a safe bet that it can be described as "medium" or average.

The taste of wine

As sensory organs go, tastebuds are pretty primitive. They can only sense five things, and only when the substance makes contact with the tongue. The five tastes are sweetness, acidity, saltiness, bitterness, and umami. In wine, only sweetness and acidity are truly important, and each is tasted in its own tongue zone (*see diagram, p45*): sweetness on the tip of the tongue, and acidity down the sides. Tastebud sensations are easy to separate from other flavors because they happen instantaneously on contact.

Evaluating sweetness

Lots of wines smell sweet, but for actual sugar to be perceptible on the tip of the tongue is rare. Since we ferment grape sugar away into alcohol, a wine's sweetness is most often expressed in terms of its absence, known as "dryness". The word "dry" is wine lingo for the opposite of "sweet". In wine tasting, the norm is dry, as standard wines have no obvious sugar content. Wines with unusually low sugar are described as "very dry" or "bone dry", a style most often seem in classic European wines. Those with high enough sugar to be perceptible on the tip of the tongue are called "off-dry", while the term "sweet" is reserved for overtly sugary specialties, like Ice Wine and Port, known as dessert wines.

Evaluating acidity

Acidity is the other crucial "taste" in evaluating wine. It is wine's secret weapon, since it provides refreshment and flatters food.

Perceived along the sides of the tongue, it tingles and makes the mouth water, like lemon juice or vinegar. While all wines have some acidity, a few are uncommonly sharp or unusually soft. Mildly acidic wines (considered to have low acid levels) have a creamy taste to them. Normal or medium-acid wines taste crisp. Highly acidic wines will stand out because they are tart and bracingly intense.

The feeling of wine

The way a particular wine feels in your mouth should not be underestimated. In tasting wine, there are two key sensations that are informed by our sense of touch: the body or "thickness" of a wine, and also its astringency.

Evaluating body

Alcohol is thicker than water—the stronger the wine, the more viscous and mouth-coating it will feel. We call this textural quality in wine "body". Body does not refer to quality, color, or flavor intensity, although it often fluctuates along with them. Body is the thickness, or texture, of wine, and it can be felt in the mouth or observed in the "legs" that slide down the inside of the glass after swirling. Since alcohol is wine's main source of thickness, body is directly connected to a wine's alcohol content. Light-bodied wines have a delicate, sheer mouthfeel, and tend to be low in alcohol. Medium-bodied wines have a bit more alcohol, and leave a moderate coating on the palate. Full-bodied wines tend to have the highest alcohol content, and produce a thick, rich mouthfeel.

Evaluating astringency

Astringency is another important sensation informed by touch. This is produced by a wine component called tannin, which is perceived as a drying sensation on the tongue, gums, and palate. It is found only in red wines, since it comes from the same source as red color—grape skins. Tannin also comes from other grape solids, such as seeds, and stems. In white winemaking these are discarded, but they are the essential source of color and flavor for reds.

Tannin is odorless and flavorless, but it is physically felt by the flesh of the mouth. Its astringency blocks salivation, triggering a creeping "dry-mouth" sensation—similar to the tacky feeling you get from drinking a mug of oversteeped tea. Wine that is low in tannin produces a lush, velvety feeling in the mouth; wines with medium or moderate tannin have a suedey mouthfeel. And, finally, wines with high or aggressive tannin leave a rasping "sandpapery" feel in the mouth.

The smell of wine

Believe it or not, what we call flavor is almost always perceived by our sense of smell, and not by our tastebuds. When we eat or drink, aromatic components are channeled up the passage that connects the nose and the throat, delivering flavor messages to the brain. (Try tasting something with your nose plugged, and you'll see how this works immediately.)

Olfactory flavor

Unlike limited tastebud sensations, we can recognize thousands of different olfactory aromas, which are perceived as flavors when we eat or drink. Subjective descriptors are used for these qualities, usually by comparing a wine's aroma and flavor to other food experiences. However, intensity of flavor is often more important than individual character in selecting wine. We will separate wine's flavor into two categories depending on their source—the fermented fruit or oak barrels.

Evaluating fruit

"Fruit" is an umbrella term used to encompass all such olfactory flavors. Many wines deliver flavors of fruit, such as berries or apples. But, the fruit component includes many other flavors, too—from herbal to earthy to floral flavors. Think of fruit as a scale of intensity of "flavor per square inch" (like from water to espresso). A wine with low fruit concentration would have a subtle, mild flavor. A wine ranked as medium in fruit component would have normal flavor concentration, while one rated as high would offer bold, intense flavor.

Evaluating oak

New oak barrels are a winemaker's only seasoning, adding spicy depth and richness to wine. Aging or fermenting wine in new oak imparts a distinctive flavor, reminiscent of vanilla, dessert spices, or smoke, described again on an intensity scale. Not all wines get barrel treatment, and fewer see new oak, so many whites and some reds have no perceptible oak qualities. Others have only a suggestion of oak, reflecting the moderate norm. Some wines—mostly strong reds and rich whites—exhibit intense, bold, oaky flavors.

TASTING AND EVALUATING WINE:
a step-by-step summary

1. LOOK AT THE WINE.
Is it white, red, or pink? Does it have bubbles?

2. SWIRL THE WINE IN YOUR GLASS.
This intensifies wine aromas dramatically.

3. TAKE A FEW DEEP SNIFFS.
Is it mild or intense? Does it remind you of anything?
Fruits? Spices? Vegetables? Flowers?

4. TASTE THE WINE.
Take a mouthful of wine and swish it around, as if it were mouthwash.

5. EVALUATE THE CHARACTERISTICS BELOW AS LOW, MEDIUM, OR HIGH.

TASTE
SWEETNESS Is there perceptible sweetness or is the wine "dry"?
ACIDITY   Is the wine tart and sharp or round and creamy?

SMELL
FRUIT Is the wine's overall flavor subtle or is it bold?
OAK   Is there evidence of new oak flavor? (Think of the toasty, spicy flavor of cognac or bourbon.)

TOUCH
BODY   Does the wine feel sheer and delicate or thick and viscous?
TANNIN If red, does the wine feel soft and velvety or astringent and leathery?

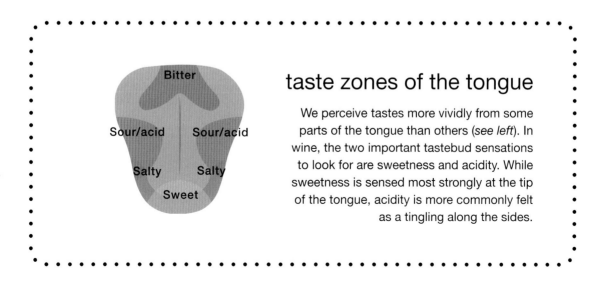

taste zones of the tongue

We perceive tastes more vividly from some parts of the tongue than others (*see left*). In wine, the two important tastebud sensations to look for are sweetness and acidity. While sweetness is sensed most strongly at the tip of the tongue, acidity is more commonly felt as a tingling along the sides.

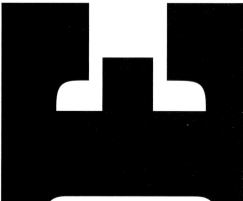

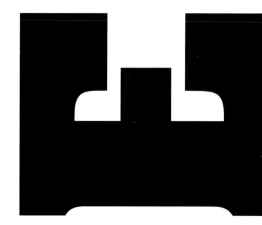
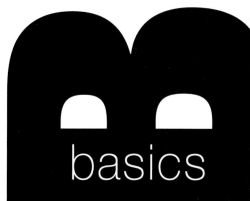

BEER

basics

what is
beer?

By its loosest, most simplistic definition, beer is an alcoholic beverage made from malted grains. Other ingredients that are key to the beer "recipe" are water, hops, and yeast. Now, just because there is a basic list of essential ingredients that doesn't mean that all beers are the same. There's a whole lot more to it than that.

The essentials
According to the US government, beer is only beer if it is made with four main ingredients: hops, yeast, water, and grain. But these basic ingredients are just the starting point for brewers. Because the crafting of beer is primarily controlled by human choices (unlike wine, which is heavily influenced by climate), this means that brewers can (and do) tinker with the types of grains, hops, and yeasts they use, and they also may add other ingredients for a variety of distinct flavors. Even though brewers have been making world-class beers from these four main ingredients for centuries, there is also a great tradition of brewing with exotic items, such as fruits, herbs, spices, wood, and wild yeast.

Fermentation: ales and lagers
As in winemaking, fermentation is essential to the production of beer. In beermaking, this is the process by which yeast, a fungus, converts the sugars in the grains (and other ingredients) into alcohol. The two main categories of beer—ales and lagers—are delineated by the types of yeast used for fermentation, and also how they are fermented. Ales are fermented quickly at warmer temperatures using ale yeast, while lagers are fermented slowly at cooler temperatures using lager yeast. Ale yeast ferments from the top, and lagers ferment from the bottom (see illustration, opposite).

A warm, fast ale fermentation makes the final beer more fruity and spicy, whereas a slow, cool lager fermentation makes the beer more crisp, neutral, and clean. Because of the way in which they are fermented, lagers tend to be more mellow and refined, and ales tend to be more robust and complex.

Some traditional breweries in Belgium make beers simply by pulling back the roofs of their breweries and letting wild airborne yeast ferment their beer naturally. This is called "spontaneous fermentation" and the beers— Lambics and Gueuzes—are usually tart, complex, and acidic.

Diversity in beer
Beer has been around for longer than wine, and it also has more potential for diversity (as we will prove mathematically in the section on

"There is a great tradition of brewing with exotic items, such as fruits, herbs, spices, wood, and wild yeast."

48

beer ingredients on pages 52–55). From the days of the Ancients up until recent history, beer was made in small batches and in a huge range of styles. For example, Belgian Kriek beers are brewed with cherries, Swedish Sahti beers are brewed with juniper berries and rye, and African Tej beers are brewed with honey. Wine is fermented grape juice and that's about it. No wonder the complexity and breadth of beer flavors, aromas, and styles far outshine their wine world counterparts.

The rise of industry, however, brought with it automation, consolidation, and distribution that dulled the vibrancy and diversity of the noble

"Wine is fermented grape juice and that's about it. No wonder beer flavors far outshine wine."

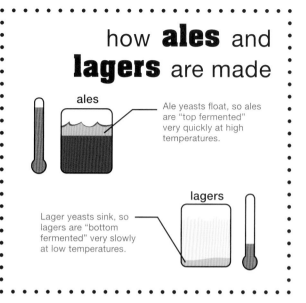

how **ales** and **lagers** are made

ales

Ale yeasts float, so ales are "top fermented" very quickly at high temperatures.

lagers

Lager yeasts sink, so lagers are "bottom fermented" very slowly at low temperatures.

art form of brewing. Brew enthusiasts in America and around the world suddenly found that the variety of beer available was very limited. We found ourselves with a few giant breweries making huge amounts of very similar beers. Because of this, beer had become homogenized and marginalized to such an extent that over 80 percent of the beer drunk all over the world was a slight variation on the exact same style: light lager.

The craft beer renaissance
The artisanal brewers who have popped up in the last 30 years and the idiosyncratic regional breweries that have survived throughout the world are changing all of that now. Old,

historic, indigenous styles are being reborn, and new styles are being invented as the craft brewing renaissance pushes us out of the dark ages of beer-style totalitarianism.

Beer is a beverage to get excited about tasting, enjoying, and sharing with friends. But, because of the proliferation of mass-produced light lager, some people still think of beer as more of a commodified staple: that is, a product like toothpaste or toilet paper, where

"New styles are being invented as the craft brewing renaissance pushes us out of the dark ages."

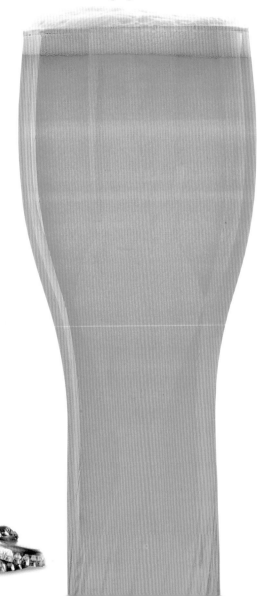

50

you pick a favorite off the shelf and stick with it throughout your entire life. This is a shame because these people haven't been exposed to the wide world of beer, and are missing out on one of the most exciting gastronomical trends coming of age around the globe today.

Quality of beer for quality of life

Today, most consumers know that a great, high-quality bottle of Pinot Noir can justifiably cost four times more than a mediocre bottle of Pinot Noir. That same consumer, the world over, is just beginning to understand that an amazing six-pack of strong, wood-aged beer, for example, can be a better value, at three times the cost, than a six-pack of cheap, mass-produced light lager. That's not to say there isn't a time and place to enjoy a light lager—all beer is good. For instance, I might pop a can of light beer after a hockey game or while mowing the lawn. But to pair with a wood-grilled steak? To celebrate an anniversary or a birthday? To pair with steamed mussels? To ring in the new year? There are as many amazing beer choices as there are celebration-worthy occasions in life.

The information in this book will help to expand your definition of what a beer can be, and how well different beers can be paired with a wide variety of foods. And, hopefully, after reading it, you will become—like me and the millions of other beer enthusiasts out there—evangelical in your passion for spreading the gospel of better beer.

beer
ingredients

The *Reinheitsgebot* or German Beer Purity Law of 1516 stated that beer must be made with only three ingredients: water, barley, and hops. Today, however, brewers in Germany and throughout the world make beer with a huge variety of ingredients—and so much the better!

Grains

The backbone of all beer is grains, since the sugars found in grains are the main source of fermentable sugars. Just within the family of grains used in brewing there is more diversity than there is in the varieties of grapes used in winemaking. Barley is the oldest and most common grain used in brewing beer. However, some beer brewers use wheat or rye as their primary ingredient, particularly when making specialties, such as wheat or rye beer.

Other grains include corn and rice, which are typically used by large-scale industrial breweries. These grains contribute less flavor than barley, wheat, or rye, and so are well-suited for making light lagers. They're also cheaper than barley, wheat, and rye.

Barley and malts

Among the grains used in beerbrewing, however, barley is considered king. Barley is also, usually, the most critical ingredient in contributing flavor to a particular beer. Through fermentation, barley contributes flavor, color, mouthfeel, body, sweetness, foaminess, and roastiness in varying levels for each different type of beer.

But unlike in winemaking, where the grape is used directly from the vine, barley cannot be used in its raw state for brewing. The barley must first be malted, which means the grains are hydrated, partially germinated, then slow-cooked to different levels of dryness and color.

This process converts the starch in the grain to sugar so that the yeast will have something yummy to eat and transform into alcohol. Malting imparts a range of depth and flavor to the grain, and it also provides enzymes which help to fuel the fermentation process.

There are many examples of malts, such as Pilsner, which gives beer a clean, sweet taste. Munich and Vienna malts impart rich flavors, such as caramel and toffee, respectively, whereas Crystal malt provides a nutty taste. Some specialty beers are brewed with highly kilned or toasted barley varieties, such as Black Patent and Chocolate (which contribute color, dryness, roastiness, and flavor reminiscent of chocolate) and Peat-smoked malt, which contributes whiskey-like smokiness to certain beers. Usually, the darker the malt is, the deeper and richer the flavor it will impart. To see what some of these malts look like, check out the table on page 53.

Sweeteners

While sweeteners, such as honey, maple syrup, or brown sugar can be added to a beer after it is boiled, the sugars of the grain itself will still be the main source of fermentable sugar in most beers. Usually, the more barley you use in a batch of beer, the more fermentable sugars will be present, and the more alcohol the final product will have. The average beer is about 4.5 percent alcohol by volume (often abbreviated in the drinks world

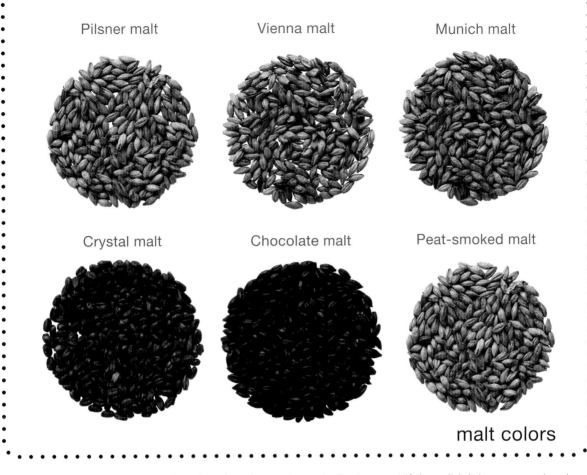

Pilsner malt

Vienna malt

Munich malt

Crystal malt

Chocolate malt

Peat-smoked malt

malt colors

as "abv"). However, there is a lot of excitement and growth in the beer industry today around stronger, more complex, food-friendly beers. And these beers typically have alcohol contents more often associated with the wine world (about 10–15 percent abv). For instance, the average beer coming out of my brewery, Dogfish Head, is over 9 percent abv, and the average beer coming out of Unibroue, a well-regarded Canadian brewery, is 7 percent abv.

Hops
A major ingredient in beer is hops. Hops *(see image, right)* are robust perennial plants with vines that sprout flowery cones. And, in the world of beer, hops are the ying to barley's yang. The spiciness and bitterness of hops counterbalances the sweetness of the barley. Even very light beers would taste cloyingly sweet if they didn't have some level of hop bitterness. A brewer uses hops in much the same way as a master chef would use salt, pepper, garlic, or herbs: as a spice.

In addition to the spiciness and bitterness hops impart, they also contribute the floral, grassy, and herbal aromas typical of beer. Hops naturally inhibit the growth of bacteria, too, which is why well-hopped beers have a longer shelf-life and are more durable than less "hoppy" beers. The earlier the hops are used in the brewing process, the more they will contribute flavor and bitterness. If hops are used later in the process, they will contribute more aroma and complexity.

All breweries add hops at the point where the beer is boiling, but many breweries also add hops to the beer after it is boiled and while it is cooling, or even after fermentation is complete. This is known as "dry-hopping".

Like hemp and nettles, hops are related to the cannabis plant. So, unsurprisingly, hops act as a mild sedative. Historically, it was not uncommon for restless sleepers to drink hop tea before bed time, or fill their pillowcases with hop leaves. So hops—and by extension, beer—literally mellow you out. I'm pretty sure that wine cannot make that same promise.

Hopping around the world

Unlike the delicate, highly particular grape vine, which can only grow well in certain exclusive regions of certain exclusive countries, the hop vine is a gregarious, outgoing, and expansive plant. There are hundreds of hop varieties that grow well throughout the world.

Some of the more prolific hop-growing parts of the world include the United States, Canada, Australia, New Zealand, the United Kingdom, the Czech Republic, France, Belgium, and Germany. A few of the more popular bittering hops include Northern Brewer, Challenger, Centennial, and Nugget. And some of the most cherished varieties of hops for aroma include Amarillo, Cascade, Fuggle, Hallertauer, Saaz, and Willamette.

Water

Okay, so water probably isn't anybody's idea of a fun ingredient (or a good time), but it has to be mentioned. This is because water is the most voluminous brewing ingredient found in beer, accounting for anywhere from 85 to 95 percent of a finished beer's volume. All breweries spend a lot of time testing, analyzing, and treating their water supply to get the perfect profile.

The mineral levels, pH balance, and salt content of the water will each have an effect on the brewing process in a different way. For instance, municipal water tends to be very high in chlorine, whereas well water tends to be high in minerals and iron. Chlorine is added to water as an antibacterial agent, but it can also slow yeast growth and its viability. Certain beer styles, such as Pilsners and Oktoberfests, taste best when made with low-mineral water, whereas other styles, such as Pale Ales and Saisons, taste the way they should when made with mineral-rich water.

Yeast

Yeast is a single-celled fungus that rapidly reproduces as it eats sugar, makes alcohol, and burps carbon dioxide. This is, in a nutshell, the process of fermentation. Sounds delicious, right? The yeasts that beer brewers use work in the same way as winemakers' yeasts. Different factors in the brewing process affect the yeast and fermentation profile of the beer in different ways. Factors that affect the beer include the amount of sugar present in the grain mash before fermentation occurs, the temperature of the beer, the volume of oxygen in the solution, the amount of and health of the yeast cells used, and the amount of alcohol in the beer as it ferments.

That's a lot to consider, but basically, when the alcohol the yeast is producing through fermentation reaches a certain strength it becomes toxic to the yeast, and kills it. This is why you don't have beer or wine that is as strong as gin or vodka. The natural process of fermentation can only take you into the high teens or early twenties as a percentage of alcohol—to get beyond this threshold, you must either distill (as with Bier Schnapps) or freeze (as with Ice Bock).

There are hundreds of different strains of yeast that have been isolated and sold by commercial yeast banks to breweries around the world. Add the hundreds of different yeast strands to the hundreds of different grains, malts, and hops, and you are now well into the hundreds of thousands of different ingredient permutations that brewers can play with in order to create a vast number of amazing, unique beers. All that, and we haven't even begun to discuss all the fun specialty ingredients yet!

Specialty ingredients

In addition to all the common brewing ingredients I've already described, there is a growing number of artisanal breweries around the world who are playing with more exotic ingredients. And this is where beer gets really exciting and leaves wine in the dust.

The tradition of spicing beers goes back to the beginning of civilization. Before hops were even domesticated and became the go-to "spice" for brewers around the world, people were using things like bog myrtle, spruce tips, grains of paradise, and saffron to spice their beers. Today, beer brewers are re-examining this tradition, and imparting their own modern twist. Some of the more common specialty ingredients used in beer making today are herbs and spices such as coriander, cloves, all-spice, nutmeg, orange peels, cinnamon, heather, and licorice. Specialty brewing ingredients, such as the few I've mentioned above, exponentially broaden the potential for complexity and diversity in beer brewing.

Extreme beers

The brewing of exotic beers is a movement from within the greater niche of craft beers. These beers are often referred to as "extreme beers". In my book of the same name, I defined extreme beers in this way: "Beers that are either brewed with an extreme volume of traditional ingredients (like Barleywines and Double IPAs), or beers that are brewed with non-traditional, exotic ingredients."

In addition to herbs and spices, many brewers are turning to exotic sugar sources to boost the alcohol content and complexity of their beers. These stronger, more intense beers are usually great replacements for wine at the dinner table since they have the body, mouthfeel, and richness of any wine you can find—and then some. Some of the popular non-grain sugar sources include honey, molasses, fruit, beet sugar, brown sugar, and maple syrup. So when you throw the hundreds of different spice, herb, fruit, and sugar possibilities and combinations onto the brewer's palette you can see that the huge range of ingredient diversity and complexity moves into the millions. As a reminder, on the wine side, grape varieties and appellations number in the thousands—at most. So now, armed with all this information, the question of whether beer or wine is the more complex and diverse beverage becomes a rhetorical one.

old & new world
brewing

With wine it is easy to draw geographical distinctions between the countries that represent the old and new world wine styles. But the idea of comparing old and new world brewing practices, traditions, and styles would seem impossible; almost impossible, but not quite. It just cannot be defined only by geography.

A state of mind, not a nation state

The difference between old and new world brewing can't be neatly summarized in a geography lesson. This is because, in Europe (a region that most Westerners would consider the old world), for example, there are countries such as Belgium, where more than 600 varieties of beer are made and centuries of innovative techniques and ingredients that have fueled a progressive beer culture. Meanwhile, not far away in Germany, beer brewing rules and regulations are much more stringently enforced, which of course, limits what brewers can do stylistically. This illustrates the great divide in beer cultures within Europe itself. This is indicative of an international reality. Old world versus new world in the context of beer brewing is more a matter of mindset than geography. In its simplest terms, old world brewing is characterized by homogeneity of style, whereas new world brewing is notable in the variety of beer

styles it offers. So, a traditional Pilsner can be a perfect example of new world brewing—as long as it's not the only style on offer by a particular brewing company.

One size does not fit all

In the context of beer brewing, I define old world as the mass-production tendency to simplify, commodify, and homogenize beer. Over time, the big breweries realized that the beer on the shelf might be cheaper, lighter, and easier to find if it didn't vary much from one six-pack to the next. And so the main result was the proliferation of the generic light lager. Big breweries got bigger, and small breweries, unable to brew with similar economies of scale, got destroyed.

In the United States, long before Prohibition, almost every town had a local brewery, in the same way that it had local butchers, bakers, and candlestick makers. Before Prohibition,

56

there were more than 1500 breweries in the United States. The beers brewed in each town reflected the ethnic background and evolving taste preferences of the townspeople. So the beers in different towns and regions were as unique and colorful as the people who lived there. Somewhat counter-intuitively, this period in pre-Prohibition era America better reflected the tenets of new beer brewing.

In the decades after Prohibition, though, the rise of mass-production and the aggressive expansion of larger breweries homogenized the styles of beer available to such an extent that, by the 1980's, there were fewer than 100 breweries in the country—and nearly all of them were selling slight variations of the same light lager. It would seem that America had all but lost its rich, diverse beer culture, and the same thing was happening around the globe. Thankfully, though, throughout the world beer drinkers revolted.

Variety is the spice of life
The new world brewer is one who is participating in, and contributing to, the movement toward fuller-flavored, diverse beers, and away from samey light lagers. The new world beer drinker is one who supports the diversity of beer and recognizes that a wide range of beers go better with different foods. Crucially, he or she realizes that size isn't everything, that small is the new big, and that handcrafted, small-batch breads, cheeses, yogurts, and beers might actually be more in line with their personal taste than mass-produced products.

Old is the new new
The craft brewing renaissance took hold in America in the late 1980's in response to this sentiment and, as a result, the beer landscape of the country changed dramatically. Soon, great craft breweries such as Sierra Nevada and Boston Beer were selling their beer all over the United States, which helped to restore a colorful spectrum of beers that reflected the diversity of the people.

And it didn't just happen in America, either. Homebrewing took off in countries around the world. A number of these homebrewers became skilled enough (and brave enough) to open their own boutique, artisanal craft breweries and fight the good fight against the dominance of light lagers. Not that light lagers are a bad thing. All beer is good, remember? But one style of beer should not dominate to such an extent that it obliterates all other styles. That just flattens the drinks landscape, and no beer enthusiast wants to see that happen.

Sea change
Organizations such as CAMRA (the Campaign for Real Ale) in the United Kingdom, the Brewer's Association in the United States, and Unionbirrai in Italy sprang up to recognize, promote, and protect the new world brewer. And importantly, the consumer stood up and said, "I'm bored as hell and I'm not going to take it any more". Beer drinkers demanded to have a choice in the kinds of beer that were available to drink and enjoy. In the same way that a person wouldn't eat the same thing day after day without eventually rebelling out of sheer boredom, beer drinkers around the world collectively revolted and demanded choice.

There will always be a big place for the old world of beer. Light lager isn't going away anytime soon—that's good news, because it's a style of beer that a lot of people enjoy. But, luckily, it isn't the only style of beer out there. And, because it is light and best served very cold, it is rarely the ideal choice to pair with food. The new world brewers, whether they run a third-generation brewhouse in Brussels or a brand new brewpub in Boston, have aligned in their passion to deliver exciting and unique beers to people throughout the world.

major
lager styles

Lagers are the world's most popular beers, inspired by Germany's exceptional brews. Lager yeasts ferment slowly at cool temperatures, and are cleaner and crisper, more clear and less fruity than ales. Lagers can range widely in color, flavor, and strength, but the vast majority are pale and light in body.

The lagers

The pale Pilsner style of lager originated in the Czech city of Plzen, where it was made with pale malts, Bavarian lager yeasts, and Saaz hops. Neighboring German brewers refined the Pilsner recipe with even paler malts and more bitter hops, and now the style is the most imitated on earth.

Amber and dark lager styles first emerged in Bavaria, in southern Germany, and largely remain regional specialties, less well-known abroad than paler Pilsners. But more and more breweries abroad are releasing darker lager styles. Most brewers follow the classic European styles, modeled on toasty amber seasonal lagers like Oktoberfest and Dunkel.

Strong lagers with more than 6 percent abv are known as Bock beers. Native to Germany, these beers are made with less water and more malt than usual. In Germany, Bocks are strong malty lagers; dark Doppelbocks and pale Maibocks are even stronger.

PALE LAGERS

STYLE PROFILE	Bright, light-bodied beers with crisp refreshing finish; pale yellow through deep gold; hop levels range widely All-barley malt brews are stronger in malt and hop flavors; large-scale brews often substitute cheaper grains, yielding more neutral flavor
FLAVOR SPECTRUM	Mass-market flavors: puffed rice, cornmeal, white bread Classic and craft flavors: cracked wheat, green herbs, black tea
TRADITIONAL STYLES	**Germany** eg: Helles, Pilsner, Lager, Dortmunder Export **Czech Republic** eg: Pilsner
MODERN STYLES	**United States and International** eg: Standard Lager, Light Beer, Steam Beer (USA), Rice Lager (Asia)

AMBER & DARK LAGERS

STYLE PROFILE	Clean-finishing mid-weight beers, ranging from amber to black As color deepens, toasty malt flavor often takes precedence over herbal hops
FLAVOR SPECTRUM	Amber flavors: toasted almond, carrot cake, honey Brown and black flavors: bran muffin, toffee, coffee
TRADITIONAL STYLES	**Germany** eg: Oktoberfest-Marzen (amber), Dunkel Lager (brown), Schwarzbier (black) **Austria** eg: Vienna Lager (amber)
MODERN STYLES	United States and International eg: Amber Lager, Dark Lager, Black Lager

STRONG LAGERS

STYLE PROFILE	Strong full-bodied, malty beers, ranging from golden to dark brown As alcohol climbs, beers get sweeter and richer in texture; hop bitterness ranges from moderate to strong
FLAVOR SPECTRUM	Pale color flavors: pound cake, crème caramel, butterscotch Dark color flavors: pecan pie, maltballs, dark rum, molasses
TRADITIONAL STYLES	**Germany** eg: Bock (dark), Maibock (pale), Doppelbock (dark)
MODERN STYLES	United States and International eg: Bock (dark), Doppelbock (dark), Imperial Pilsner (pale)

major **ale styles**

Top-fermenting ale yeasts generate a breadth of flavors and wild aromas that range from earthy to spicy, from fruity to downright funky, more like red wines. The artisanal craft beer renaissance is largely focused on ales, since these fuller-flavored, more colorful beers are remarkably complex and infinitely varied.

The ales

Copper-colored Pale Ale has a recognizable hop character and a nutty malt backbone, whereas India Pale Ale (IPA) is stronger and hoppier. American Pale Ale tends to be hoppier than the British original, while American IPA is stronger and more citrusy.

Dark Ales gain complexity and intensity from the use of dark barley malt, and they usually aren't very hoppy or strong. They range in color from reddish brown to black and can be anywhere on the sweet to bitter spectrum. Unlike Pale Ales, their bitterness usually comes from roasted barley instead of hops.

Strong Ales originally hail from Belgium and the UK. Belgian Abbey-style beers are grouped by strength: malty, caramelly Dubbels, strong, frothy Tripels, etc. British Strong Ales include potent Barleywines and Old Ales, and strong, sweet Imperial Stout. New world craft brewers use the term "Imperial" to denote turbo-charged spins on any existing style's recipe.

PALE ALES

STYLE PROFILE	Golden to copper-colored mid-weight beers, usually complex, highly hopped, fruity, and aromatic Traditional styles are more subtle, modern styles are bolder and hoppier
FLAVOR SPECTRUM	Subtle "classic" flavors: whole grain toast, dried herbs, hazelnuts Bold "modern" flavors: oatmeal cookie, citrus peel, fresh cedar
TRADITIONAL STYLES	United Kingdom eg: English Bitter, English Pale Ale, English Extra Special Bitter (ESB), English India Pale Ale (IPA) Belgium eg: Belgian Pale Ale, Farmhouse Ale, Saison
MODERN STYLES	United States and International eg: Pale Ale, India Pale Ale, Amber Ale, Cream Ale, Farmhouse Ale

DARK ALES

STYLE PROFILE	Light- and mid-weight beers ranging from garnet red to inky black, usually malty, complex, fruity, and mildly hopped *As color deepens, roasty malt flavor takes flavor precedence over herbal hops*
FLAVOR SPECTRUM	Red and brown flavors: raisin bread, sticky buns, chutney Black flavors: espresso, pumpernickel, bittersweet chocolate
TRADITIONAL STYLES	**United Kingdom** Red and brown, eg: English Mild, English Brown Ale, English Extra Special Ale (ESA), Irish Red Ale, Scottish Ale, Black, eg: English Porter, Dry Irish Stout, Sweet/Milk Stout **Belgium** Red and brown, eg: Belgian Dark Ale, Flemish Sour Ale
MODERN STYLES	**United States and International** Red and brown, eg: Red Ale, Brown Ale, Abbey Brown Ale Black, eg: Porter, Stout

STRONG ALES

STYLE PROFILE	Strong, full-bodied malty beers, usually ranging from golden yellow to inky black *As alcohol climbs, beers get sweeter and richer in texture; hop bitterness ranges widely*
FLAVOR SPECTRUM	Pale color flavors: apple cake, butterscotch, juniper berries Dark color flavors: fruit cake, chocolate caramels, mincemeat
TRADITIONAL STYLES	**United Kingdom** eg: Wee Heavy (red), Strong Ale (brown), Old Ale (amber), Barleywine (brown), Imperial Stout (black) **Belgium** eg: Strong Golden Ale (gold), Strong Dark Ale (brown), Trappist/Abbey Dubbel (brown), Trappist/Abbey Tripel (golden), Trappist/Abbey Quadrupel (brown)
MODERN STYLES	**United States and International** eg: Strong Ale, Golden Ale, Barleywine, Imperial India Pale Ale, Abbey-style Ales, Imperial Stout, Extreme Ales

specialty
beer styles

By adding special ingredients, brewers can create infinite flavor variations. Seasonality and experimentation play a greater role in the world of beer than in wine—we change the recipes because we can. Light wheat beers are incredibly refreshing on a hot day, and spiced beers banish a cold evening's chill.

Special styles

Wheat beers are ales, and they can be pale or dark, delicate or strong. Since wheat adds a refreshing snap to brews, the most popular are light-weight summer quenchers that are pale, dry, and food-friendly. Wheat brews may be hazy or downright cloudy in appearance.

The most notable spicy beers are Belgian ales, like Witbiers and Saisons. However, modern brewers are stepping outside tradition, adding exotic ingredients like chocolate or chilis, ginger or nutmeg to their beers. Since many of these ingredients are often used in cooking, they give these beers tremendous complexity and food-compatibility.

The most celebrated fruit beers, Belgian Lambics, are aged sour wheat beers made with wild yeasts. Most incorporate huge quantities of fruit, yielding a beer that tastes more like sparkling wine or cider. Elsewhere, modern brewers add fruit, like raspberries, to classic recipes, like Hefeweizens.

WHEAT BEERS

STYLE PROFILE	Cloudy beers ranging from yellow to brown, usually pale, light-weight, high in fruity yeast aromas, and refreshingly tart These ales are often low in hop character, and may be spiced or seasoned with fruit instead. Often a summer seasonal style
FLAVOR SPECTRUM	German-style flavors: banana bread, cloves, bread dough Belgian-style flavors: orange peel, coriander, soft cheese
TRADITIONAL STYLES	Germany eg: Hefeweizen (pale), Berliner Weisse (pale), Dunkel Weizen (dark), Weizenbock (strong) Belgium eg: Witbier (pale & spiced), Lambic (plain or fruited)
MODERN STYLES	United States and International eg: Wheat Beer, Hefeweizen, Wheat Wine

SPICED BEERS

STYLE PROFILE	Intense, aromatic beers ranging from golden yellow to dark brown; usually complex, full-bodied, and high in fruity yeast aromas Dessert spices are most common, but other botanicals or smoked malts may be used. Often a winter seasonal style
FLAVOR SPECTRUM	Dessert spices: nutmeg, cloves, cinnamon, all spice, star anise Other common seasonings: orange peel, coriander, peat-smoked malt
TRADITIONAL STYLES	Germany eg: Rauchbier (smoked malt) Belgium eg: Witbier (orange peel and coriander), Saison (often spiced)
MODERN STYLES	USA and International eg: Pumpkin Ale (dessert spice), Christmas Ale (dessert spice), Belgian-style Dark Ale (dessert spice), Smoked Ale (smoked malt), Experimental Ale (often spiced or seasoned)

FRUIT BEERS

STYLE PROFILE	Fruit-seasoned beers ranging from pale to dark, usually light-weight and tangy Most often wheat beers and lambics, frequently sweet, and dominated by fruit flavor and color
FLAVOR SPECTRUM	Traditional fruit flavors: raspberry, cherry, peach, blackcurrant Modern fruit flavors: raisin, pumpkin, apple, blueberry
TRADITIONAL STYLES	Belgium eg: Framboise Lambic (raspberry), Kriek Lambic (sour cherry), Pêche Lambic (peach), Cassis Lambic (blackcurrant)
MODERN STYLES	United States and International eg: Fruit-Wheat Beer, Fruit-Sour Ales, Experimental Ale, Pumpkin Ale, Cherry Stout

beer styles
by region

While any type of beer can be made well anywhere, it is interesting to see which beer styles are most strongly associated with particular regions of the world. The chart below is intended to give a very general idea of where some of the major beers styles are most commonly produced. (Note: this is not intended to be a comprehensive list.)

COUNTRIES	BEER STYLES — LAGERS	Pale/Pilsner	Steam Beer	Amber/Oktoberfest	Dark/Dunkel	Black/Schwarzbier	Bock/Doppelbock
UNITED KINGDOM	●						
CZECH REPUBLIC	●						
GERMANY	●		●	●	●	●	
BELGIUM	●						
FRANCE	●						
THE NETHERLANDS	●				●		
NORWAY/DENMARK	●						
ITALY	●		●				
AUSTRIA	●		●	●			
CANADA	●		●	●		●	
UNITED STATES	●	●	●	●	●	●	
MEXICO	●			●			
BRAZIL	●						
JAPAN	●			●	●		

64

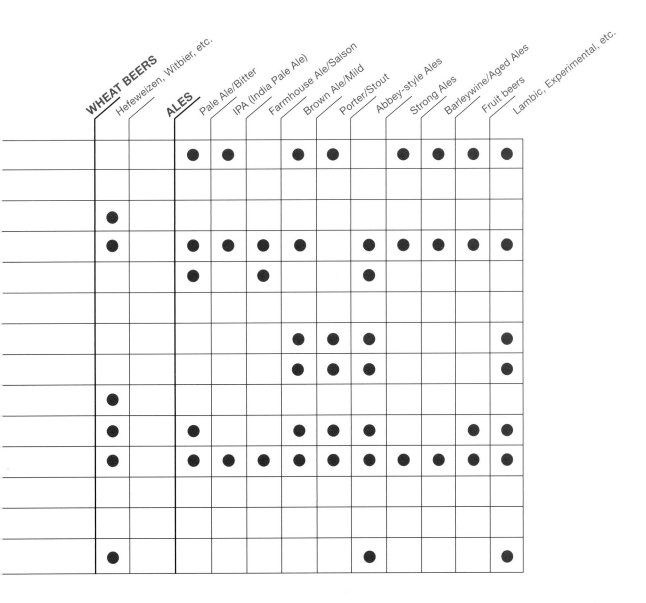

beer
tasting 101

The enjoyment of beer is, by nature, a subjective thing. If it weren't, the world would only need one style of beer to satisfy everyone. Thankfully, "that ain't happening", but there are some universal characteristics our senses recognize that can help guide us as we evaluate beer styles.

Setting up shop

When tasting a beer, it's important to remember that it is both a physical and psychological experience. This is why it's essential to consider atmosphere before moving on to the actual tasting.

Environment is important. You should aim to be in a neutral environment, which means no loud noise, obnoxious smells, uncomfortable temperature, or, most importantly, annoying people. Remember that drinking beer, at its best, is meant to be a relaxing and inviting social lubricant. Great beer is best enjoyed with great friends or, at least, with people you like. If you are surrounded by people you don't know (or, worse, those you dislike!), you may be too anxious or too unsettled to properly evaluate what you are drinking. Any of these environmental factors can interfere with your beer tasting.

Skip the background check

I don't think it's necessary to read up on a beer before you try it. The bottle's label will often give you the style of beer, and sometimes the alcohol content as well, and that should be a sufficient amount of information. You don't need to research a beer to fully enjoy it. Doing so will only tell you how other people perceive the beer, and not how you will experience it. In fact, it could even create a bias, thereby preventing you from forming your own opinion.

The five senses

Human beings have five major senses: sight, hearing, touch, taste, and smell. How these senses act and interact helps us to formulate our perception and evaluation of the beer we are tasting. Most of our perceptions are more or less objective, meaning everyone experiences them pretty much the same way. Whether a beer looks pale or dark, tastes sweet or bitter, feels thin or thick, fizzy or flat—these can all be ascertained by anyone.

Describing the smells and flavors our olfactory sense delivers can be more slippery, though. Two people will usually agree on whether a beer is bland or packed with flavor. But, if one describes the flavor as "clovey" and another says "cinnamony"—they're both right. Everyone's experience is subjective, or unique to themselves, when it comes to identifying

"I don't think it's necessary to read up on a beer. The label will give you a sufficient amount of information."

smells, but judging power is less nebulous. As Marnie already pointed out, when eating or drinking, the "flavor" we experience isn't "taste" alone—we simultaneously process stimuli through our sense of taste and smell. So when describing beer qualities in this book, we'll stick to objective territory—relatively constant qualities that are easy to identify, such as color, sweetness, and body. We'll throw in maltiness and yeastiness, but will assess them on an overall scale of intensity.

Touch—that's cold!

On to the heavenly liquid itself. First, you'll want to make sure you taste a beer at its ideal temperature. If the beer is served too cold, it will numb your tastebuds and impede your ability to perceive the subtle and enjoyable nuances of the beer. If the beer is served too warm, then the carbonation will quickly fade and the beer will go flat. Either one of these scenarios will interfere with your beer tasting.

While there may be specific stylistic exceptions, in general, the ideal temperature at which to enjoy a lager is going to be in the low 50's and the ideal temperature for an ale is going to be in the low 60's. You'll want to have water on hand to cleanse the palate and, if you're not doing the tasting in conjunction with a meal, some unsalted crackers, too. This small amount of food can be a big help for two major reasons: firstly, it helps to clear the palate between tasting beers, and secondly, it gets a bit of food in your stomach to absorb some of the alcohol.

Sound—listen to your beer

Hearing is probably the least important of your five senses in the context of a beer tasting, but even so, it's not irrelevant. Get your ear close to the bottle when you open it. As you open the bottle, you should hear that telltale "pop" or "ffft" that lets you know the beer has maintained its carbonation. If you don't hear that sound, it means the beer is low in carbonation—either intentionally or unintentionally. It will be thinner on the tongue and less effervescent, so it won't

taste or smell as good. In this way, it will be more like a wine than a beer. Beyond this, listening to your beer won't tell you much. There is no such thing as a beer-whisperer: someone who can glean everything you'd want to know about a beer by putting his ear next to the glass.

Sight—look at your beer

I can't think of any situation where drinking beer from the bottle or can makes more sense than drinking it from a glass—except where legal restrictions apply! While different breweries from different regions of the world will have differing opinions regarding the ideal glass for their beer, you can't go wrong with a red wine glass or a brandy snifter. The balloon shape of these glasses captures the aromas of the beer more effectively than traditional straight-side pint glasses—plus it reminds you that what you are drinking is a pretty damn special beverage, and therefore deserving of a special glass.

As you pour the beer, it's important to look for color (is it light or dark, red, yellow, or brown?) and also clarity. Some styles, such as Hefeweizen or Gueuze, are best served unfiltered, and so do have a desirable haze, but most beers should be quite clear. If you see chunks in your beer, then that's a pretty good indicator that it has spoiled. Some beers, however, are bottle-conditioned (carbonated naturally in the bottle with yeast) and will have a film or flakes of yeast on the bottom of a settled bottle. While the sediment isn't going to hurt you, it is usually a good idea to decant the beer in order to separate it from the yeast.

Smell—sniff your snifter

As you bring the glass of beer up to your nose, give it a slight swirl so that it coats the inside of the glass. This will help increase the surface area that the beer covers, which will make it easier to smell. Once you've done that, take a few short, sharp sniffs. The nose of the beer is going to be a compass toward the taste perception. Does the beer smell citrusy, grassy, or floral? If so, it will most likely be higher in hops than malt. If the beer smells toasty, sweet, or caramelly, then the brewer will have probably accentuated the malt component more than the hops.

It's important to bear in mind that different yeast strains can contribute vastly different aroma components to the beer. For example, Hefeweizens are notable for their banana, bready aroma. Belgian-style Ales, on the other hand, tend to have spicy notes due to the unique yeast strains they feature.

Touch—how a beer "feels"

The sense of touch is critical when evaluating things such as the body and carbonation of the beer. Take your first sip and actually chew the beer. I know this sounds weird, but close your lips and move your jaw and tongue a bit to make sure that beer coats the entire surface of the inside of your mouth. Through touch our brains are processing the body, or thickness, of the beer compared to the average drink we'd have, and also the heat or alcohol content, the carbonation, and the temperature of the beer.

Taste—sweet, sour, bitter

Take your second sip and this time breathe in at the same time that you pull the beer into your mouth. By doing this you are activating your smell and touch senses simultaneously, and maximizing your experience of the beer. Does the beer taste sweet, sour, or bitter? Taste is an objective sense concentrated in zones of the tongue (see diagram, opposite). Bitterness is most strongly perceived at the back of the tongue, while sweetness is more vividly tasted on the tip of the tongue, and acidity or sourness is experienced down the sides. (While some recent research suggests there may be more to it, it's generally accepted that this is how taste is perceived.)

Any nuance you detect beyond the above falls into the subjective realm of flavor. It might be perceived as taste, but in reality, your sense of smell is in the driver's seat. Even though the beer is now in your mouth, your olfactory glands are working hard to help you qualify the sensation: is the beer fruity, spicy, yeasty, or something else? Relax and enjoy sipping and smelling the beer that remains in your glass, and your mind will continue to process the experience as it warms your heart and soul.

Practice makes perfect

No one is born an expert at tasting beer. It is a matter of nurture over nature, and you can condition your palate and your brain to improve your ability. The more different beers you try, the more your memory has to work with as it puts a new beer experience into context.

As you try a new beer your brain searches its memory for similar taste experiences. So the more different beers you try, the more you expand your mental library of beer experiences and the better a taster you become; just another reason why life is too short to be married to the same old beer. Cheating on your go-to beer is actually good for you!

TASTING AND EVALUATING BEER:
a step-by-step summary

1. LISTEN TO YOUR BEER AS YOU OPEN IT
What kind of sound does it make when you open the bottle or can?

2. LOOK AT THE BEER IN YOUR GLASS
What color is it? Is it hazy or clear? Does it have chunks or sediment in it?

3. SWIRL THE BEER IN THE GLASS AND TAKE A FEW SHARP SNIFFS
Is it mild or intense? Does it remind you of anything? Does it smell citrusy, grassy, or flowery? Or does it smell fruity, sweet, or caramelly?

4. TAKE YOUR FIRST SIP
Take a mouthful of beer and "chew on it". Make sure it coats the entire inside of your mouth—tongue, palate, and gums. Is it very fizzy or less so? Does it feel watery or more "thick" and viscous?

5. TAKE YOUR SECOND SIP
Take a mouthful of beer, while breathing in at the same time. Which parts of your tongue (*see diagram below*) feel most stimulated: the back (bitterness), the sides (sourness or acidity), or the tip (sweetness)? What flavors emerge from the interplay between your senses of taste and smell?

6. DO IT AGAIN WITH ANOTHER BEER SOON
Practice will make you even better!

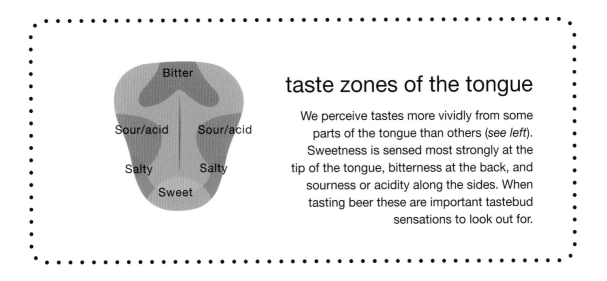

taste zones of the tongue

We perceive tastes more vividly from some parts of the tongue than others (*see left*). Sweetness is sensed most strongly at the tip of the tongue, bitterness at the back, and sourness or acidity along the sides. When tasting beer these are important tastebud sensations to look out for.

the food debate

about
food pairing

Old adages like "white wine with fish, red wine with meat" should be taken as friendly advice, rather than restrictions. Most foods taste great with most quality wines and beers. But many people feel bewildered when faced with pairing food and drink. Experimenting is delicious fun, but here are some useful guidelines on how to choose what to drink with your meal.

Flattering partnerships

The culinary world abounds with classic pairings. But tastes are not universal, and there is no definitive list of the perfect combinations that will suit everyone's subjective preferences. However, every bite or sip we take changes the way we perceive the next flavor, often in predictable ways. There are objective patterns to the sensory interactions that beverages have with food. A few guidelines can help improve the odds of finding great food and drink pairings.

Matching intensity

When food pairing, we must first assess the dish's lightness or heaviness (based on its fat content) and flavor intensity. Beverages should be matched to the strongest flavors on the plate, and most often the sauce and preparation are the dominant features. For example, roasted chicken will be less intense than curried chicken.

Next, we need to choose a wine or beer style that is similar in intensity to our dish. The overall intensity of a wine is based primarily on its body and the power of its olfactory flavor components: fruit and oak. A low- to high-intensity spectrum of wines would range as follows: sparkling wine (the least intense), white wines, red wines, and fortified wines (the most intense).

Overall intensity in beer is based on its body and flavor strength (which can come from malt and hops). Sweetness can make brews seem stronger, while sourness can make them seem lighter. A low- to high-intensity spectrum of styles would range as follows: wheat beers (the least intense), Lambics, lagers, ales, Stouts, and Strong Ales (the most intense).

How the senses operate

When similar elements are present in the flavor of both the beverage and the food, they tend to balance rather than amplify one another. This generally has a flattering, harmonizing effect. For example, when acidic wine is served with an acidic food, it softens, rather than intensifies, the total impression of acidity. When a sweet, malty beer is served with sweet food, both seem less sweet together than they do alone. Olfactory sensations and physical sensations interact in a similar fashion. For example, smoked foods served with oaky wines or roasty beers seem less extreme together than they do alone; herbal sauces served with wines with herbal aromatics or highly hopped beers seem less "green" together; rich foods served with full-bodied wines or rich, strong beers feel less "thick" together than they do alone. This pattern is useful to remember when matching beverages with foods.

Some exceptions to remember

Among taste sensations, saltiness neutralizes our perception of sourness and vice versa. So, beverages taste less acidic paired with salty foods and foods seem less salty served with acidic wines and beers. Sugar, on the other hand, has nearly the opposite effect, making acidity seem more prominent. Beverages served with sugary foods taste more sour and less sweet; foods served with sugary drinks seem more sour and less sweet too.

Since salt and sugar are such kitchen staples, this helps explain why wines can seem so different with and without food, while beers tend to experience a less dramatic flavor shift. All wines are acidic, while most beers aren't. Many wines seem a little too "sour" when tasted alone, and even more so with sugary foods. Most wines are designed with

" Every bite or sip we take changes the way we perceive the next flavor, often in predictable ways. "

savory foods in mind, whose salt will soften their sharp acidity. Beers, which are generally low in acid, are not affected as strongly by either salt or sugar. This allows a beer to retain flavors more consistent with its first impression when paired with food.

Fatty foods pair best with wines and beers that provide a counterbalancing effect. In red wines, tannin is the key (derived from grape skins and stems), imparting an astringency that helps rich foods seem less oily. In beer, hops have a similar influence, cutting the perceived greasiness of a rich dish. Lastly, since alcohol intensifies the "burning" sensation of spicy heat, spicy foods are difficult to pair with the strongest drinks. Averaging less than half of wine's alcohol content, beer is a traditional partner with the spiciest cuisines.

wine,

beer

& cheese

Cheese is its own universe, encompassing flavors as different as night and day. From intensely pungent Roquefort to mild goat cheese, the tastes and textures of cheeses run the culinary gamut. Luckily, wine and beer are just as diverse, and can offer enough range to keep pace. Whether it's an aged Cheddar or an earthy Brie, rest assured that there is always a perfect beer and wine to complement any cheese you choose. All you have to do is discover which flavor combinations you like best. What better way to spend an afternoon or spark conversation?

wine & cheese

Wine and cheese are classic partners, like Bogart and Bacall or Hepburn and Tracy. They are so thoroughly awesome together that we've named special parties after the fabulous "wine and cheese" combo. Few foods can flatter wine as dramatically as cheese, and wine can return the favor. Beer should be so lucky!

The x-factor
It shouldn't be a surprise that wine and cheese, two famously fermented products, go so well together: the flavors that are created in the process of making wine and making cheese certainly have some things in common. However, that alone doesn't explain the incredible synergy found between cheese and wine. If that were all there was to it, beer would be just as good a cheese partner, but the truth is, it can't quite measure up.

Perfect chemistry
The secret to the legendary affinity of wine and cheese is rooted in sensory science, and it is easy to understand if you think back to high school chemistry. Wine is bracingly tart and refreshing thanks to the acidity of its raw material—tangy fresh grapes. Cheese, on the other hand, is a salty food, a property that gets stronger as cheese ages.

If you remember the pH scale, acidity is the exact opposite of saltiness, since all salts are "bases". It makes sense, then, that wine provides the perfect balancing opposition to refresh the palate. Not only do salt and

acid neutralize one another in nature, but our senses follow suit. Saltiness and acidity, two of the five things we can actually "taste" with the tongue alone (*see pp42–45*), are both perceived by the tastebuds. But salt and acid seem to block one another on the palate, as if both were competing for the attention of the same receptors. When we taste both cheese and wine back and forth, the salt in the cheese counteracts wine's acidity and the acid in wine blocks cheese's saltiness. The overall effect mellows the flavor of both in one of the all-time classic pairings of wine and food. Beer's greatest failing as a food partner is its lack of acidity, the characteristic that gives wine its food-friendly edge and long lingering finish.

Fat is not a four-letter word
The other universal cheese component is dairy fat, which gives cheeses their luxurious texture. Wine's snappy tang and dry finish are perfect foils for rich foods like cheese, and cheese can do even better in return. Red wines can have a mouth-drying quality that comes from grape skins and oak barrels. Tannin is the compound responsible, a phenol

"From the mildest Brie to the fiercest blue, all CHEESES TASTE TERRIFIC with most wines."

that's also found in things like walnuts and tea. This sensation can be unpleasant, almost a flavor barrier, when tannic wines are paired with low-fat foods. But, in the presence of oils or fats, like those found in cheese, tannin can act to pleasantly balance the "greasy" sensation of eating rich foods.

With wine's refreshingly sharp acidity and the tannic "grip" of reds, there's a natural harmony found between wine and cheese. From the mildest Brie to the fiercest blue, all cheeses taste terrific with most wines, but some combinations are simply mind-blowing. Beer with cheese may taste good, but it cannot compete with the riveting, almost electric stimulation found with wine and cheese. And, as with all of history's classic partnerships, you can feel the sparks fly.

Pairing particulars

While most people think of cheese as calling for strong red wine, that combination most often flatters the wine more than the cheese, whose nuances can get lost. As with most wine and food pairings, the first step is to gauge the flavor intensity of the food, and then pair like with like. So, the most delicate cheeses call for the most subtle wines, and the most intense cheeses need far bolder wine flavors. Lighter, brighter wines, and unoaked white wines in particular, can be a sound choice when tasting a sampling of different cheeses.

Young, fresh cheeses typically fare best with young, fresh wines. On the other end of the spectrum, the caramelization of flavor that occurs as hard cheeses mature tends to pair well with wines that have spent time aging on their lees or in oak barrels.

Picking a winner

If you're unsure about which wine to choose for cheese, white wines and medium-bodied reds are generally the best all-around performers. High-acid wines, such as white wines, "old world" wines (see pp32–33), and cool climate wines, have a natural advantage as cheese partners. And while dry wines tend to be the standard choice for cheese, sweet dessert wines paired with extremely salty, fatty cheeses can be a revelation.

rules of thumb
wine for cheese

The dots on this chart represent some simplified rules on the characteristics to look out for when pairing wine with cheese. There can be exceptions to the rules and, where applicable, these are mentioned in the text below each entry. On a scale of one to five the dots below represent the suggested intensity of a wine's objective characteristics. Five dots indicate a very strong characteristic, while one dot means that the property is less prominent.

BODY ● ● ● ●
Exception: Young, mild cheeses can pair well with lighter wines.

SWEET ● ●
Exception: Salty, fatty blue cheeses can pair well with sweet wines.

ACID ● ● ● ●

FRUIT ● ● ●

OAK ● ● ●

*TANNIN ● ● ●

*Tannin is only found in red wine.

wine & cheese pairings

In the world of food pairing, wine and cheese are superstars. They both benefit from their huge variety of styles and flavors. Because of this incredible range (and because they are so well-suited to one another), the permutations for wine and cheese pairings are almost endless, but here are a few of my top pairing picks.

1 | MOZZARELLA &
Maschio Brut Prosecco

For a subtle mozzarella whose pleasures are mostly in its mouthfeel, my first choice is a wine that mirrors these qualities—a subtle wine whose bubbles provide delightful texture. Maschio's Prosecco is a bright, light-bodied sparkling wine from northern Italy with flavors reminiscent of fresh-picked apples.
This works too: Australian Unwooded Chardonnay

2 | GOAT CHEESE &
Jolivet Chateau du Nozay Sancerre

Goat cheese's yogurty sourness needs an extra-sharp wine to stand up to it. This Sauvignon Blanc from the French town of Sancerre is bracingly tart, bone-dry, medium-bodied, and full of stony, herbal aromatics, free from toasty oak. Hard-edged and lean when tasted alone, this Sancerre from Jolivet blooms with goat cheeses, particularly aged versions.
This works too: California Pinot Noir Rosé

BRIE & | 3
Chehalem Reserve Pinot Gris

Brie's opulent texture and "bloomy" rind is delightful when paired with white wines aged on their lees to boost flavor. The ample body of Chehalem's gorgeous Pinot Gris from Oregon combines a luscious mouthfeel with flavors of orchard fruits such as nectarine, and the faint accents of freshly baked bread echo Brie's yeasty flavor beautifully.
This works too: French Champagne

4 | SHARP AGED CHEDDAR &
Blandy's 10 Year Old Malmsey Madeira

Aged cheddar is one of the world's most stunning cheeses. Sharp and salty, it shines with a vast range of wines. My favorite is sweet fortified Malmsey from the island of Madeira off North Africa. Blandy's tasty 10 Year Old combines the vibrancy of tangerines with the caramelized goodness of hard toffee.

This works too: Chilean Cabernet Sauvignon

5 | PARMIGIANO REGGIANO &
McWilliam's Cabernet Sauvignon

Australia's cool coastal zones produce Cabernets, such as this one by McWilliam's, with "tart and tannic" Italianate qualities that shine with "real Parm". This savory cheese bounces off the wild and woodsy berry flavors of the Cabernet brilliantly, and both compete for your attention in a game of gastronomic ping pong.

This works too: Italian Chianti

6 | ROQUEFORT &
Zenato Amarone

Blue cheeses, such as Roquefort, have epic concentrations of flavor, salt, and fat, and can easily overwhelm "normal" wines. I choose freakishly intense wines to match, like this full-bodied Italian Amarone from Zenato. Its dense fig and molasses flavors give Amarone a fighting chance to tame the wild "bleu".

This works too: French Sauternes

specific wines
objective characteristics

This chart lists each suggested wine's objective characteristics, as described by the number of dots used. Five dots indicate a very strong characteristic, while one dot means that the property is less prominent. Zero dots indicate that the characteristic is not present.

1. Maschio Brut Prosecco
Pairs well with mozzarella.

Body	●
Sweet	● ● ● ●
Acid	● ● ● ●
Fruit	● ●
Oak	

2. Jolivet Chateau du Nozay Sancerre
Pairs well with goat cheese.

Body	● ● ●
Sweet	●
Acid	● ● ● ●
Fruit	● ●
Oak	

3. Chehalem Reserve Pinot Gris
Pairs well with Brie.

Body	● ● ● ●
Sweet	● ● ●
Acid	● ● ●
Fruit	● ● ● ●
Oak	●

4. Blandy's 10 Year Old Madeira
Pairs well with sharp aged Cheddar.

Body	● ● ● ● ●
Sweet	● ● ● ●
Acid	● ● ● ●
Fruit	● ● ● ●
Oak	● ● ●

5. McWilliam's Cabernet Sauvignon
Pairs well with Parmigiano Reggiano.

Body	● ● ● ●
Sweet	● ●
Acid	● ● ●
Fruit	● ● ● ●
Oak	● ● ●
Tannin	● ● ● ●

6. Zenato Amarone
Pairs well with Roquefort.

Body	● ● ● ●
Sweet	● ● ●
Acid	● ● ●
Fruit	● ● ● ● ●
Oak	● ● ●
Tannin	● ● ● ●

beer
& cheese

Beer with cheese is a classic flavor combination, and the two are closely tied—something that the wisest Christian monks knew long ago. Historically, some Western European monasteries often made both beers and cheeses, and today, many modern breweries make and sell their own cheeses and beers.

A pairing made in heaven
It's not just the European monks who have all the fun! People all over the world have cottoned on to the sublime combination of beer and cheese. In the United States, for example, there are many breweries that also produce cheese.

Perhaps the most well-known American hybrid artisanal producer is Fritz Maytag, the owner of Anchor Brewing Company in San Francisco. This brewing company produces fantastic beer, but is also responsible for making the well-respected Maytag Blue Cheese.

Similarities: the pros and the cons
There is good reason that beer and cheese pair so well together. As with wine, there are similarities in the way cheese and beer are made. There are basically three stages in both beer and cheese production. In brewing beer there is mashing, boiling, and fermenting. In cheese-making, the process involves production, reduction, and ripening. The higher a beer is in alcohol, the longer its finish will last. And similarly, the harder a cheese is,

the longer it, too, will last. Unfortunately the trend toward giant, industrial, multinational beer producers is mirrored in the world of cheese as well. Big beer and cheese producers tend to pasteurize and homogenize their products. Pasteurization—the process of heating something up to a temperature at which no bacteria can survive—does extend the shelf life of a beer or a cheese. Unfortunately, it also neuters its flavor and complexity.

Think high-quality, low volume
Industrially processed cheeses also tend to contain cheap filler ingredients, in much the same way that some big breweries skimp on high-quality ingredients and use cheaper filler grains. However, as the craft brewing renaissance has taken hold around the globe, support for high-quality, artisanal cheeses is surging too. So seek out these kinds of beers and cheeses for optimum pairing results. And remember, the best way to buy your cheese is fresh from the block or wheel, sliced right before your eyes.

"My favorite cheeses come from Belgium, Italy, and America—three countries with fantastic beer cultures."

My favorite cheeses come from Belgium, Italy, and America—three countries with fantastic beer cultures. Coincidence? I think not. It almost goes without saying that if you can pair your cheese with a beer from the same country, you're on to a winner.

Gauging intensity

A good rule of thumb is to pair beer and cheese of similar intensities. So, light, soft cheeses, such as goat cheese or Mascarpone work well with lighter beers like Hefeweizens, Pilsners, or Belgian Wit beers. Sharp, hard cheeses like Cheddar work nicely with well-hopped beer styles like India Pale Ale, English Brown Ale, or American Amber Ale. Soft-ripened, but flavorful and velvety Brie or Camembert pair nicely with fruit beers. Both sweet and sour fruit beers work equally well with these cheeses. Look for sweet fruit beers, such as raspberry wheat beers, and sour fruit beers, such as Belgian Lambic fruit beer or Berliner Weisse.

The big guns

When you amp up the flavor intensity of your cheese, you'll need a more assertive beer style. For example, smoky cheeses, such as Gouda, need a dark, roasty beer, such as a Porter or a Dry Stout. For the strongest cheeses available, which include stinky, blue-veined varieties such as Roquefort, Stilton, and Gorgonzola, you should opt for very powerful beers. Match these cheeses with beers such as English Barleywines or Double Pilsners, and the pairing won't let you down. Having said that, a Russian Imperial Stout is also burly enough to stand up to and complement the flavors found in these strong cheeses.

rules of thumb
beer for cheese

The dots on this chart represent some simplified rules on the characteristics to look out for when pairing beer with cheese. There can be exceptions to the rules and, where applicable, these are mentioned in the text below each entry. On a scale of one to five the dots below represent the suggested intensity of a beer's objective characteristics. Five dots indicate a very strong characteristic, while one dot means that the property is less prominent.

COLOR ● ●

SWEET ● ● ● ●
Exception: Rich, aged cheeses can pair well with sweeter beers.

BODY ● ● ●
Exception: Young, fresh cheeses can pair well with lighter-bodied beers.

YEAST ● ●

HOPS ● ●

beer & cheese pairings

When pairing beer with cheese, start with the most subtle combinations and progressively work your way up to the more full-flavored pairings in order to avoid overwhelming your palate. For maximum flavor, serve your beer cool, but not cold, and your cheese at room temperature.

1

MOZZARELLA &
Wittekerke White Beer

Mozzarella is one of the lighter cheeses, both in flavor and fat content. So, it makes sense that it tastes great with a lighter beer style, such as Belgian White Beer. Bavik Wittekerke White Beer is a mildly spicy, light-bodied beer. Its clean, snappy finish will complement, rather than overpower, the subtle flavor of the mozzarella.
This works too: Hefeweizen

2

GOAT CHEESE &
Penn Hefeweizen

Goat cheese is another type of cheese that has a delicate flavor, so choose a lighter beer style, such as an American Hefeweizen. A great one to try is Pennsylvania Brewing Company's Penn Hefeweizen. This beer succeeds because it's crisp and light-bodied with a hint of sweetness and spice that perfectly offset the mellow goat cheese.
This works too: Continental Pilsner

3

BRIE &
Cantillon Kriek Lambic

A flavorful, ripe, and velvety cheese such as Brie (and Camembert, too) will almost always pair very nicely with fruit beers, both sweet and tart. My favorite flavor combination, however, is Brie with Cantillon Kriek Lambic, a Belgian Lambic fruit beer. This dry cherry beer is tart, rather than sweet, and its astringency counterbalances the rich creaminess of the Brie.
This works too: Berliner Weisse

4

SHARP AGED CHEDDAR &
Harpoon IPA

Hard, sharp cheeses such as Cheddar require a beer style that can really stand up to strong flavors. India Pale Ales work a treat in this department. A great pairing partner is Harpoon IPA, which is hoppy and slightly sweet, with subtle apple flavors.
This works too: English Brown Ale

5

PARMIGIANO REGGIANO &
Anderson Valley Boont Amber

For intensely flavored, hard cheeses, such as Parmigiano Reggiano, an American Amber Ale is an ideal partner. A good one to try is Anderson Valley Boont Amber, which is roasty and rich, but smooth at the same time. It's also malty enough to handle the strong flavors present in the cheese.
This works too: India Pale Ale

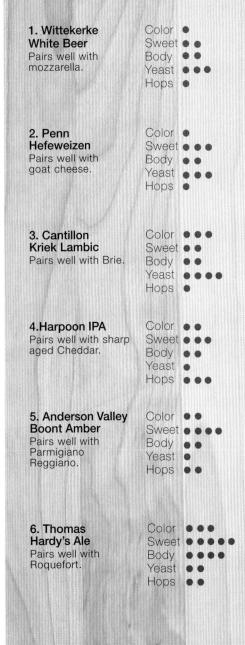

6

ROQUEFORT &
Thomas Hardy's Ale

Big, stinky cheeses such as Roquefort (as well as Gorgonzola and Stilton) are not for the faint of heart, and definitely not for subtle beers. These cheeses can be tamed, though, by a powerful, flavorful beer style such as British Strong or Old Ale. Full bodied, smoky, and fruity, Thomas Hardy's Ale is a great match for a really strong Roquefort.
This works too: Russian Imperial Stout

specific beers
objective characteristics

The chart below lists each suggested beer's objective characteristics, as described by the number of dots used. Five dots indicate a very strong characteristic, while one dot means that the property is less prominent.

1. Wittekerke White Beer
Pairs well with mozzarella.

Color	●
Sweet	● ●
Body	● ● ●
Yeast	● ● ● ●
Hops	●

2. Penn Hefeweizen
Pairs well with goat cheese.

Color	●
Sweet	● ● ●
Body	● ●
Yeast	● ● ●
Hops	●

3. Cantillon Kriek Lambic
Pairs well with Brie.

Color	● ● ●
Sweet	● ●
Body	● ●
Yeast	● ● ● ● ●
Hops	●

4. Harpoon IPA
Pairs well with sharp aged Cheddar.

Color	● ●
Sweet	● ● ●
Body	● ●
Yeast	●
Hops	● ● ●

5. Anderson Valley Boont Amber
Pairs well with Parmigiano Reggiano.

Color	● ● ● ●
Sweet	● ● ● ●
Body	● ● ●
Yeast	●
Hops	● ●

6. Thomas Hardy's Ale
Pairs well with Roquefort.

Color	● ● ●
Sweet	● ● ● ● ●
Body	● ● ● ●
Yeast	● ●
Hops	● ●

which **drink** wins

Marnie and Sam will each state their case for wine or beer, but there has to be a winner for each pairing. Conduct your own beer, wine, and food tasting, and choose which drink wins on the score card at right.

There are no more **PERFECT PARTNERS** in the realm of food and beverage pairing than wine and cheese. There's a reason we have "wine and cheese" parties, and not "beer and cheese" parties!

Yeah, we do have beer and cheese parties—what do you drink with pizza when your friends come over to watch the game? I'll give you a hint—**it isn't wine.** Pizza is nothing more than a giant melted cheese sandwich.

Nice, Sam, lots of nuance. We're talking about real cheese, not Cheez with a "z"! Natural cheeses come in a huge range of flavors, but all have two wine-friendly components—salt and fat. Wine has a sharp, **acidic backbone** (sadly lacking in beer) that provides an ideal counterpoint for cheese.

While the traditional light lager can't cut the cheese with grace and aplomb, there are some **AMAZINGLY TART,** "acidic" beers that are up to the task. Belgian Lambics, Berliner Weisses, and American wheat beers come immediately to mind.

Marnie

So your argument is that only rare, wine-like beers stand up to a good cheese? May I quote you on that? All wine is terrific with all cheese, while, as you say, only rare, specialty beers make for **outstanding pairings.**

These beer styles have been **around for centuries** and are hardly rare. Beer and cheese are such great partners that there are world-famous cheeses made by beer brewers, such as Maytag Blue from California's Anchor Brewing company.

There's not one winery whose claim to fame is cheese, but if brewers **have to resort** to making cheese to earn a living...

Okay, Marnie, there is an overlap between wine and cheese production—that processed, **port-wine-esque shwag.** Of course, the overlap between beer and cheese is more perfect and pure: the Trappist monks (who make both) certainly think so.

Sam

you choose
which wins

After you've tasted each cheese with every wine and beer, use this score card to keep track of which combinations you prefer.

	Wine	**Beer**
Mozzarella	☐	☐
Goat cheese	☐	☐
Brie	☐	☐
Sharp aged Cheddar	☐	☐
Parmigiano Reggiano	☐	☐
Roquefort	☐	☐

wine, beer & vegetables

Vegetables are the crowning jewel in Mother Nature's crown. They come in a rainbow of colors, and a vast range of flavors and textures. And the vegetable kingdom is full of surprises. Each season brings something new, from light, peppery arugula and sweet, ripe tomatoes in the warmer months to hearty butternut squash and meaty eggplant in the cooler months. In fact, the only way you can improve on a delicious, nutritious vegetable dish is to pair it with a perfect beer or wine.

wine
& vegetables

Fruits and vegetables are plant foods and, since wine is made from fruit, it's not surprising that it's a terrific partner for most vegetables. Most often, in fact, wine and vegetables taste better together than they do on their own, from simple salads to vegetarian entrées.

Like with like
Which style of wine works best with a particular vegetable will depend on factors such as the vegetable's flavor and color. It will also depend on whether the vegetable is cooked or served raw, as well as how the dish is seasoned. As with all the food groups, our natural instinct to pair light with light and heavy with heavy is right on the money. Bright, tangy vegetable dishes work best with bright, tangy wines. On the flipside, richer, more flavorful recipes merit deeper, richer wine partners.

The naturals
Some vegetables are so wine-friendly that it's hard to go wrong. For example, most wines are superb with Mediterranean staples such as tomatoes, onions, and olives, while other vegetables, such as potatoes and squash, are more of a blank slate, over which cooking methods and seasonings assert their dominance. In these circumstances, we take our wine cues from the dish's strongest flavors, often from the sauce more than from the "neutral" main ingredient—that is, the vegetable itself.

Temperamental veggies
To be honest, though, not all marriages between wine and vegetables are blissful. A few vegetables, such as those in the cabbage family, can be finicky, requiring patience to find pleasing combinations. And, in a cruel

twist of fate, a couple of the very worst veggie offenders rank among the culinary elite of vegetables. Both the slender asparagus and the portly artichoke can be self-centered, often leaving their wine partners tasting strangely off-balance and askew.

Family ties
Fruits and vegetables are such close relations within the plant family that lines can blur in distinguishing the two. Most fruits, like grapes and oranges, are a plant's reproductive organ, usually tasty edible flesh cushioning precious seeds. Vegetables, on the other hand, run the gamut of "plant parts".

Vegetables can be leaves like lettuce, stems like celery, roots like turnips, or flowers like broccoli. Some are even technically the "fruits" of their plants, like cucumbers and bell peppers. In practice, though, the fruit-vegetable boundary is drawn between dinner and dessert. In other words, it is based more on how we eat them rather than by their botanical classification. We generally consider plant foods to be "fruits" when they taste sweet and "vegetables" when they don't.

Color coordinating

Believe it or not, our fashion instincts for matching colors can produce terrific results in matching wines to vegetable dishes. For example, golden yellow corn shines with golden white wines like Chardonnay. Beets taste "purple", and work beautifully with young violet-tinged red wines like Beaujolais.

Harmonizing flavors

In addition to color, we can add the sound strategies we use with any food group—pairing wines whose aromas are in sync with the "taste" of our veggies. It follows, then, that earthy wines like Pinot Noir, for instance, are brilliant with the funky fungus flavors of wild mushrooms. However, as noted earlier, sometimes the preparation or seasoning of a dish will trump the main ingredient. One example of a vegetable's pairing partner being determined by the preparation method is the humble pea. A tart Sauvignon Blanc is absolutely lovely with a snappy snow pea salad, while pea soup with ham can hold its own with deeper, darker reds like Bordeaux blends.

Cooking method matters

Fresh, raw vegetables tend to favor "fresh" young wines, especially those with bright, primary fruit flavors, like whites fermented in stainless steel rather than oak barrels. Vegetables that are cooked in butter or caramelized will be more in tune with wines enriched in oak barrels than veggies we serve raw. These factors can lead us to choose radically different wines for dishes based on the same vegetable. Whether a white or red wine is a better choice for a food will largely depend on the specific dish and how it is made.

rules of thumb
wine for vegetables

The dots on this chart represent some simplified rules on the characteristics to look out for when pairing wine with vegetables. There can be exceptions to the rules and, where applicable, these are mentioned in the text below each entry. On a scale of one to five the dots below represent the suggested intensity of a wine's objective characteristics. Five dots indicate a very strong characteristic, while one dot means that the property is less prominent.

BODY ● ●
Exception: Rich vegetable dishes can pair well with stronger wines.

SWEET ● ●
Exception: Sweet vegetable dishes can pair well with sweeter wines.

ACID ● ● ● ●
Exception: Sweet vegetable dishes can pair well with less acidic wines.

FRUIT ● ● ●

OAK ●
Exception: Grilled or buttered vegetables can pair well with oakier wines.

*TANNIN ●
Exception: Oily vegetable dishes can pair well with more tannic reds.

*Tannin is only found in red wine.

wine &
vegetable pairings

Vegetables come in a rainbow of flavors, quite literally. We can "taste" color, and nowhere more vividly than among vegetables. Keep this in mind when looking for a vegetable's perfect wine partner. Below, I've applied this same logic for some of my favorite wine and vegetable pairings.

1 GREEN SALAD &
Nora Albariño

A light, acidic dish like this one requires a light, acidic wine. This Spanish Albariño hails from cool, moist Galicia, or "Green Spain", where low ripeness yields spritzy white wines with low alcohol and zingy acidity. Nora is one of my favorite green salad wines, thanks to its faintly "green" flavors: green apple with herbal accents.
This works too: New Zealand Sauvignon Blanc

2 TOMATO SALAD &
Tiefenbrunner
Pinot Grigio

Both sweet and tart, tomatoes can be unkind to lean, bone-dry wines, favoring riper styles instead. While many wines are tomato-friendly, I prefer understated whites that won't upstage these juicy little divas, such as Tiefenbrunner Pinot Grigio from northern Italy. As subtly refreshing as a fresh-picked pear, the best Pinot Grigios have delicate aromas of pine nuts and white tea.
This works too:
Washington Merlot

CAESAR SALAD & 3
Sterling Vintner's Collection
Sauvignon Blanc

Caesar dressing boosts the intensity of crisp romaine lettuce. Mid-weight white wines with bold aromatics are terrific partners for this classic. My favorite pairing is a Sauvignon Blanc from warm, sunny California, where this grape ripens fully. This one from Sterling has a citrusy backbone and herbal aromas that are softened by a melon-like richness.
This works too:
French Macon-Villages

4 | EGGPLANT PARMESAN &
Concha y Toro Casillero del Diablo Merlot

With this dish, it is the tomato sauce and melted cheese that give us our wine pairing cues. Chilean Merlots are exceptionally well-suited to vegetables in herbed tomato sauces. This value from Concha y Toro combines the dark sweet berry notes with savory aromas of black olive and fire-roasted peppers.
This works too: Italian Barbera

5 | FRENCH FRIES &
Domaine Carneros Sparkling Wine

For French fries, nothing beats "Champagne method" sparkling wine, especially this one from California. Not as dry as French Champagne, this wine has a more generous mouthfeel. A bracing contrast of cold bubbles to the fries' hot oil, this "yeast-aged" wine harmonizes well with toasty fried starch.
This works too: Australian Chardonnay

6 | GARLICKY SPINACH &
Schloss Gobelsburg Gobelsburger Grüner Veltliner

Few wines are as game for greens like sautéed garlicky spinach as Austria's tongue-twisting Grüner Veltliner. Similar to Sauvignon Blanc in many ways, this one has aromatics that evoke martini olives, celery seed, and white pepper.
This works too: French Red Bordeaux

---

specific wines
objective characteristics

This chart lists each suggested wine's objective characteristics, as described by the number of dots used. Five dots indicate a very strong characteristic, while one dot means that the property is less prominent. Zero dots indicate that the characteristic is not present.

1. Nora Albariño
Pairs well with green salad.

	Dots
Body	●●
Sweet	●●●
Acid	●●●●
Fruit	●●●
Oak	

2. Tiefenbrunner Pinot Grigio
Pairs well with tomato salad.

	Dots
Body	●●●
Sweet	●●
Acid	●●●●
Fruit	●●●●
Oak	

3. Sterling Vintner's Collection Sauvignon Blanc
Pairs well with Caesar salad.

	Dots
Body	●●●
Sweet	●●
Acid	●●●●
Fruit	●●●●
Oak	●●●

4. Concha y Toro Casillero del Diablo Merlot
Pairs well with eggplant Parmesan.

	Dots
Body	●●●●
Sweet	●●
Acid	●●●
Fruit	●●●●
Oak	●●●
Tannin	●●

5. Domaine Carneros Sparkling Wine
Pairs well with french fries.

	Dots
Body	●●●
Sweet	●●●
Acid	●●●●
Fruit	●
Oak	

6. Schloss Gobelsburg Gobelsburger Grüner Veltliner
Pairs well with garlicky spinach.

	Dots
Body	●●●
Sweet	●●
Acid	●●●●
Fruit	●●●
Oak	

beer
& vegetables

Both beer and vegetables are loaded with healthy stuff. In ancient Egypt, beer was actually administered as medicine; and, in recent centuries, doctors would recommend that patients drink Stout, which is relatively low in alcohol but high in nutrients. As two nutritious, delicious treats, beer and vegetables just go together.

An acquired taste

Whenever my wife reminds me that I should eat my vegetables "because they're good for me", I have a cringe-inducing childhood flashback. Kids' palates just seem to be naturally calibrated to prefer sweet flavors, rather than bitter ones.

Generally speaking, vegetables (especially when raw) are less sweet than other foods. However, as we get older and our tastes become more sophisticated, we begin to appreciate the subtle nuances of vegetables. Luckily for adults, vegetables are perfect partners for healthy, vibrant beers.

The vegetable's dominant flavor

All beers and foods have dominant sensual characteristics that come from their flavor and texture or body. And vegetables are no exception. From astringent, light-bodied spinach to lush, creamy, and heavy winter squashes, vegetables come in a huge variety of flavors and textures. When you cook a vegetable, and season it with sauces and preparations, this will also affect the vegetable's dominant sensual characteristics.

It's these most prominent flavors and textures in a dish that you should consider when seeking out a beer partner. And a good rule of thumb is to pair like with like. Since beer styles are as diverse as any food category out there, there will always be an appropriate beer for a given vegetable dish.

Fresh, light, and tangy vegetables

Light, fresh vegetables—especially those that are high in acid, such as tomatoes or onions—call for a beer with similar properties. Tart Lambic beers, such as Lindeman's Cuvée René, generally have a refreshing and mouth-watering acidic component, so they will flatter your vegetable dish—and vice versa.

But, that's not to say that Lambics are the only appropriate beer style for acidic vegetables. A nice wheat beer will fare just as well—and sometimes better, in certain instances. For example, the most common component in salad dressings is vinegar, which is extremely acidic. Vinegar and wheat beers, such as Berliner Weisse, couldn't get along better. This is because the food and the beer share a dominant central component of tart and acidic dryness, so they harmonize well with one another. (Just an aside for salad fans: vinegar and wine fight like cats and dogs!)

Preparation is key

When a vegetable is roasted, smoked, or caramelized, its flavor profile changes dramatically. You only need to compare a fresh bell pepper with a roasted one, or a fresh onion with a caramelized one to taste the difference.

The process of roasting and caramelizing actually makes a vegetable taste sweeter, while smoking imparts a rich, hearty flavor. So, not surprisingly, the criteria for a good beer partner change accordingly. A Porter has the right stuff for these types of dishes. Porters are typically made with dark malted barley, which gives them a deep, dry, roasty character. These rich, smoky beers echo the flavors found in roasted, smoked, and caramelized vegetables, and pair impressively with them.

Hearty vegetables

Some vegetables are meatier and heartier than others, especially when they are baked or stuffed with an ingredient like cheese. These vegetable dishes, which include stuffed mushrooms and baked eggplant Parmesan, are best paired with stronger, "meatier" lagers and ales. Strong, dark lagers and ales will be complex enough to do these sorts of dishes justice. This type of balanced pairing will also ensure that neither the dish nor the beer will be overwhelmed.

rules of thumb
beer for vegetables

The dots on this chart represent some simplified rules on the characteristics to look out for when pairing beer with vegetables. There can be exceptions to the rules and, where applicable, these are mentioned in the text below each entry. On a scale of one to five the dots below represent the suggested intensity of a beer's objective characteristics. Five dots indicate a very strong characteristic, while one dot means that the property is less prominent.

COLOR ● ●

SWEET ● ●
Exception: Vegetable dishes with sweeter sauces can pair well with sweeter beers.

BODY ● ●
Exception: Richer vegetable dishes can pair well with stronger beers.

YEAST ● ● ● ●
Exception: Crisp, raw vegetables can pair well with low-yeast beers.

HOPS ● ● ●

beer & vegetable pairings

The world of beer can offer a perfect partner for any kind of vegetable. For the best pairings, always consider the properties of the vegetable itself (light or meaty, astringent or sweet), and how it has been prepared (raw or roasted, caramelized or cooked). Then choose your beer to match like with like.

1

GREEN SALAD &
Rodenbach Red
A green salad, chock full of astringent, bitter lettuce leaves and drizzled with a vinegar-based dressing, needs a flavorful beer that is high in acidity. For simple salads like this one, a Belgian Red Ale can work wonderfully. This Belgian Ale from Rodenbach is tart and acidic, and infused with the flavor of sour cherries.
This works too:
Bière de Garde

2

TOMATO SALAD &
Lindeman's Cuvée René
The tomato, the veggie star of this salad, is fresh and sweet, but also acidic. Mirroring both of these properties in your beer selection is a good pairing tactic. Try Cuvée René, a well-respected and highly coveted Belgian Gueuze Lambic from Lindemans.
This works too: Belgian Sour Brown Ale

3

CAESAR SALAD &
Dogfish Head Festina Pêche
The hallmark of a good Caesar salad is its piquant dressing. Its anchovies also make it quite a salty treat. Festina Pêche, a tart Berliner Weisse from Dogfish Head, will heighten this dish's flavors.
This works too: American Brown Ale

4
EGGPLANT PARMESAN &
Negra Modelo

Eggplant Parmesan is a hearty vegetable recipe, rich with baked, cheesy goodness. A dish like this one needs an equally assertive and complex beer. Try Negra Modelo, a dark lager from Mexico.
This works too: English Brown Ale

5
FRENCH FRIES &
Short's Anniversary Ale

Believe it or not, the crisp, starchy French fry is actually a member of the veggie food group. Nothing complements a side of freshly made fries quite as well as a malty Imperial IPA, such as Anniversary Ale from Short's Brewing Company.
This works too: Dry Stout

6
GARLICKY SPINACH &
Allagash White

Spinach and garlic are wonderfully healthy foods. But, since they're both naturally astringent, they'll need a beer that harmonizes rather than competes with them. A spicy Belgian-style wheat beer fits the bill. A good one to try is Allagash White from the Allagash Brewing Company.
This works too: Berliner Weisse

specific beers
objective characteristics

The chart below lists each suggested beer's objective characteristics, as described by the number of dots used. Five dots indicate a very strong characteristic, while one dot means that the property is less prominent.

1. Rodenbach Red
Pairs well with green salad.

Color	••
Sweet	•••
Body	•••
Yeast	•••
Hops	•

2. Lindeman's Cuvée René
Pairs well with tomato salad.

Color	•••
Sweet	••
Body	••
Yeast	•••••
Hops	•

3. Dogfish Head Festina Pêche
Pairs well with Caesar salad.

Color	•
Sweet	•
Body	••
Yeast	••••
Hops	•

4. Negra Modelo
Pairs well with eggplant Parmesan.

Color	•••
Sweet	•••
Body	•
Yeast	•
Hops	•

5. Short's Anniversary Ale
Pairs well with French fries.

Color	••
Sweet	••
Body	•••
Yeast	••
Hops	••••

6. Allagash White
Pairs well with garlicky spinach.

Color	•
Sweet	••
Body	•••
Yeast	••••
Hops	•

which **drink** wins

Marnie and Sam will each state their case for wine or beer, but there has to be a winner for each pairing. Conduct your own beer, wine, and food tasting, and choose which drink wins on the score card at right.

Beer is a cold, mind-altering, vegetarian barley soup—it's **like GUY-spacho**. Besides, all beer contains a certain amount of vegetation: hops.

Whether it's corn, tomatoes, or beans, wine showcases vegetables' fresh-picked flavors better than beer, since **wine's vibrancy** comes from the natural preservative action of fresh fruit acidity.

Marnie, beer is all about freshness. After all, beer, not wine, comes with freshness dating. And which beverage commands **more cooler space** at the store—wine or beer?

Just because a product spoils faster doesn't mean it tastes fresher! Beer is made with dried grain and dried hops, and its taste evokes the dry goods shelf, not the produce aisle. The only reason you guys get more cooler space is that **unsold beer takes up so much room**.

Sam

Yes, beer particularly takes up a lot of room at the dinner table when it's time to find the perfect partner for a veggie dish. All wine geeks know that vegetables and wine are **mortal enemies**.

Those antiquated rules are SO last century! All food is fresher now, and most modern wines are vibrant and tangy. Unoaked whites and young reds are **remarkably good** with veggies.

These new-age wines may now be welcome in the veggie kingdom, but beer is still sitting on the **veggie throne**.

Live in the past all you like, Sam. Blando beer may be fine with blando vegetables, but for those of us hooked on flavor complexity, **wine wins hands down**. Achieving similar results with beer would amount to a royal pain in the arse, your highness.

Marnie

you choose
which wins

After you've tasted each dish with every wine and beer, use this score card to keep track of which combinations you prefer.

	Wine	**Beer**
Green salad	☐	☐
Tomato salad	☐	☐
Caesar salad	☐	☐
Eggplant Parmesan	☐	☐
French fries	☐	☐
Garlicky spinach	☐	☐

wine, beer
& sandwiches

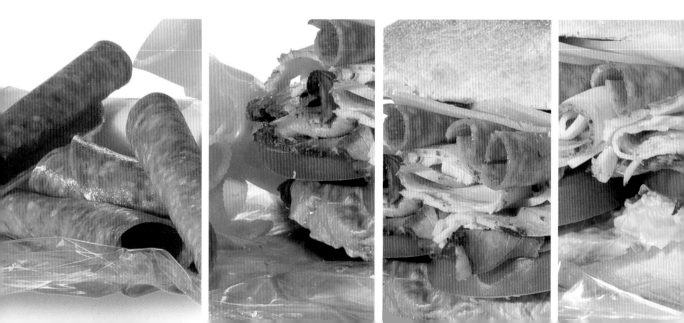

Ah, the sandwich—what an ingenious triumph of food engineering! Since they encase even the messiest foods in a nutritious edible "wrapper" and free us from the pesky need for utensils, sandwiches may qualify as the world's most convenient food. Easy to make, easy to pack, and easy to eat, they adapt as well to the dinner table as they do to a mountain peak. Bread can be layered around just about anything good to eat. Other than soup, it's tough to find a food you can't make into a sandwich. From burgers to falafel, it's difficult to think of a more popular food category than the sandwich.

wine & sandwiches

Sandwiches are as varied as the world of food itself—you can put almost anything between two slices of bread. From sprouts to barbequed pork, the humble sandwich does it all. And wherever there's bread, you'll find some local variation on this simple dish. Luckily, wine is varied enough to complement any sandwich.

A perfect combo

Wine has proven itself to be the ultimate food partner among alcoholic beverages. Neither beer nor distilled spirits can match wine's ability to balance food's myriad components. Wine can both satiate and pique the appetite, and it can also taste terrific and flatter food at the same time.

No other beverage can match wine's capacity for amplifying the gastronomic pleasures of eating and drinking. That said, there seems to be a widespread misconception that wine is not the best partner for sandwiches. I hate to disappoint all the nay-sayers out there, but this couldn't be further from the truth.

It's only logical

It's unclear to me how anyone could doubt that wine's superiority extends to the realm of sandwiches. Why would it matter where the bread is—wrapped around the meat or on the side, or whether you need a fork to get the food into your mouth? If wine is the best food partner, then wine must clearly be best with sandwiches as well.

But, many people fall into a trap when it comes to pairing drinks with sandwiches. They focus on the casual one-handed delivery system, the absence of utensils, and then decide that wine is too "fancy" to serve with a sandwich. Nonsense. This is faulty logic—an outdated bias whose usefulness is long past.

Changing perceptions

Wines may once have been a rare and costly delicacy, reserved for special occasions. But, the wine world has changed dramatically in recent decades. Where affordable wines were once dire, now delicious fruit-forward wines are widely available at prices per serving that rival cheap beer. Preconceptions about the high price and rarity of "decent wine" no longer reflect the reality of the 21st century.

Yes, sandwiches conjure images of paper plates and tables without cloths in the mind's eye. But, that is no reason to rule out wine as a great sandwich partner. One bite of a meatball sandwich with a yummy red wine, or a BLT with a toasty white wine, and all our prejudices melt away.

So, if wine is a more appetizing food partner (as we know it is), and better equipped than other beverages to flatter savory flavors and refresh between bites, then why punish the palate with beer? Go ahead—pull a cork; pour some wine. You deserve the best.

The filling's the thing

Since virtually all foods are wine-friendly, it makes sense that virtually all sandwiches will work well with wine. Of course, bread may be what makes a sandwich a sandwich, but in pairing wines it's important to look at the ingredients that lie between the buns for cues. Because of the vast range of sandwich fillings, there are no hard and fast rules for choosing wines to serve with them. Having said that, though, there are some general guidelines worth considering.

Identify the strongest flavor

The most dominant flavor is always what guides us as we make wine choices, and sandwiches are no exception. Among sandwiches, the core flavors are usually the protein component, such as meat, fish, or fowl, but also (and especially) the sauces or preparations used to "season" it. As with all wine and food pairing, we generally put the lightest wines with the lightest foods; that is, foods low in fats or oils and subtle in overall flavor. As richness and flavor both increase, we can look to stronger and more flavorful wines.

Compare and contrast

Other standard wine pairing patterns, such as if and how the food is cooked, hold true as well. So, for example, toasted or grilled sandwiches, or those with smoked fillings, are those most suited to oaky wines, white or red. For sandwich fillings seasoned with sharp,

> **❝Why punish the palate with beer? Go ahead—pull a cork; pour some wine. You deserve the best.❞**

tangy sauces such as mustard or balsamic vinegar, you should opt for equally sharp wine partners. And, of course, the saltier a sandwich is, the more acidic its wine partner needs to be. (Remember from the cheese pairing section on pages 76–79 that salt and acids act to balance and mellow one another.)

Fillings that have sweet flavors, such as ketchup, barbeque sauce, jams, and chutneys favor wines that are not fully dry. Most often, shooting to "echo" the sandwich flavors with similar tastes in the wine is a sound strategy. However, for a refreshing change of pace, sometimes a direct contrast can work, too.

rules of thumb
wine for sandwiches

The dots on this chart represent some simplified rules on the characteristics to look out for when pairing wine with sandwiches. There can be exceptions to the rules and, where applicable, these are mentioned in the text below each entry. On a scale of one to five the dots below represent the suggested intensity of a wine's objective characteristics. Five dots indicate a very strong characteristic, while one dot means that the property is less prominent.

BODY ● ● ●
Exception: Hot sandwiches can pair well with stronger wines.

SWEET ● ●
Exception: Sugary sandwich sauces can pair well with sweeter wines.

ACID ● ●

FRUIT ● ● ●

OAK ● ● ●
Exception: Smoked flavors can pair well with oakier wines.

*TANNIN ● ●

*Tannin is only found in red wine.

wine & sandwich pairings

Once you try wine as a sandwich partner, you'll never go back. Any kind of food can go in the middle of a sandwich. Since wine is the world's finest food partner, wine and sandwiches are a terrific match. Once we bring wine down off its pedestal, it can show us how well it suits any kind of sandwich you can imagine.

1 | TRADITIONAL BURGER &
Penfolds Thomas Hyland Shiraz

Australian Shiraz is dense with dark, rich, spiced fruit flavors, balanced with a quenching tang. This modest offering from iconic Penfolds is quintessential Shiraz, so dark it looks more aggressive than it really is. Soft and plump in the mouth, packed with blackberry jam flavors, it is an ideal pairing for burgers and their sweet-tart condiments, like ketchup and pickles.
This works too: California Petite Sirah

2 | TURKEY CLUB &
Casa Lapostolle Chardonnay

The delicacy of low-fat turkey calls for a white wine partner, and the smoky bacon always leads me toward barrel-fermented wines with a touch of toasty oak, such as a cool climate Chardonnay. I favor the snappy, refreshing styles that hail from coastal Chile, like this Casa Lapostolle. They are as bright and crisp as Golden Delicious apples and fresh white corn.
This works too: Italian Chardonnay

FALAFEL PITA & | 3
Vega Sindoa El Chaparral

Falafel can work with white or red wine, depending on your toppings. A red wine, Spanish Garnacha, is a favorite, though. Multi-dimensional in flavor, wines like El Chaparral combine a sweet core of stewed red fruit with aromas of Moroccan spices that embrace falafel's garlicky goodness.
This works too: Australian Semillon/Chardonnay

4 | ITALIAN SUB &
M. Chapoutier Belleruche Côtes-du-Rhône
Few wines are as well-suited to this sandwich as a simple Côtes-du-Rhône, like this one from Michel Chapoutier. Its "cured meaty" aromas aren't far removed from those of your cold cuts. Savory without feeling heavy, this red delivers flavor and refreshment in equal measure.
This works too: Italian Salice Salentino

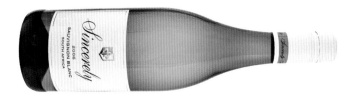

5 | TUNA SALAD &
Neil Ellis Sincerely Sauvignon Blanc
Tuna salad needs a sharp partner to cut through its mayo base. Citrusy South African Sauvignon Blancs, like this one from Neil Ellis, are my favorites. South Africa's take on this grape is less austere than the Loire Valley's, and less tropical than New Zealand's. Its grapefruity edge of acidity is bracing between bites.
This works too: Italian Prosecco

6 | ROAST BEEF &
Hogue Genesis Cabernet Sauvignon
Beef needs a muscular red wine like Cabernet Sauvignon. If served cold with horseradish, wines from the cooler end of the grape's climate range, where cedary Cabernet retains its "herbal" edge, fare best. In Washington State, "fruity" and "woodsy" coexist in harmony, as this Cabernet from Hogue shows so well.
This works too: French St. Emilion

---

specific wines
objective characteristics

This chart lists each suggested wine's objective characteristics, as described by the number of dots used. Five dots indicate a very strong characteristic, while one dot means that the property is less prominent. Zero dots indicate that the characteristic is not present.

1. Penfolds Thomas Hyland Shiraz
Pairs well with a traditional burger.

Body	••••
Sweet	••
Acid	•••
Fruit	•••••
Oak	•••
Tannin	••

2. Casa Lapostolle Chardonnay
Pairs well with a turkey club.

Body	••••
Sweet	••
Acid	•••
Fruit	•••
Oak	•••

3. Vega Sindoa El Chaparral
Pairs well with a falafel pita.

Body	•••
Sweet	•
Acid	•••
Fruit	••••
Oak	•••
Tannin	••

4. M. Chapoutier Belleruche Côtes-du-Rhône
Pairs well with an Italian sub.

Body	••••
Sweet	•
Acid	•••
Fruit	•••
Oak	••
Tannin	••

5. Neil Ellis Sincerely Sauvignon Blanc
Pairs well with a tuna salad sandwich.

Body	•••
Sweet	•
Acid	•••••
Fruit	••••
Oak	

6. Hogue Genesis Cabernet Sauvignon
Pairs well with a roast beef sandwich.

Body	••••
Sweet	•
Acid	•••
Fruit	•••
Oak	•••
Tannin	•••••

beer
& sandwiches

At my restaurant, we serve all kinds of food, but our sandwiches are best-sellers—even at dinner time. And, of course, everybody orders beer with their burgers. This combination is so popular because sandwiches and beer go together like, well, sandwiches and beer. In other words, it's an instinctive pairing.

Match point
Sandwiches are all about uncomplicated but pleasurable eating. And sandwiches just work with the uncomplicated but pleasurable quaffing of beer. I'd feel weird swirling and sipping a fancy wine then chomping on a cheesesteak and I doubt I'm alone. But there's more to this no-brainer pairing than instinct.

Bread is the common ingredient for almost every kind of sandwich. It's baked from the flour of grain—barley, wheat, rye, you name it. When made well, bread is pure, simple, sumptuous sustenance. Grain is also common to the beverage that pairs best with sandwiches. You guessed it—beer. Grain is the principle building block of sandwiches and beer, the platform from which additional ingredients stage their assault.

Start with the bread
In the realm of bread, there are yeasty breads (such as sourdough), spicy breads (such as rye), and bitter-flavored breads (such as pumpernickel). Similarly, there are yeasty, spicy, and bitter beers. Wine can't bond with sandwiches in the way beer can because it doesn't speak the language of grain.

Once you know which kind of bread you'll be using with your sandwich, you have your first cue for which beer to choose. With the bread element, pairing similar flavors is a sound strategy—so, a yeasty bread with yeasty beer, a spicy bread with a spicy beer, and so on.

The filling: light-weight or heavy?
The next step is to gauge the heaviness or lightness of the sandwich filling, and match it to that of the beer. So, a fatty grilled burger will require a big, full-flavored beer, such as an English Brown Ale. On the flipside, light fare, such as a watercress sandwich, will pair best with a light-bodied beer, such as a Hefeweizen. On the light-to-heavy scale, a chicken salad sandwich would fall somewhere between these two, and a mid-weight Pale Ale would be a good partner.

104

Contrasting and matching flavors

In addition to the filling's heaviness, the most forward-flavor component of your sandwich will lead you to the ultimate beer partner. Many sandwiches incorporate condiments, relishes, or other ingredients beyond the main protein component. When the primary flavor is a subtle one, try a beer with contrasting flavors for exciting results. For example, a simple lobster roll is usually made with a dash of mayonnaise, but the dominant flavor comes from the subtly sweet, salty lobster meat itself. In this case, the sandwich will benefit from a contrasting pairing, such as a well-hopped (but light) IPA.

Pairing beer and sandwiches with similar flavors will work better if the most dominant flavor of the dish comes from a strong, pungent

"I'd feel weird swirling and sipping a fancy wine then CHOMPING ON A CHEESESTEAK and I doubt I'm alone."

sauce or condiment. So, a sweet Texas-style barbeque sandwich will nestle right up to a sweet, strong Belgian Dubbel. With the more sour and acidic Carolina-style barbeque sandwich, look to a more sour and acidic beer, such as a Flemish Red Ale.

The wonderstuff

Hops and grain are the keys to great food and beer pairings. Depending on the variety, hops can add spicy, citrusy, grassy, or even cheesy complexity to a beer, and specialty grains impart a roasty or chocolatey character. Once you're able to identify these flavors, they can be coordinated with the flavors of the protein, sauces, and condiments in your sandwich for sublime results.

rules of thumb
beer for sandwiches

The dots on this chart represent some simplified rules on the characteristics to look out for when pairing beer with sandwiches. There can be exceptions to the rules and, where applicable, these are mentioned in the text below each entry. On a scale of one to five the dots below represent the suggested intensity of a beer's objective characteristics. Five dots indicate a very strong characteristic, while one dot means that the property is less prominent.

COLOR ● ●

SWEET ● ●

BODY ● ● ●
Exception: Hot sandwiches can pair well with stronger beers.

YEAST ● ●

HOPS ● ●

beer & sandwich pairings

A sandwich is a wonderful partner for beer. When choosing a beer for a sandwich, consider both the heaviness of the filling, as well as the flavoring of the filling. Subtle filling flavors warrant a beer with contrasting flavors, while powerful, assertive flavors should be matched with a similarly strong beer partner.

1
TRADITIONAL BURGER &
Dogfish Head Indian Brown Ale

The best burgers are a bit greasy, so you need a beer with more color and alcohol than a light lager. The alcohol cuts through the fat, and the color, derived from dark malted barley, gives the beer both sweetness and dryness. Dogfish Head Indian Brown Ale has the caramelized character of a Scotch Ale, a dark chocolatey hue derived from specialty barleys, the hops of an IPA, and nearly twice the alcohol of a light lager.

This works too: Munich Lager

2
TURKEY CLUB &
Stoudt's Blonde Double Maibock

A turkey club is lighter and more acidic than a burger, so you don't want to go too dark or too bitter with your beer choice. For a great complementary pairing, try the smooth, nutty-sweet Double Maibock from Stoudt's Brewery in Pennsylvania.

This works too: Dunkelweisse

3
FALAFEL AND PITA &
Trappistes Rochefort 8

With falafel, the accompanying sauce is key to its overall flavor. I have seen falafels garnished with a sesame Tahini sauce, but the most popular topping tends to be a mint-yogurt sauce. The creaminess of the yogurt is tough on most wines, but a well-carbonated beer is just the thing to de-coat your tongue between bites. The Belgian Abbey Ale, Rochefort 8, is robust, dry, and fruity—the perfect contrast to the creamy sweetness of the yogurt sauce.

This works too: Czech Pilsner

106

4
ITALIAN SUB &
Warsteiner Premium Verum

To complement the Italian sub's herbal and peppery components, opt for a drier, lighter beer with a subtle hop spice. A lighter Continental Pilsner, Warsteiner Premium Verum is hoppy and dry enough to bring the varying flavors of this sandwich into harmony.

This works too: Scotch Ale

5
TUNA SALAD SANDWICH &
XX Bitter Golden Ale

A beer brimming with hops and alcohol will reign in the creamy mayonnaise in tuna salad. The De Ranke XX Bitter is super-hoppy, but it's not a one-trick hop-pony. It has a yeasty note that works well with the bread, and an acidic note that nestles up to the celery in the salad, too.

This works too: Belgian-style White Beer

6
ROAST BEEF SANDWICH &
Great Lakes Eliot Ness Vienna Lager

With this rich sandwich, opt for a Vienna-style Lager like the famous Eliot Ness lager. It offers the caramelized notes of darker malts and a palate-cleansing dryness from the healthy addition of noble hops.

This works too: Rye Ale

specific beers
objective characteristics

The chart below lists each suggested beer's objective characteristics, as described by the number of dots used. Five dots indicate a very strong characteristic, while one dot means that the property is less prominent.

1. Dogfish Head Indian Brown Ale
Pairs well with a traditional burger.

Color	● ● ●
Sweet	● ● ●
Body	● ● ●
Yeast	● ●
Hops	● ● ●

2. Stoudt's Blonde Double Maibock
Pairs well with a turkey club.

Color	● ●
Sweet	● ● ●
Body	● ● ●
Yeast	● ●
Hops	● ●

3. Trappistes Rochefort 8
Pairs well with a falafel and pita.

Color	● ●
Sweet	● ●
Body	● ● ●
Yeast	● ● ●
Hops	● ●

4. Warsteiner Premium Verum
Pairs well with an Italian sub.

Color	●
Sweet	● ●
Body	● ●
Yeast	● ● ●
Hops	● ●

5. XX Bitter Golden Ale
Pairs well with a tuna salad sandwich.

Color	● ●
Sweet	●
Body	● ● ●
Yeast	● ● ●
Hops	● ● ● ●

6. Great Lakes Eliot Ness Vienna Lager
Pairs well with a roast beef sandwich.

Color	● ●
Sweet	● ●
Body	● ●
Yeast	●
Hops	● ●

which **drink** wins

Marnie and Sam will each state their case for wine or beer, but there has to be a winner for each pairing. Conduct your own beer, wine, and food tasting, and choose which drink wins on the score card at right.

It used to be that wine was only for fancy food, but as we make better sandwiches, it's no wonder people are choosing better beverages, too. Wine is a **natural upgrade** for sandwiches— as comfy with a burger as a BLT.

What could be more comfy than a beer, a burger, and a football game on the TV? Sandwiches all have one thing in common— bread. Beer is **liquid bread**. 'Nuff said.

I'll freely grant sandwiches to the beer column as long as you stick to **baloney** on processed white bread. But, bun or no bun, juicy hamburgers cry out for rich red wine.

A red wine might work with a burger, but not as well as a roasty brown ale. And when you go the classic sub route, a wheat beer can hang with all that oil and vinegar, while wine just **wimps out**.

Marnie

108

Sam

Beer will do with a sandwich when there's no good wine around. Sure, beer is cheaper and more widely available than wine, but life is short. **Why settle** for second best?

Then I guess most people around the world are making the wrong choice? From panini and Peroni in Pisa to sausage sandwiches and Späten in Stuttgart, a beer in one hand and a sandwich in the other is the perfectly **balanced meal**.

This is a debate about quality, not quantity. And if we're going by majority rule, you'd have us all **drinking water**.

Actually, this is a debate about quality and quantity. The quantity of beer choices that **work perfectly** with sandwiches is only exceeded by the level of quality you'll find in those choices.

you choose
which wins

After you've tasted each dish with every wine and beer, use this score card to keep track of which combinations you prefer.

	Wine	**Beer**
Traditional burger	☐	☐
Turkey club	☐	☐
Falafel and pita	☐	☐
Italian sub	☐	☐
Tuna salad sandwich	☐	☐
Roast beef sandwich	☐	☐

wine, beer
& pizza & pasta

Pizza and pasta, two Italian dietary staples that have been embraced the world over, are amazingly versatile foods. Their bases, crust and noodles, are pretty ordinary on their own, but when you throw cheese, garlic, and vibrant sauces into the mix, that's when pizza and pasta get really exciting. You can top them with anything under the sun—and that's exactly what people do. So no matter where you go in the world, there are almost always fantastic local twists on these classics.

wine
& pizza & pasta

Pizza and pasta are Italian classics that have earned rock star status. Both rank among the most popular foods on earth, but deep down, pizza and pasta are like fraternal twins. They may look different, but they're just two kinds of "dough" topped with flavorful sauce and tasty toppings.

Pizza: the locals know best
Italy is home to one of the world's great gastronomic cultures, where one can "eat well and drink better" as Giuseppe Garibaldi famously put it. I really hate to be the one to break it to Sam, but Italy is the world's number one producer of wine, not beer.

Eating pasta or pizza without a glass of "vino" is like wearing jeans without pockets— it's just not right. But, this is hardly a surprise, is it? Italian wine is made in every corner of the country, in every color, style, and strength. In Italy, wine and food go hand in hand—it comes with every meal like an intoxicating "sauce on the side".

Do the right thing
Pizza is street food straight to its core, perfectly designed for one-handed, utensil-free munching. It takes the joys of mopping your plate with a crust of bread to its logical conclusion. But just because pizza isn't "fancy" food there's still no reason to abandon it to a lesser beverage like beer. No, no, no—every single one of pizza's layers have a natural synergy with wine.

The toasty pizza crust echoes the oak flavor of wines that have been mellowed by time in barrels. Sweet and tart, that herb-spiked tomato sauce cries out for a bright, tangy red wine to do it justice. Meltingly delicious mozzarella cheese tops the whole thing off with a big helping of gooey richness. And as

we already know, because of its acidity, wine is cheese's natural ally—sure to make any pizza taste better than it does alone.

Pasta: past to present
Pasta, on the other hand, can be as simple or as ambitious as the chef wants it to be. Silken noodles tossed with any one of a rainbow of sauces and herbs, pastas are also often enriched, stuffed, or topped with cheese. Once a humble agrarian staple, pasta is a peasant's dish where flour and water stand in for proteins, such as meat or fish. But, crucially, the peasants drank wine with their pasta. Today, pasta is served at the world's top restaurants, and guess what? The diners still order a bottle of wine to go with it.

Once we admit that the sauce is where the flavor is, we can recognize pasta as the pinnacle of haute cuisine, where preparation and seasoning trump the primary ingredient. Pasta is even more wine-oriented than pizza, assuming that's possible. Where pizza tends to stick to the tomato and mozzarella model, pasta ranges free of such constraints, from delicate sauces of white wine and clams to dense ragoûts of oxtail. As you can imagine, the wine pairing possibilities are endless.

Pairing notes for pizza
Tomato sauce and cheese are the center of the pizza universe, and they are the primary flavors for pairing purposes.

Both of these components need the bracing acidity of wine to provide balance (which is so sadly missing in beer).

Generally, the more salty (think cheese) and the more tangy (think tomato) a dish tastes, the sharper a wine we choose as a partner. This means that pizza is a natural match for refreshing wines of all colors, especially those from cool climate regions.

In circumstances where the pizza's toppings are going to be the strongest flavor, it's a good idea to orient your wine pairing to the topping. So, for mushrooms, for example, think earthy wines like Pinot Noir, while ham and pineapple will work better with something more smoky and fruity, like a snappy Chardonnay.

Pairing notes for pasta

Pasta covers far more ground than pizza. Pizza rarely strays from the tomato-cheese orbit, but variations in pasta sauce are explored more often, and are virtually infinite. Wine matching principles for pasta are as difficult to pin down as a buttered noodle. However, there are some handy rules of thumb.

When it comes to weight and intensity, pastas hug the middle ground—that is, pastas are not as light as a leafy salad, but they're not as hefty as a loin of venison. This means that pastas are most likely to pair well with medium-bodied wine, rather than those at the extremes of a style. With low-fat sauces, aim to stay on the lighter, whiter side of the wine spectrum. And remember that as the color, flavor, and richness of the pasta dish increases (as with a baked ziti, for example), you can push into darker, bigger, or stronger wines, such as a rich Cabernet Sauvignon.

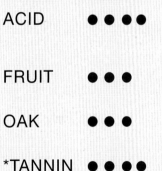

rules of thumb
wine for pizza & pasta

The dots on this chart represent some simplified rules on the characteristics to look out for when pairing wine with pizza and pasta. There can be exceptions to the rules and, where applicable, these are mentioned in the text below each entry. On a scale of one to five the dots below represent the suggested intensity of a wine's objective characteristics. Five dots indicate a very strong characteristic, while one dot means that the property is less prominent.

BODY ● ● ●
Exception: Rich pasta dishes can pair well with stronger wines.

SWEET ●
Exception: Sweet toppings or sauces can pair well with sweeter wines.

ACID ● ● ● ●

FRUIT ● ● ●

OAK ● ● ●

*TANNIN ● ● ● ●
Exception: Low-fat pastas will need less tannic red wines.

*Tannin is only found in red wine.

wine & pizza & pasta pairings

Just about any medium-bodied wine will pair well with pizza and pasta, but feel free to change it up based on the weather and the mood. For light fare, opt for lighter wines, both paler and lower in alcohol. Heartier dishes, or those loaded down with meat or extra cheese, can handle denser, more concentrated wines.

1 | CLASSIC CHEESE PIZZA &
Antinori Pèppoli Chianti Classico
There is no better partner for the classic cheese pizza than Italy's most famous alcoholic export, Chianti. This mid-weight red wine provides a backbone of sharp acidity that can stand up to tangy tomato sauce just as well as it can cut through salty cheese. The Chianti district of Tuscany now makes deep, rich wines, largely thanks to visionary producers like Antinori.
This works too: Chilean Merlot

2 | PEPPERONI PIZZA &
Beringer Napa Valley Merlot
Pepperoni is one snazzy sausage, and, on pizza, it calls out for red wine. Juicy and forward in mixed berry flavors, Merlot is a real crowd pleaser—neither too acidic nor too astringent. Napa Valley's ample sunshine coaxes out Merlot's best, as with this icon from Beringer, whose sweet cherry-vanilla core is accented with dark olive notes that evoke the Mediterranean.
This works too: French Côtes-du-Rhône Rouge

WHITE GARLIC PIZZA & | 3
Anselmi San Vincenzo
White pie is all about the dough, glistening with garlicky oil, and dusted with grated Parmesan. I love to echo this dominant flavor with a glass of Soave, a yeasty white wine made in northern Italy. This stellar spin on Soave from Anselmi is oddly reminiscent of pears poached in wheat beer.
This works too: Australian Sparkling White Wine

114

4 | SPAGHETTI BOLOGNESE &
Secco-Bertani Valpolicella Ripasso

Bolognese is the ultimate meat sauce and can carry a hefty wine. Pair it with an Italian red that's as soft, plump, and meaty as the pasta. Try the "Ripasso" style Valpolicella, pioneered by Bertani, where light Valpolicella wine is "refermented" with leftover Amarone skins, which revs up its flavor and color.
This works too: California Zinfandel

5 | PASTA CARBONARA &
Ken Forrester Chenin Blanc

I like to pair this dish with lushly textured white wines with toasty qualities, like those imparted by oak barrel fermentation. Chenin Blanc is an aromatic grape best known for making light Vouvray. But in sunny South Africa, producers like Ken Forrester produce Chenin Blancs with honeyed opulence and buttery richness.
This works too: Spanish Cava

6 | PENNE WITH PESTO &
Hacienda Araucano Cabernet Sauvignon

Pesto's herbal flavors can tame the wild cedary edge of the Bordeaux grape family, which includes Cabernet Sauvignon and Sauvignon Blanc. A traditionalist might go white, but red works too. Grapes ripen slowly in coastal Chile, retaining a woodsy aromatic quality. Wines like this sleek Araucano offer Cabernet flavors without the ponderous weight.
This works too: French White Bordeaux

---

specific wines
objective characteristics

This chart lists each suggested wine's objective characteristics, as described by the number of dots used. Five dots indicate a very strong characteristic, while one dot means that the property is less prominent. Zero dots indicate that the characteristic is not present.

1. Antinori Pèppoli Chianti Classico
Pairs well with classic cheese pizza.

Body	●●●
Sweet	●
Acid	●●●●
Fruit	●●●●
Oak	●●●
Tannin	●●●

2. Beringer Napa Valley Merlot
Pairs well with pepperoni pizza.

Body	●●●●
Sweet	●●●
Acid	●●●
Fruit	●●●●
Oak	●●●●
Tannin	●●

3. Anselmi San Vincenzo
Pairs well with white garlic pizza.

Body	●●
Sweet	●●
Acid	●●●
Fruit	●●
Oak	

4. Secco-Bertani Valpolicella Ripasso
Pairs well with spaghetti Bolognese.

Body	●●●
Sweet	●●
Acid	●●●
Fruit	●●●
Oak	●●
Tannin	●●●

5. Ken Forrester Chenin Blanc
Pairs well with pasta Carbonara.

Body	●●●●
Sweet	●●
Acid	●●●
Fruit	●●●●
Oak	●●●●

6. Hacienda Araucano Cabernet Sauvignon
Pairs well with penne with pesto.

Body	●●●●
Sweet	●●
Acid	●●●
Fruit	●●●●
Oak	●●●●
Tannin	●●●●

beer
& pizza & pasta

Just as DNA is the building block of life, grain is the building block of nutrition. Nowhere is that more apparent than in the explosive popularity of pasta, pizza, and beer throughout the world. Once regional phenomena, today all three of these nutritious staples can be found in nearly every corner of every country.

The common denominator

Pasta, pizza, and beer can each come in myriad flavors and styles. All three can be as complex or as simple as a chef or brewer wants them to be, but they all begin with the same basic building blocks: yeast, grain, and water. Since the flavors and textures of grain-based foods harmonize best with grain-based beverages, it's no surprise that beer, pizza, and pasta go so well together. And whereas the high acidity of tomato-based sauces used in pizza and pasta can be unwieldy and unpleasant with some wines, it is ideally suited for matching with an array of beer styles.

Italy's beer renaissance

The Italians have centered their gastronomic tradition around pasta for nearly a millennium. While this county is better known for its wine than its beer, this is quickly changing. Today, the Italian craft beer renaissance is in full-bloom, and it is recognized as one of the most exciting and innovative brewing locales in the world. And the beers the Italian craft brewers are producing happen to pair perfectly with the staples of the Italian diet. Since beer-making involves recipes devised and implemented by brewers, it's much easier for beer to be tailor-made to suit a wide variety of food, including pizza and pasta.

Pointers for beer with pasta

The grain-base that pasta and beer share is enough to give beer a leg up as a good pairing partner. However, when looking for the perfect beer for a pasta dish, you shouldn't focus too much on the pasta itself. It's a solid starting point, but what's more important is the pasta's sauce and how the dish is prepared. As with most pairings, it's essential to consider the dominant flavor of the sauce's ingredients, and how heavy or light the dish is as a whole.

Lighter pasta sauces will usually pair best with lighter beers, while heavier, spicier, and meatier sauces will usually do better with heavier and darker beers. Baked pastas, such as lasagne and ziti, are typically considered heavy dishes that will fare best with darker, more robust beers.

That said, there are exceptions to the rule. In some instances, the sauce itself may technically be light, while its flavor is strong.

"The Italian craft beer renaissance is in full-bloom, and is one of the most exciting and innovative in the world."

For example, most pesto dishes are served without meat and might therefore fall near the lighter end of the flavor spectrum. However, many pesto dishes incorporate a boatload of flavor from garlic. This pungent vegetable explodes on the tastebuds and can overwhelm many lighter beers. So, a super-garlicky pasta dish such as pasta with pesto would be best paired with bolder, darker beers, such as a Belgian Trappist Tripel.

"Pizza is a much-loved meal, but with the right beer, the flavors in both can be amplified and expanded upon."

Pointers for beer with pizza

Pizza is a much-loved meal the world over, but when it is enjoyed with the right beer, the flavors in both can be amplified and expanded upon. Pizza crust has become a platform for creative interpretation to a degree above and beyond the world of pasta. Since beer is more diverse than wine, it's no wonder so many different beers are up to the challenge of matching the huge range of pizzas available today.

A classic pizza's tomato sauce is usually seasoned with herbs such as oregano, parsley, and basil, which give it an earthy quality. A beer that has both heightened herbal and malty notes can perfectly balance the herbs and the acidity found in the tomato sauce. Styles like Pilsners and IPAs feature the herbal tang of hops, as well as a malty backbone to keep the pizza's acidity in check.

White pizzas, on the other hand, do not have the acidic tomato component of classic pizzas. Cheese and garlic feature more prominently in these dishes. White pizzas are milder, but heavier pies, so they fare best when paired with dark, heavy beers such as Porters or Maibocks.

rules of thumb
beer for pizza & pasta

The dots on this chart represent some simplified rules on the characteristics to look out for when pairing beer with pizza and pasta. There can be exceptions to the rules and, where applicable, these are mentioned in the text below each entry. On a scale of one to five the dots below represent the suggested intensity of a beer's objective characteristics. Five dots indicate a very strong characteristic, while one dot means that the property is less prominent.

COLOR ● ●
Exception: Garlicky pizzas and pastas can pair well with paler beers.

SWEET ● ● ●

BODY ● ●
Exception: Richer pizzas and pastas can pair well with stronger beers.

YEAST ●

HOPS ● ●

beer & pizza & pasta pairings

When pairing beer with pizza and pasta, look to the dish's sauces and toppings for your pairing cues. In most instances, the flavor intensity and heaviness of your dish should be on a par with that of your beer. However, for some meals, such as spicy pepperoni pizza, choosing a beer with contrasting flavors can work wonders.

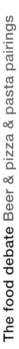

1

CLASSIC CHEESE PIZZA &
Dogfish Head 60 Minute IPA

Some of the best meals I have ever enjoyed have featured classic cheese pizzas. When prepared with fresh tomatoes, hand-picked herbs, and authentic Italian cheeses, the simple cheese pizza can be mind-bending in flavor. Classic, herb-forward pizzas deserve a classic hop-forward beer like our Dogfish Head 60 Minute IPA.

This works too: Belgian Golden Strong Ale

2

PEPPERONI PIZZA &
Brooklyn Brown Ale

This is a pizza that is better paired with a contrasting beer style than a matching one. The spicier the sausage on your pizza, the less hoppy or spicy your beer choice should be. A malty, sweet beer, like an American Brown Ale, will effectively quell the spicy bite of the pepperoni. Try a Brooklyn Brown Ale from New York City.

This works too: Dunkelweisse

3

WHITE GARLIC PIZZA &
Paulaner Hefe-Weizen

White pizza is a dish that is always better paired with beer than wine. These pizzas tend to be heavy and fatty and coat your tastebuds. Where wine just kind of bounces off this coating, beer's carbonation cuts through the film on your tongue and prepares you for your next bite. Try Paulaner Hefe-Weizen with your next white pizza, and you'll see exactly what I mean.

This works too: Double Bock

4
SPAGHETTI BOLOGNESE &
Newcastle Brown Ale
The sweetness and complexity of this Italian dish are best aligned with the caramelly, nutty, and roasty flavors of a medium-bodied brown ale. The classic Newcastle Brown Ale from England is always a satisfying choice.
This works too: Belgian Gueuze

5
PASTA CARBONARA &
Brasserie Ellezelloise Hercule Stout
The pancetta or bacon used in preparing traditional pasta Carbonara contributes a smoky depth to this dish, while generous lashings of cream make it quite heavy. A great match would be Hercule Stout, a full-bodied beer from Brasserie Ellezelloise in Belgium.
This works too: Irish Stout

6
PENNE WITH PESTO &
Westmalle Tripel
This light dish can be heavy on the garlic, so you'll need a beer that's not too light. Try a Belgian Trappist Ale, such as Westmalle Tripel, whose yeasty spice will magnify the complexity of your dish without overwhelming it.
This works too: German Bock

specific beers
objective characteristics
The chart below lists each suggested beer's objective characteristics, as described by the number of dots used. Five dots indicate a very strong characteristic, while one dot means that the property is less prominent.

1. Dogfish Head 60 Minute IPA
Pairs well with classic cheese pizza.

Color	● ●
Sweet	● ● ●
Body	● ● ●
Yeast	●
Hops	● ● ● ●

2. Brooklyn Brown Ale
Pairs well with pepperoni pizza.

Color	● ● ●
Sweet	● ● ●
Body	● ●
Yeast	● ●
Hops	● ●

3. Paulaner Hefe-Weizen
Pairs well with white cheese pizza.

Color	●
Sweet	● ●
Body	● ●
Yeast	● ● ●
Hops	●

4. Newcastle Brown Ale
Pairs well with spaghetti Bolognese.

Color	● ●
Sweet	● ●
Body	● ● ●
Yeast	●
Hops	●

5. Brasserie Ellezelloise Hercule Stout
Pairs well with pasta Carbonara.

Color	● ● ● ●
Sweet	● ● ●
Body	● ● ●
Yeast	● ● ●
Hops	● ●

6. Westmalle Tripel
Pairs well with penne with pesto.

Color	● ●
Sweet	● ● ●
Body	● ● ●
Yeast	● ●
Hops	● ● ●

which **drink** wins

Marnie and Sam will each state their case for wine or beer, but there has to be a winner for each pairing. Conduct your own beer, wine, and food tasting, and choose which drink wins on the score card below.

Both pizza and pasta are built on a base of grains—just like beer—and the best pizza and pasta dishes also incorporate spicy and herbal components. Thanks to **our friend the hop leaf**, this holds true for beer as well. Similar ingredients and similar flavor profiles make for singularly perfect pairing scenarios.

Who cares about noodles or crust? Any foodie will tell you that when it comes to perfect pairings, it's all about the sauces and the toppings. Wine is like the **ultimate sauce on the side**. It brings out the best in everything from pesto to puttanesca and pepperoni to pineapple.

you choose
which wins

After you've tasted each dish with every wine and beer, use this score card to keep track of which combinations you prefer.

The way different hops can accentuate the flavors in any sauce or topping, from spicy to citrusy, cheesy to herbal, guarantees that you'll always find the perfect partner for any pasta or pizza dish within the **wide world of beer**.

	Wine	**Beer**
Classic cheese pizza	☐	☐
Pepperoni pizza	☐	☐
White garlic pizza	☐	☐
Spaghetti Bolognese	☐	☐
Pasta Carbonara	☐	☐
Penne with pesto	☐	☐

Earth to Sam—this is Italian food we are talking about here. It's not a coincidence that Italy's most popular foods taste best paired with wine. After all, Italy is **synonymous with wine**, not beer. It is the world's largest wine producer, despite being smaller than the state of California.

Um, Marnie? You do know my full name is Santos Antonio Mastroianni Calagione III, right? My father and my grandfather made wine, but they worked hard so that I might have the opportunity to produce a **superior beverage**. Let it suffice to say that they are very proud of what we've accomplished at Dogfish Head Craft Brewery.

No wonder your beer is decent—centuries of winemaking tradition flow through your veins! But I bet the family still **tugs on the vino rosso** when you're not looking. And if the American dream of children outdoing their parents holds true, then maybe the Calagiones will get back to fermenting grapes instead of barley mash.

I wouldn't wish that on my worst enemy, much less my own flesh and blood! The family tradition has been **elevated to beer** and we all acknowledge and honor that tradition. They know that bringing wine instead of beer to a pizza party is like showing up at a gun fight with a knife.

Sam

Don't underestimate my knife-skills, Sam. Wine is such a natural with tomatoes and cheese and mushrooms and olive oil, it's a **slice of heaven** with almost any pizza or pasta. I can only conclude that beer-guy parties must be more about the buzz and less about the meal than those I attend.

Marnie

The food debate Which drink wins

wine,

beer
& spicy food

Herbs, spices, sauces, and rubs are the gastronomic decorations made possible by human experience, and they elevate food from the primal to the sublime. In the wild, food is a naked need, consumed raw, and sometimes quivering. Yet, perhaps there is nostalgia for the harsh life we've left behind. How else can we explain our fascination with foods that cause physical discomfort? The "heat" found in spicy sauces causes sensations that bear a distinct resemblance to pain. Like skydiving and horror movies, hot sauces get the heart pounding and remind us that we're alive.

wine
& spicy food

Wine can be a remarkable partner for spicy foods. Few drinks can match wine's flavor intensity per sip, which is a great advantage in standing up to highly seasoned dishes, as well as those that only use a light, warming dash of spice. A range of wine styles can flatter these dishes, from delicate whites to muscular reds.

Think big
Highly seasoned foods call for concentrated, flavorful wines since, next to curry or chili, subtle wines can fade into the background. Flavor in fruit is driven by sunshine and warmth, which are deeply connected to ripeness. So, it makes sense that the most intensely flavored wines are those grown in the warmest and sunniest regions of the world. When multiple spices are competing for attention but the actual "heat" of the dish is moderate, big wines with big flavors can be terrific partners.

A caveat
However, I must confess—it's true that the very hottest sauces can be a challenge to pair with wine, unless you're a bit of a masochist. (Not that there's anything wrong with that, of course.) Spicy heat is not really a taste or a smell, you see. Spiciness is not even technically heat. It is actually an inflammation of the lips, tongue, or other points of contact that is perceived as a physical sensation of burning.

Hot peppers cause pain, a feeling similar to that of a scrape or a burn that sends our nerve endings into panic mode. The nerves bombard the brain with emergency signals that translate roughly as "Fire!" or "Help!"—their version of calling the fire department. You may begin to sweat or feel your pulse race. Instinctively, you grab a glass of water to douse the flames, only to discover that you can't rinse away the spicy heat. You just have to wait for it to burn itself out.

An alcohol conundrum
The difficulty in pairing wines with extremely spicy foods comes from one of the very qualities that make wine superior with so many other foods. Compared to other fermented beverages, such as beer, wine's alcohol content is extraordinarily high.

Flavor-wise, this is a good thing: it's what makes wine so aromatic and flavorful. But alcohol makes scrapes and burns hurt more, not less. If you've ever cleaned a wound with rubbing alcohol, you'll know what I mean. Since wine is much stronger than beer, it can be a more painful accompaniment to the very spiciest of foods. In fact, ordering really fiery food may be the only good excuse I can think of to choose beer over wine—not because beer is superior in flavor, but simply because it is a much weaker drink.

Hot or highly seasoned?
When we think of spicy foods, there are two main groups that come to mind. There are those dominated by "spicy heat", like that of hot peppers, ginger, and chilies. These foods trigger the familiar burning sensation of hot sauce. Then there are others that may be better described as "highly seasoned", where multiple spices compete for attention.

These tend to be less fiery overall, but far more intensely flavored than standard fare. Each of these categories require a slightly different pairing strategy.

Hot stuff

With food that is seriously hot, such as a lamb vindaloo, we need to factor in wine's alcohol content in our pairing decisions. There's a reason we don't drink martinis in Mexican or Indian restaurants—it's because they make your mouth hurt more. Light-bodied wines have the lowest alcohol, most often sparkling wines, whites, and some rosés. Best of all are those where fermentation was interrupted, suppressing alcohol and retaining grapey sweetness, as found in styles such as German Riesling and Italian Asti. Sugar, like starch, can tame the heat and these wines deliver ample flavor as well.

More mild than wild

When the spicy heat of a dish is mild, as with a chicken korma, the only factor to consider is the seasoning of a dish. In these cases, the pairing strategy is almost the complete reverse of the super-hot scenario. It's also much easier to find a great wine partner—and more fun.

In these situations, we look to wines whose intensity of flavor is similar to that of the dish itself. Since it is the sunshine in the vineyard that develops the flavor of the grapes, we tend to look to warm regions to provide wines of adequate concentration and whose flavors echo the "exotic" spiciness of the food. From full-bodied whites to overtly spicy smelling reds, the wine world abounds with a range of styles that are up to the task.

rules of thumb
wine for spicy food

The dots on this chart represent some simplified rules on the characteristics to look out for when pairing wine with spicy food. There can be exceptions to the rules and, where applicable, these are mentioned in the text below each entry. On a scale of one to five the dots below represent the suggested intensity of a wine's objective characteristics. Five dots indicate a very strong characteristic, while one dot means that the property is less prominent.

BODY ● ●
Exception: Mildly hot foods can pair well with stronger wines.

SWEET ● ● ● ●
Exception: Mildly hot foods can pair well with drier wines.

ACID ● ● ●

FRUIT ● ● ● ●

OAK ●
Exception: Smoked or grilled foods can pair well with oakier wines.

*TANNIN ●
Exception: Fattier dishes can pair well with more tannic red wines.

*Tannin is only found in red wine.

wine &
spicy food pairings

Cultures around the globe spike their dishes with a dash of "heat". Fresh, young wines, especially vibrantly fruity whites, can tame this heat, and are often the best partners for fiery cuisine. When the seasoning is more complex, as in more spices rather than more heat, more intense wines are needed to step up to the plate.

1 | **KUNG PAO CHICKEN &**
Cave Spring Riesling
Potent dried chilies put the "pow!" in kung pao. Since its sauce has both heat and sweetness, this dish needs a light-bodied wine with a palpable hint of sugar. Riesling delivers delicious flavor with low alcohol. This Riesling from Canada's Cave Spring is perfectly balanced, and is as sweet-tart as a Granny Smith apple.
This works too: California White Zinfandel

2 | **GRILLED CHORIZO &**
Bodega Norton Malbec
There's something about sausage that ups the flavor ante, and spicy Spanish chorizo is no exception. But its "heat" is an accent, not the main event, so we can go whole hog, pairing a red as intense as our dish. Hot and desert-dry, Argentina is known for its dense, dark wines from the under-estimated Malbec grape. Bodegas like Norton make classically styled Malbec, whose earthy "dried spice" flavors echo the chorizo's smoky paprika.
This works too: Spanish Rioja

JAMBALAYA & | **3**
Domaine Longval
Tavel Rosé
Jambalaya, a fiery Cajun stew of meats, vegetables, and rice, is both hot and complex. It needs a wine that combines both refreshment and flavor density, like the dry rosés of southern France. Longval's gorgeous wine from the "pink-only" village of Tavel is ideal, packed with peppered raspberry flavors.
This works too: South African Pinotage Rosé

4 | TOM YUM SOUP &
Dr. Loosen Dr. L Riesling

The citrusy tang of this spicy soup needs a wine just as sharp to keep up with it. Classic "off-dry" German Riesling fits the bill beautifully, with its piercing aromatics and racy acidity. Snappy and fresh, this entry-level offering from a top producer, Dr. Loosen, displays the astonishing purity and verve of the style.
This works too: French Vouvray

5 | SCALLOP CEVICHE &
Kim Crawford Sauvignon Blanc

Ceviche has such forceful acidity that a wine partner needs as much or more "tang" for the buck. A bright, zesty, and tart New Zealand Sauvignon Blanc can go toe to toe with citrus-drenched dishes any day. Kim Crawford's is electric with grapefruit and passionfruit flavors, threaded with graceful herbal aromatics.
This works too: Portuguese Vinho Verde

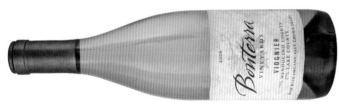

6 | COCONUT CURRIED SHRIMP &
Bonterra Viognier

My pairing preference for a mild, fragrant coconut curry is a rich, aromatic white wine, such as a Viognier. It combines a golden opulence reminiscent of Chardonnay with floral aromas. This Viognier from Bonterra is lush in the mouth, and tastes like apricots poached in orange flower water.
This works too: Italian Fiano di Avellino

specific wines
objective characteristics

This chart lists each suggested wine's objective characteristics, as described by the number of dots used. Five dots indicate a very strong characteristic, while one dot means that the property is less prominent. Zero dots indicate that the characteristic is not present.

1. Cave Spring Riesling
Pairs well with kung pao chicken.

Body	●●
Sweet	●●●●
Acid	●●●●
Fruit	●●●
Oak	

2. Bodega Norton Malbec
Pairs well with grilled chorizo.

Body	●●●●●
Sweet	●●
Acid	●●●
Fruit	●●●●●
Oak	●●●●
Tannin	●●●●

3. Domaine Longval Tavel Rosé
Pairs well with jambalaya.

Body	●●●
Sweet	●
Acid	●●●●
Fruit	●●●
Oak	

4. Dr. Loosen Dr. L Riesling
Pairs well with tom yum soup.

Body	●
Sweet	●●●●
Acid	●●●●●
Fruit	●●●
Oak	

5. Kim Crawford Sauvignon Blanc
Pairs well with scallop ceviche.

Body	●●●
Sweet	●
Acid	●●●●●
Fruit	●●●●
Oak	

6. Bonterra Viognier
Pairs well with coconut curried shrimp.

Body	●●●●
Sweet	●●
Acid	●●
Fruit	●●●●
Oak	●●●

beer
& spicy food

Spicy food and cold beer is a popular partnership: from hot enchiladas to fiery curry, the alcoholic beverage of choice is nearly always a cold beer. Like yin and yang, hot food and cold beer come together at dinner tables around the world. This makes sense, since wine is simply ill-equipped to stand up to spicy foods.

Cold comfort

Spicy foods can have the effect of setting your mouth on fire, which means a nice cold beverage is required to put out the flames. It's rare to find a wine with an ideal serving temperature bordering on freezing cold. While white wines are more often drunk cold than reds, they are still served at recommended serving temperatures that are well above those required for beers. Luckily for beer drinkers, many light lagers find their sweet spot when served around 48°F (9°C).

These cold, light beers work a treat with spicy foods for more than one reason. To start with, the act of eating spicy foods actually stimulates your tastebuds. However, when you drink ice-cold liquid (such as a delicious lager) you numb your tastebuds, canceling out a fraction of the discomfort they are perceiving as "heat". In addition to this, light lagers are light (obviously), which means they are refreshing and thirst-quenching—important qualities, since eating spicy food can make you thirsty. Wine falls flat on its face here, since nobody considers quaffing a room-temperature Merlot refreshing.

One more reason that beer beats wine for pairing with spicy foods is alcohol content. Alcohol magnifies the "heat" of spicy food, but even strong beers are lower in alcohol than most wines.

Sweet and lowdown

So the light, ice-cold lager has earned its rightful place at the dining table next to spicy food, but there are many other beer styles to consider. For spicy foods you can go in two directions when looking for an alternative to light lagers: sweeter beers (which tone down the heat) or spicier beers (which harmonize with the spice).

We'll start with the sweet beers, since sugar content is another key reason that beers work better than wines do with hot foods. The sweetness in beer is derived from the unfermented sugars in grains such as barley, wheat, rye, rice, and corn. The grain-based sweetness found in beer seems to counteract the capsaicin (found in spices such as chili peppers) more readily than wines, since many wines (though not all) are a lot "drier" than beers.

Lagers and ales

Generally, lagers pair better than ales with spicy foods, but as an alternative to the standard light lager, you can choose a sweeter variety. Seek out bigger, sweeter lagers like

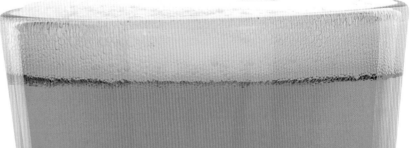

Doppelbocks or Dortmunder-style German Lagers. If you feel that those are too heavy for a summer meal served al fresco, look for a Kölsch-style beer. Although this is an ale, it's actually similar in body to a light lager. That said, Kölsch-style ales don't need to be served as cold as light lagers in order to be enjoyable.

The spice route

Numb tastebuds and subtle spiciness are not for everyone, though. If you really like spicy food, and you really like beer, then aren't you going to want to taste what you're eating? Of course, you can't do that so well with frozen tastebuds, can you? So, for the brave spice-masochists out there, I urge you to explore other types of beers that harmonize with (rather than downplay) the flavors of spicy foods. If you choose to explore spicier beers, then your beverage choices rapidly multiply. There are basically two ways spiciness can be built into a beer: through hops and through yeast.

Hops and yeast

As we have discussed, hops give a beer its bitterness. Certain varieties of hops can create spicy, herbal notes that will intensify and play off the spicy attributes of certain dishes. Stronger, sweeter, hoppy beers, such as Imperial IPAs or robust Pilsners can be wonderful, flavor-enhancing partners for a whole range of spicy dishes.

If you take the yeast-spice route instead, check out a strong Belgian-style Golden Ale, which will balance the flavors of your spicy meal beautifully. Instead of deriving its spiciness from hops, these yeasty beers gain their spice-character from potent Belgian yeast strains, which impart complex aromas and flavors.

One of the most memorable meals I've ever had was at a beer restaurant in Brussels called Bier Circus, where a really fresh, local Duvel Strong Golden Ale was paired with a spicy dish of curried mussels—it was pure and simple beer-food marital bliss. But it's worth noting that, today, Belgian yeast strains aren't only found in beers brewed in Belgium. The world is a smaller place than it once was, and now there are many other countries producing strong ales that incorporate Belgian yeast.

rules of thumb
beer for spicy food

The dots on this chart represent some simplified rules on the characteristics to look out for when pairing beer with spicy food. There can be exceptions to the rules and, where applicable, these are mentioned in the text below each entry. On a scale of one to five the dots below represent the suggested intensity of a beer's objective characteristics. Five dots indicate a very strong characteristic, while one dot means that the property is less prominent.

COLOR ● ●

SWEET ● ● ● ●

BODY ● ● ●
Exception: Very hot and spicy dishes can pair well with lighter beers.

YEAST ● ● ● ●

HOPS ● ● ● ●
Exception: Mildly hot dishes can pair well with less hoppy beers.

beer & spicy food pairings

With spicy foods, it's all about what you want to get out of your pairing. If you want to dampen the spiciness of intense dishes, choose a big, sweet beer that has a relatively low alcohol content. If you're a spice fan, then choose a yeasty or hoppy beer that will harmonize with the dish's heat.

1

KUNG PAO CHICKEN &
Schloss Eggenberg Urbock 23°
In China, this dish's country of origin, light lager still rules supreme. But this intensely spicy dish needs a big, sweet lager to reign in the spice. So, for a less traditional, but more flavorful, pairing with kung pao chicken, try an Austrian Doppelbock like Schloss Eggenberg Urbock 23°.
This works too: English Brown Ale

GRILLED CHORIZO &
Bluebird Bitter
This delicious sausage dish originally hails from Spain, but today it's enjoyed all over the world. Since the grilled sausage has a sweetly spicy character, you'll need a malty style of beer to pair with it. Try an English Ale like Bluebird Bitter from the Coniston Brewing Company.
This works too: German Helles

2

3

JAMBALAYA &
Dogfish Head 90 Minute IPA
Jambalaya is a thick, rich dish that has a pronounced spice intensity. Here is where you will need a big, bold, hoppy beer to stand up to the richness of the dish. I would recommend an Imperial IPA (also known as Double IPA), such as my own Dogfish Head 90 Minute IPA.
This works too: Baltic Porter

4 TOM YUM SOUP & **Dab Original**

The spices found in a tom yum soup are typically more subtle and nuanced than those in other Thai dishes. Try a more delicate and less boozy beer like a light lager or a Dortmunder with a bit of color and roastiness. A great one for this occasion would be Dab Original from Germany.

This works too: English Mild

SCALLOP CEVICHE & **Full Sail Session Lager** 5

The heat of ceviche is not very intense, but its vibrant flavors are. This light, warm-weather dish is best completed with a light, warm-weather beer, so reach for a traditional light lager or a new world interpretation such as Full Sail Session Lager from Oregon.

This works too: German Kölsch

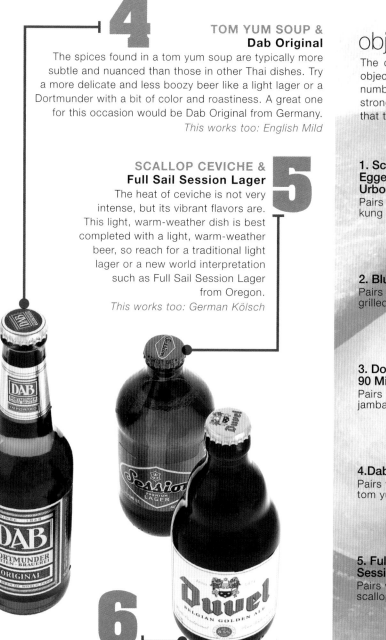

6

COCONUT CURRIED SHRIMP & **Moortgat Duvel**

This dish has flavor complexity beyond its heat, and pairs best with a spicy, full-bodied beer. Try a Strong Golden Ale, such as Duvel from the Moortgat brewery in Belgium, and you won't be disappointed.

This works too: Russian Imperial Stout

specific beers
objective characteristics

The chart below lists each suggested beer's objective characteristics, as described by the number of dots used. Five dots indicate a very strong characteristic, while one dot means that the property is less prominent.

1. Schloss Eggenberg Urbock 23°
Pairs well with kung pao chicken.

Color	●●
Sweet	●●●
Body	●●●●
Yeast	●●
Hops	●●

2. Bluebird Bitter
Pairs well with grilled chorizo.

Color	●
Sweet	●
Body	●
Yeast	●●
Hops	●●

3. Dogfish Head 90 Minute IPA
Pairs well with jambalaya.

Color	●●
Sweet	●●●
Body	●●●
Yeast	●
Hops	●●●●

4. Dab Original
Pairs well with tom yum soup.

Color	●●
Sweet	●●●
Body	●●●
Yeast	●●
Hops	●●

5. Full Sail Session Lager
Pairs well with scallop ceviche.

Color	●●
Sweet	●●
Body	●●
Yeast	●
Hops	●

6. Moortgat Duvel
Pairs well with coconut curried shrimp.

Color	●●
Sweet	●●
Body	●●●●
Yeast	●●
Hops	●●

which **drink** wins

Marnie and Sam will each state their case for wine or beer, but there has to be a winner for each pairing. Conduct your own beer, wine, and food tasting, and choose which drink wins on the score card at right.

Wine gets overlooked as a partner for spicy food, but the combination can be terrific. Light, off-dry whites **calm the flames** of spicy heat, while aromatic reds can provide a complex counterpoint to layered flavors and seasonings.

Nope, we both know that spicy food is a major **Achilles heel** for wine. The carbonation, maltiness, and alcohol content of beer makes it the perfect partner for even the spiciest dishes. To be fair, though, I once used a Riesling to put out a grease-fire.

Beer geeks like you just want to find a chink in wine's armor! Spicy heat can be a challenge for wine, but no, I'm not going to start ordering beer with fiery foods! **I'll revel in my Riesling**, whether or not the world sees the light.

The world DOES see the light—the light lager, that is—and the dark Porter, the malty Amber Ale, the Belgian Tripel, and the English Mild. In fact, each of these sweeter beer styles, and others too numerous to name here, **do a body good** when called upon to rescue over-heated tastebuds.

Sam

Marnie

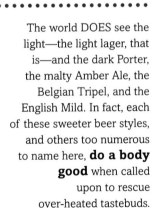

There are plenty of sweeter wine styles that fit the bill. When wines are not fermented fully dry, the result is **a boon** for pairing with spicy foods: higher in sugar and lower in alcohol.

You're dying on the vine, here. Please name a few of these wine styles for our intrepid readers. I shared a whole laundry list of appropriate beer style choices for spicy foods, while you've stubbornly clung to your **lonely Riesling**.

No problem—there's also French Vouvray, Italian Moscato, Alsace Pinot Gris, and California Viognier to name but a few...

...Cream Stout, Doppelbock, Marzen, English Bitter, Dubbel, Baltic Porter, Kölsch, Old Ale, Helles, Bière de Garde, Scotch Ale.... oops, sorry—while you were thinking of a few exceptions to the rule, I've been jotting down a partial list of many more beer styles that work **amazingly well** with spicy food.

you choose
which wins

After you've tasted each dish with every wine and beer, use this score card to keep track of which combinations you prefer.

	Wine	**Beer**
Kung pao chicken	☐	☐
Grilled chorizo	☐	☐
Jambalaya	☐	☐
Tom yum soup	☐	☐
Scallop ceviche	☐	☐
Coconut curried shrimp	☐	☐

The shellfish family includes foods that are among the most prized on earth. Tender shellfish are delicate in flavor and highly perishable. Great care must be taken to preserve them at their peak freshness. The clock is ticking from the time they leave the ocean, since the natural sweetness of fresh seafood fades quickly. The French have a delightful phrase for describing this group of non-fish seafood delicacies—*fruits de mer*, or "fruits of the sea".

wine, beer
& shellfish

wine
& shellfish

Shellfish range from simple mullusks, such as meaty clams and succulent oysters, through to more complex creatures, such as sweet-fleshed crabs and shrimp. But, whatever shellfish is on the menu, wine is an ideal partner for them all, whether they're served pristinely raw, or cooked and splashed with savory sauces.

A balancing act

The briny taste of the ocean can be found in virtually all seafood, and shellfish is no exception. Fortunately, the acidity found in wine is well-suited to complement that salty tang. This acidity acts to balance the saltwater taste and focus the attention on the natural sweetness of fresh seafood.

Salt and acid lie at either end of the pH scale, opposing one another in nature. At the dinner table, these two qualities create a delightful tension, point and counterpoint, but we know this instinctively. For example, it's not coincidental that so many of our favorite seafood sauces are sharply acidic, from cocktail sauce to simple salt and vinegar. Like these sauces and seasonings, wine is inherently tangy. The natural acidity of fruit provides wine's tart edge, which is ideally suited to seafood. Beer simply lacks wine's bracing, acidic qualities, and therefore falls flat in pairing with shellfish.

Age matters

Freshness is particularly important in retaining peak flavor in shellfish. So, as you might expect, aged wines aren't the best choice for shellfish served fresh from the sea. The nutty, dried fruit, and tea-like qualities that emerge in mature wines simply do not flatter shellfish dishes. Instead, brighter and more youthful wines tend to reward the fresh, bright, and tangy flavors found in shellfish. Overall, white

wines, whether still or sparkling, are the best choices for shellfish dishes. As nuanced as the seafood itself, whites can brilliantly showcase the subtleties of shellfish. White wine's snappy backbone of acidity and cleansing finish acts to perk up each bite, much as a squeeze of lemon might do. The varied flavors of whites are perfectly suited to coaxing out the best qualities in shellfish dishes.

The problem with red wines

However, shellfish seem at odds with red wines on many levels. On the surface, pale-fleshed seafood is rarely strong enough in taste to benefit from the dense, dark fruit flavors of red wine. More fundamentally, shellfish are vulnerable to the tannin component found in reds, that faint "drying" sensation that can prickle on the palate. Perceived as an arid astringent quality, tannin occurs in significant levels only among red wines, since its primary source is grape skins. Tannic wines clash with seafood, in general, and shellfish, in particular. The combination is flattering to neither partner, leaving the wine feeling brittle in the mouth and the seafood tasting less than fresh.

When reds can work

There are a few cases when red wine can flatter a shellfish dish, but they are uncommon. These tend to involve the use of an intense seasoning, like blackening spices or barbeque sauce, or a cooking method that enriches and deepens the flavor of the seafood, such as grilling or slow braising. But since shellfish is naturally so delicate, such recipes and preparations are rarely used, and therefore tend to be the exception rather than the rule.

Raw and simple

When selecting a wine to pair with shellfish, the primary cues should be taken from the cooking method, or lack thereof. As mentioned earlier, the vast majority of shellfish dishes are better suited to white wines than reds. But nowhere is this more true than with raw shellfish, such as oysters on the half shell.

Raw seafood is incredibly delicate and calls for the lightest, most subtle wines. Understated wine styles, such as cool climate whites and sparkling wines, like French Chablis or Italian Prosecco, would be swamped if paired with a steak. However, these wines have a simplicity that can be stunning with raw bar delicacies.

Rich sauces

When shellfish is cooked, and as sauces get stronger, we look to whites with more aromatic intensity. Vibrantly aromatic, unoaked white wines, such as dry Riesling and Sauvignon Blanc, are brilliant with tangy flavors like citrus or capers, and are adept at cutting through melted butter. Or, if the shellfish dish is served with a creamy Alfredo or buttery Hollandaise sauce, then textural opulence becomes a central pairing cue. In these cases, the richness of the dish should be echoed in the wine chosen. Try a lush, opulent Chardonnay from a warm climate, such as California.

Deeper flavors

Only when the sauce or preparation is tilted toward deep, dark flavors do we even consider moving away from white wines. When shellfish hits the grill or encounters complex seasonings, rosés can be an excellent compromise. But, if flavors deepen with stewed tomatoes or cured meats like chorizo, a red wine may be in order. However, stick to lighter reds, like mid-weight styles with lower alcohol contents and paler colors that hail from cool climates.

rules of thumb
wine for shellfish

The dots on this chart represent some simplified rules on the characteristics to look out for when pairing wine with shellfish. There can be exceptions to the rules and, where applicable, these are mentioned in the text below each entry. On a scale of one to five the dots below represent the suggested intensity of a wine's objective characteristics. Five dots indicate a very strong characteristic, while one dot means that the property is less prominent.

BODY ● ●
Exception: Rich, oily shellfish dishes can pair well with stronger wines.

SWEET ●
Exception: Sweet sauces can pair well with sweeter wines.

ACID ● ● ● ●

FRUIT ● ● ●

OAK ●
Exception: Grilled or buttered shellfish can pair well with oakier wines.

*TANNIN ●

*Tannin is only found in red wine.

wine &
shellfish pairings

Within the seafood family, shellfish are the cream of the crop, holding a place of honor in international cuisine. Tender and sweet, they can be just as tasty in the raw as when they're lightly cooked. But they achieve true nobility when paired with a great wine that helps their naturally dainty flavors to shine through.

1 | OYSTERS ON THE HALF SHELL &
Domaine Laroche St. Martin Chablis

Delicate raw oysters have a briny tang and a creamy finish. Lean, mineral-scented French Chablis is tailor-made for them. This classic wine is rarely oaked and is widely misunderstood. Chablis can seem austere alone, but wines like this one from Domaine Laroche are designed with subtle pleasures, like oysters, in mind.
This works too: Spanish Albariño

2 | MUSSELS MARINARA &
Banfi Centine
Toscana Rosso

Black-shelled mussels do have a deeper flavor than most mollusks, but here, the sauce directs the pairing. This young Italian red complements the spicy tomato kick of the sauce. Banfi's "Centine" is a vibrant Sangiovese blend, whose tart red-cherry flavors are *simpatico* with tangy tomato. Youthful and mid-weight, it won't overpower our succulent shellfish.
This works too: Canadian Pinot Noir

NEW ENGLAND CLAM CHOWDER & | 3
Geyser Peak Chardonnay

Rich shellfish dishes favor plump, full-bodied whites like Chardonnay, especially those spiced with new oak, like this blonde bombshell from California's Geyser Peak. This wine achieves mango ripeness without losing citrus freshness. A deft winemaker's hand ensures its "buttered toast" qualities from barrel fermentation are pleasantly balanced.
This works too: Italian Greco di Tufo

4 | GARLIC SHRIMP &
Hermanos Lurton Rueda Blanco

Garlic shrimp shines with bright, snappy white wines, especially sharp unoaked whites, which cut through oil or butter. Rueda from Spain is a lively white made from fragrant Verdejo grapes. This one from Hermanos Lurton is like a Latin spin on Sauvignon Blanc. Its aromas evoke green apples, white lillies, and cilantro.

This works too: Argentine Torrontes

5 | OLD BAY CRABS &
Trimbach Reserve Pinot Gris

For pungent, smoky dishes like this one, I turn to Alsace in northern France. Trimbach is a region known for white wines that effortlessly combine prodigious aromatics and sinewy finesse. Only in Alsace does the Pinot Gris grape offer up flavors of peaches and cream, or honeyed aromas of mimosa and cinnamon.

This works too: South African Chenin Blanc

6 | LOBSTER &
Domaine Matrot Meursault

Lobster's sweet, creamy flesh needs a white wine of noble breeding like white Burgundy. This Meursault from Matrot hails from one of three French villages that have set the standard for Chardonnays. It is complex—sharp and rich, bright and deep, and redolent of tart apples and toasted hazelnuts that thrum on the palate.

This works too: Tasmanian Sparkling Wine

specific wines
objective characteristics

This chart lists each suggested wine's objective characteristics, as described by the number of dots used. Five dots indicate a very strong characteristic, while one dot means that the property is less prominent. Zero dots indicate that the characteristic is not present.

1. Domaine Laroche St. Martin Chablis
Pairs well with oysters on the half shell.

Body	● ● ●
Sweet	
Acid	● ● ● ●
Fruit	●
Oak	

2. Banfi Centine Toscana Rosso
Pairs well with mussels Marinara.

Body	● ● ●
Sweet	●
Acid	● ● ●
Fruit	● ● ●
Oak	● ●
Tannin	● ● ●

3. Geyser Peak Chardonnay
Pairs well with New England clam chowder.

Body	● ● ● ●
Sweet	● ●
Acid	● ● ●
Fruit	● ● ● ●
Oak	● ● ● ●

4. Hermanos Lurton Rueda Blanco
Pairs well with garlic shrimp.

Body	● ● ●
Sweet	●
Acid	● ● ● ●
Fruit	● ● ●
Oak	

5. Trimbach Reserve Pinot Gris
Pairs well with Old Bay crabs.

Body	● ● ●
Sweet	● ● ●
Acid	● ● ● ●
Fruit	● ● ● ●
Oak	● ● ● ●

6. Domaine Matrot Meursault
Pairs well with lobster.

Body	● ● ● ●
Sweet	●
Acid	● ● ●
Fruit	● ● ●
Oak	● ● ●

beer
& shellfish

My brewpub, Dogfish Head Brewings & Eats, focuses on recipes made from fresh local seafood, and dishes like our Chesapeake Bay crab cakes are among our best sellers. We've done a lot of research on which drinks to pair with our shellfish menu items, and we've discovered that beer almost always works best.

The steamed mussels rule

These days, almost every bistro and gastro-pub worth checking out is going to have some version of a steamed mussel appetizer or entrée on its menu. You can quickly gauge how enlightened the establishment's chef is by whether he or she chooses to steam the mussels in beer or wine. I could go for the obvious wisecrack and say that the dish should be cooked in wine so that you can save your precious beer for the more important task of drinking. But that wouldn't be true. If

> **"If you discover that the chef chose to steam the mussels in wine...you should order the steak."**

the chef has steamed the mussels in beer, then you can rest assured that he or she knows how to combine flavors for maximum enjoyment, and appreciates how perfectly the briny tang of mussels complements the spicy sweetness of beer styles like Bière de Garde. However, if you do discover that the chef in question chose to steam the mussels in wine...you should order the steak.

Beer and shellfish just go together

So far I've only outlined why beer is a superior ingredient to wine when used to cook shellfish. This plus is small potatoes compared to the meat of the matter, though: the best beverage to enjoy drinking with shellfish. The culinary advantage may seem irrelevant, but the reason beer is best for cooking shellfish is that beer pairs best with every single kind of shellfish. Some beer styles work better than others, depending on the dish, but you'll find a perfect malt-based food partner every time, if you look hard enough.

Pairing tricks

With seafood in general, and shellfish in particular, you should be conscious of the richness of the dish and try to balance it against the body of the beer. But let's start with a general, but useful, rule of thumb: when pairing beer with shellfish you can almost never go wrong with a light, crisp, straw-hued ale or lager.

If, however, the shellfish is incorporated into a dish that is spicy or bitter, you'll want to pair it with a maltier beer like a Dubbel or an Amber Ale. This is because malty sweetness in beer tones down a food's spiciness and counterbalances its bitterness. If, on the other hand, the dish is laden with butter or a rich cream sauce, then you'll need a beer that can cut through the heaviness, so seek out a hoppier (but still light) Pilsner or Pale Ale.

A lot of foodies like to squirt some fresh lemon juice over their shellfish. If your dish is doused in lemon juice, then it will be mildly acidic, so opt for a lighter, drier, more acidic beer like a German Hefeweizen or a Belgian Gueuze.

Regional specialties

Fruitier beers—like the blueberry ales made at so many of the wonderful brewpubs in New England—harmonize well with the flavors of sweeter shellfish meat like lobster. And, in the Mid-Atlantic region of the country, many of the great local craft breweries make Porters and Stouts that are as dark as they are delicate and dry—perfect for the indigenous crab feast. Isn't it interesting how regional cooking and brewing trends often mirror and complement one another? It's just one of many examples of how great cooking and great beer brewing influence one another and enhance our enjoyment.

A poetic partnership

The crab shacks of coastal Delaware and the Lobster-roll shacks near Dogfish Head in Maine are some of my favorite haunts in the world. I love simple restaurants that specialize in local, fresh, straightforward recipes. Compared to wine, beer is the simple, fresh, straightforward beverage—no wonder it makes the perfect partner for shellfish. I've lived within walking distance of the sea for most of my life, and have noticed that breweries dot the coastlines of nearly every country. Brewing and the sea come together most poetically when a simple, fresh shellfish dish meets its perfect mate in a pint glass of beer.

rules of thumb
beer for shellfish

The dots on this chart represent some simplified rules on the characteristics to look out for when pairing beer with shellfish. There can be exceptions to the rules and, where applicable, these are mentioned in the text below each entry. On a scale of one to five the dots below represent the suggested intensity of a beer's objective characteristics. Five dots indicate a very strong characteristic, while one dot means that the property is less prominent.

COLOR ● ●
Exception: Oysters and clams can pair well with darker beers.

SWEET ● ● ●

BODY ● ●
Exception: Richer shellfish dishes can pair well with stronger beers.

YEAST ● ●

HOPS ● ● ●

beer & shellfish pairings

When pairing beer with shellfish, it's always important to consider the most prominent flavor of the dish. It may be the shellfish itself, as with sweet crab or lobster meat, but it could just as easily be the sauces, seasonings, and spices used to prepare the dish. Here are some examples of shellfish and beer combinations that work beautifully.

1 OYSTERS ON THE HALF SHELL & Cooper's Sparkling Ale

I "studied" in Sydney, Australia for a semester of college, and the restaurants down by the harbor served the most succulent oysters on the half shell. They were usually served with Cooper's Sparkling Ale—a light, spritzy, but flavorful beer. Both the oysters and the beer were light in body and richness, but big on flavor and zest.

This works too: Dry Stout

2 MUSSELS MARINARA & Birra Moretti La Rossa

I grew up pairing my grandmother's steamed mussels with Birra Moretti La Rossa. It's a mahogany-hued brown ale that has a nice sweetness and caramelly flavors that stand up to both the acidic red sauce and the briny mussels themselves.

This works too: Oktoberfest

3 NEW ENGLAND CLAM CHOWDER & Murphy's Irish Stout

This thick, rich soup has a lot of tongue-coating cream, and its briny clams give it a salty flavor. Chowder can be overwhelmed by beers that are high in alcohol, so opt for beer that is relatively low in alcohol, like a Porter or Stout. Murphy's Irish Stout has enough flavor and roastiness to punch through the thickness of the chowder, but it isn't as strong and sweet as a Double Stout, which would stifle the chowder's flavors.

This works too: Scotch Ale

4 GARLIC SHRIMP &
Victory Prima Pils

In this situation, choose your beer to stand up to the flavor of the garlic sauce rather than the shrimp. Prima Pils from Victory Brewing in Pennsylvania is a stellar option. It has a bracing hop bite, but a nice bready sweet character as well. This dish is going to be a bit on the bitter side, but the balancing subtle sweetness of the beer makes it the perfect partner.

This works too: English Brown Ale

5 OLD BAY CRABS &
Jever Friesland Pilsner

This dish is not only spicy, but it's also sweet from the crabmeat. Cracking and smashing claws is a bit of a workout, too, and a heavy, dark, or strong beer will just slow you down. Opt for a light, thirst-quenching, well-carbonated pilsner—something with less body and even less hops than the Prima Pils. Check out Jever Friesland Pilsner.

This works too: Golden Ale

6 LOBSTER &
Heineken Lager

You'll need a light, effervescent ale or lager that's low in bitterness to pair with succulent, dense sweet lobster meat. Even though the local lobster "pound" in Maine has Dogfish Head 60 Minute IPA on tap, I often opt for a Heineken when I order lobster there. The signature grassy, skunky flavor in this beer perfectly contrasts with the sweetness of the lobster meat.

This works too: Porter

specific beers
objective characteristics

The chart below lists each suggested beer's objective characteristics, as described by the number of dots used. Five dots indicate a very strong characteristic, while one dot means that the property is less prominent.

1. Cooper's Sparkling Ale
Pairs well with oysters on the half shell.

Color	●
Sweet	● ●
Body	● ●
Yeast	● ● ●
Hops	● ●

2. Birra Moretti La Rossa
Pairs well with mussels Marinara.

Color	● ● ●
Sweet	● ● ●
Body	● ●
Yeast	●
Hops	●

3. Murphy's Irish Stout
Pairs well with New England clam chowder.

Color	● ● ● ●
Sweet	● ● ●
Body	● ● ●
Yeast	● ●
Hops	● ●

4. Victory Prima Pils
Pairs well with garlic shrimp.

Color	●
Sweet	● ●
Body	● ● ●
Yeast	● ● ●
Hops	● ● ●

5. Jever Friesland Pilsner
Pairs well with Old Bay crabs.

Color	●
Sweet	● ● ●
Body	● ● ●
Yeast	●
Hops	● ●

6. Heineken Lager
Pairs well with lobster.

Color	●
Sweet	● ●
Body	●
Yeast	●
Hops	●

which **drink** wins

Marnie and Sam will each state their case for wine or beer, but there has to be a winner for each pairing. Conduct your own beer, wine, and food tasting, and choose which drink wins on the score card at right.

The quintessential shellfish and beverage pairing is oysters and Stout. No wait, crabs and lager. No wait, mussels and wheat beer...boy, **it's hard to choose** just one—but I guess I'll go with the mussels. And even if the mussels are prepared with wine, they'll taste better paired with a beer.

No, no, no. Oysters go with Chablis, crabs with Chardonnay, and mussels are tailor-made for a crisp wine whose color matches the sauce. The only reason for pairing raw oysters with a Stout is to **disguise their flavor** if they're not fresh enough.

At one time, the snooty gentry wouldn't touch oysters in much the same way that they sneered at beer. But the pairing is such a strong and popular one that now **oysters and Stout** are served in the snootiest restaurants AND the local pub. Isn't Darwinism cool?

Not quite. Truth is, foods were always cheapest where they came from. But today, we've got the ability to import lobsters from Maine, mussels from Prince Edward Island, and oysters from the Pacific Northwest. **You're just sore** that people go to greater lengths to bring in fine wines than they do beer.

Marnie

The food debate Which drink wins

Funny you mention Maine and the Pacific Northwest: two renowned American brewing regions! People want the freshest beverage to wash down the freshest shellfish. It's always best to think globally, but **DRINK LOCALLY**.

If fresh is always best, then how do you explain the ultimate shellfish partner: French Champagne? The best ones can spend a decade aging before they hit the market, and to many, shellfish has **no better accompaniment** than Champagne.

Ohmagawd—I love Champagne! It's my second favorite ingredient in a Black Velvet: a refreshing, shellfish-friendly drink made with Stout and Champagne.

Sam

you choose
which wins

After you've tasted each dish with every wine and beer, use this score card to keep track of which combinations you prefer.

	Wine	**Beer**
Oysters on the half shell	☐	☐
Mussels Marinara	☐	☐
New England clam chowder	☐	☐
Garlic shrimp	☐	☐
Old Bay crabs	☐	☐
Lobster	☐	☐

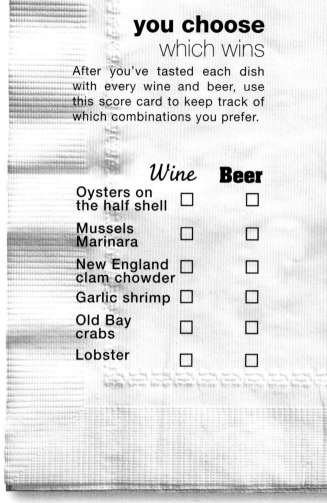

Now that's just flat wrong, Sam. Beer can be passable with shellfish, I'll admit. I've downed a few myself with raw bar treats when the wine wasn't cold enough. But to pollute a **noble glass** of Champagne with nasty burnt barley is unforgivable.

wine, beer & fish

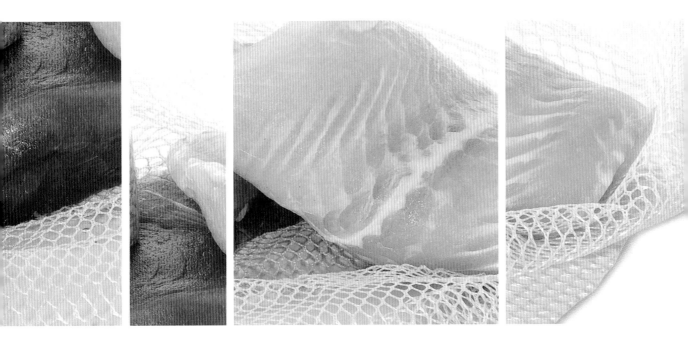

Fish is a boon from the sea. The tasty rainbow of fish flavors provides ample opportunities for pairing with delicious beverages. From freshwater to saltwater, from flaky fish to steaky fish, the possibilities are virtually endless. Fish recipes vary far more widely than those of meats, since virtually all fish can be served raw or cooked. Few foods are so impeccably healthy, loaded with nutrients and healthful oils, while also being low in artery-clogging fats.

wine & fish

While most foods are wine-friendly, fish is just one of those food groups that happen to be tailor-made for enjoying with wine. Chefs routinely poach fish in wine and top it with white wine sauces. If beer were as strong a partner for fish, wouldn't we see fish in beer sauce on more menus?

The acid test

Most of the fish we eat live in saltwater, and when preparing fish dishes, cooks tend to lean heavily toward the salty side of the seasoning spectrum. This saltiness gives fish a natural synergy with the sharp and tangy bite of dry wines, especially bracing whites and tart reds. Wine is naturally high in acidity, which balances out the saltiness in the fish.

The saltiness of most fish dishes is a huge advantage for wine lovers. But wine can perform just as well for fish lovers in return. Tangy flavors, like those found in wine, are so remarkably fish-friendly that they make regular appearances in fish recipes.

We routinely rely on acidic citrus and vinegar to liven up our fish. Much like these cooking staples, wine itself is a ready source of appetizing acidity, so it's small wonder wine is such a common ingredient when we cook with fish. Wine simply makes fish taste better.

Special sauce

Beverage pairings are like any other sauce, just served on the side. Just as a squeeze of lemon perks up your snapper, so will a sip of crisp Sauvignon Blanc. If a drizzle of vinegar flatters your fried halibut, so will a mouthful of sharp Champagne. As we move toward fattier fish, such as salmon and tuna, our dishes and sauces get deeper and more intense in flavor. Pink- and red-fleshed fish are naturally suited to the flavors of pink rosés and delicate red wines. However, the biggest reds are best saved for fattier meats and cheeses that can better handle astringent tannins.

Think white

"White wine with fish, red wine with meat" is a wine pairing adage that most people are familiar with. It isn't a hard and fast principle, but it certainly has a firm basis in food chemistry. As mentioned before, the dominant feature of white wine is its refreshing acidity. As a category, white wines also tend to be more understated in overall flavor. Both of these qualities are ideal for bringing out the best in fish.

Tart white wines do an amazing job of energizing the flavor of fish. And, since most fish are more subtle than meats in flavor, they need less intense accompaniments, both in their sauces and in their beverage partners. Even the meatiest bluefin tuna is delicate compared to beef or lamb.

Tricky tannin

There is another consideration that favors whites with fish—namely the presence of tannin in most red wines. Red wines get their color from grape skins. During the winemaking process, while color and flavor are being extracted from these skins, an astringent component called "tannin" comes along too. Tannin imparts no taste or smell, but gives red wine its distinctive "grip", a lingering leathery drying sensation not unlike what you experience after drinking a cup of over-steeped tea. Tannin is perfectly appropriate for rich and meaty foods, but it can present a challenge for delicate seafood—both fish and shellfish.

And if you must have red wine...

Generally, only the strongest, most highly seasoned preparations of the fattiest fish can handle red wines. Even then, it's best to choose red wines with the softest tannins, such as Pinot Noir. Intense, tannic reds, such as Cabernet Sauvignon should be avoided since this pairing flatters neither the food nor drink.

It bears repeating that white wines are almost always best for fish dishes. It's the path of least resistance and the pairings can be outstanding. But, if you're really set on serving red, you'll need to take a multi-pronged approach to this ambitious pairing. First, make sure you choose the fattiest fish you can, and then prepare it in a "meat-like" fashion. That is, you should cook and season it using more fat and stronger seasonings than usual. Then, choose a red wine that is as "white-like" in profile as possible. Go for reds that are paler in color, lower in alcohol, and higher in acidity than usual.

rules of thumb
wine for fish

The dots on this chart represent some simplified rules on the characteristics to look out for when pairing wine with fish. There can be exceptions to the rules and, where applicable, these are mentioned in the text below each entry. On a scale of one to five the dots below represent the suggested intensity of a wine's objective characteristics. Five dots indicate a very strong characteristic, while one dot means that the property is less prominent.

BODY ● ● ●
Exception: Rich, oily fish dishes can pair well with stronger wines.

SWEET ●
Exception: Sweet sauces can pair well with sweeter wines.

ACID ● ● ●

FRUIT ● ● ●

OAK ●
Exception: Grilled or smoked fish can pair well with oakier wines.

*TANNIN ●
Exception: Fattier fish sauces can pair well with more tannic red wines.

*Tannin is only found in red wine.

wine & fish pairings

Fish are delicate and prefer to swim with the light end of the wine family. Sommeliers tend to choose wines that are light in color, flavor, or body—and sometimes all three. Raw or rare fish call for subtle wine partners, while stronger-tasting cooking methods and concentrated sauces merit more powerful wine flavors.

1 | SUSHI/SASHIMI &
Perrier-Jouët Grand Brut Champagne

Impeccably fresh sushi and sashimi are succulently sweet. These dainty morsels offer finely etched flavors that are easily overwhelmed. French Champagne is an ideal partner, offering a shimmering array of disparate flavors in their complex finish. Carefully aged Champagnes, like this subtle stunner from Perrier-Jouët, manage to combine bracing lemony sharpness and toasty opulence.
This works too: Italian Pinot Bianco

2 | FRIED FISH AND CHIPS &
Jacob's Creek Reserve Riesling

For this battered and fried English seafood classic, look to a wine as bracing as the vinegar we sprinkle on it, such as Australian Riesling. This bone-dry example from Jacob's Creek is a startling departure from the sugary Riesling style, and it's packed with piercing lime and green apple flavors.
This works too: French Muscadet

SMOKED SALMON & | 3
Mumm Napa Blanc de Noirs Sparkling Rosé

Rich and salty smoked salmon needs a bracingly tart wine companion to scour the palate clean. With its tongue-tingling bubbles, this California sparkling rosé from Mumm Napa is just the ticket. It has a generous texture, and conjures flavors of tart red fruit, like sour cherries and raspberries, as a bracing counterpoint to the smoked fish.
This works too: French Alsace Riesling

4 | GRILLED SARDINES &
Tio Pepe Fino Sherry

Grilled sardines with dry Fino Sherry is a gastronomic pleasure of southern Spain. To create your own Mediterranean moment, the fish must be very fresh and the Tio Pepe very cold. Fino looks delicate, pale, and very dry, but it is very strong and pungent with aromas of green almonds and apple skins.

This works too: Australian Semillon

5 | SOLE WITH LEMON BUTTER &
Chateau Villa Bel-Air Graves Blanc

This delicate dish needs a dry white wine that is subtle yet rich, with a zing of balancing acidity. This white Bordeaux from Chateau Villa Bel-Air is a graceful example of the Graves district's style. Its oak adds a silky vanilla-tinged richness to finely etched fruit flavors of green plum, honeydew melon, and lemon.

This works too: California Chardonnay

6 | GRILLED TUNA &
Sokol-Blosser Pinot Noir

Tuna's red flesh has both the depth of flavor and fatty richness befitting a soft and supple red wine. An Oregon Pinot Noir, like this classic from Sokol-Blosser, is a perfect match. It's bright with cherry flavors and seductive earthy aromas, with Pinot's distinctive fish-friendly combination of low tannin and tangy acidity.

This works too: Italian Barbera

specific wines
objective characteristics

This chart lists each suggested wine's objective characteristics, as described by the number of dots used. Five dots indicate a very strong characteristic, while one dot means that the property is less prominent. Zero dots indicate that the characteristic is not present.

1. Perrier-Jouët Grand Brut Champagn
Pairs well with sushi/sashimi.

Characteristic	Dots
Body	●●
Sweet	●
Acid	●●●●●
Fruit	●●●
Oak	

2. Jacob's Creek Reserve Riesling
Pairs well with fried fish and chips.

Characteristic	Dots
Body	●●●
Sweet	●
Acid	●●●●●
Fruit	●●●
Oak	

3. Mumm Napa Blanc de Noirs Sparkling Rosé
Pairs well with smoked salmon.

Characteristic	Dots
Body	●●
Sweet	●●
Acid	●●●●
Fruit	●●●
Oak	

4. Tio Pepe Fino Sherry
Pairs well with grilled sardines.

Characteristic	Dots
Body	●●●●●
Sweet	
Acid	●●●
Fruit	●●●
Oak	

5. Chateau Villa Bel-Air Graves Blanc
Pairs well with sole with lemon butter.

Characteristic	Dots
Body	●●●
Sweet	
Acid	●●●
Fruit	●●●
Oak	●●●

6. Sokol-Blosser Pinot Noir
Pairs well with grilled tuna.

Characteristic	Dots
Body	●●●●
Sweet	●
Acid	●●●●
Fruit	●●●●●
Oak	●●●●
Tannin	●

beer
& fish

Within the world of beer there exists a sturdy stereotype that ales go best with red meat, while lagers pair best with fish. In some ways, this is a very helpful axiom to remember when choosing which beers to partner with fish. But, while this combination will typically produce good results, it's not the whole story, either.

Testing the paradigm

Light lagers will work well with many delicate, simple fish dishes. However, there is a huge variety of flavors within the world of fish, and not all fish are lightweight and mild-tasting. Species can be freshwater or saltwater, steak-like or flaky, light or oily. These are variables you'll need to consider from the get-go, as they will affect which beer you choose. And, while we will discuss lagers as we explore ideal partners for fish, an ale or three will inevitably shine through in many cases.

Seeing the light

When picking the best beer styles to pair with fish dishes, lager tends to be the natural choice. This is because most fish are less rich and fatty than other proteins, such as beef, game, and poultry. So, if you have a light, flaky fish that is prepared simply or served with a light, mild sauce, any choice within the vast range of light lagers will flatter the dish. The lighter and flakier the fish, the lower in fat it will be, and the lighter you should go with your lager. If it's a freshwater fish, such as trout, then there are lots of lager choices open to you, but if you have a saltwater fish, choose a malty lager that can handle its briny flavor.

When fish get heavy

As I've already mentioned, lager with fish can work as a food-pairing mantra (much like the wine world version—white wine with fish), but

there are exceptions to every rule—even this one. The flesh of some fish, such as fresh tuna and mako shark, actually have a meat-like consistency and flavor. (If you don't believe me, try a fresh cut of medium-rare grilled tuna, and you'll see what I mean.) Other fish, such as salmon and Chilean sea bass, are actually quite oily, and their fat content approaches those of some meats. In these instances, a light lager simply won't do. The flavor profile of the fish will dominate that of the beer.

So, when fish gets more dense and oily, or if it has been smoked, fried, or doused with a heavy or creamy sauce, then your ideal pairing choice will be a beer style of similar density and flavor. In these cases, ale will almost certainly be the better beer partner than lager. And, remember, saltwater fish typically have a briny taste to them, so choose a sweeter, malty ale for these types of fish.

Thinking globally

Fish is incredibly versatile, especially when you consider all the traditional dishes from every corner of the world. From fish curries to sushi, this internationally beloved food deserves the most international of beverages: beer. And beer is a particularly stellar partner for spicy fish dishes, such as wasabi-laced sushi. In their

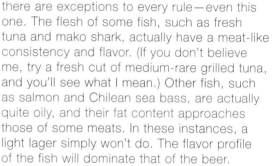

countries of origin, most regional specialties are paired best with indigenous beers, and this is a fine alternative model to use when pairing beer with fish dishes. You can have a lot of fun

"This internationally beloved food deserves the most international of beverages: beer."

discovering the global beer choices available at your local liquor store. For example, try a Japanese lager with your sushi; or try an Pale Ale from the United Kingdom with your fried fish and chips.

For unexpected results you could even pair fish dishes from one country with beers from another. For example, Alaskan smoked salmon works beautifully with a strong, roasty Stout from the Caribbean. At a World War II-themed beer dinner we once hosted we paired Axis nation dishes with Allied nation beers. Who would have thought a malty English Brown Ale could go so well with spaghetti and meatballs?

rules of thumb
beer for fish

The dots on this chart represent some simplified rules on the characteristics to look out for when pairing beer with fish. There can be exceptions to the rules and, where applicable, these are mentioned in the text below each entry. On a scale of one to five the dots below represent the suggested intensity of a beer's objective characteristics. Five dots indicate a very strong characteristic, while one dot means that the property is less prominent.

COLOR ● ●
Exception: Grilled steak fish can pair well with darker beers.

SWEET ● ● ●

BODY ● ●
Exception: Fish dishes with richer sauces can pair well with stronger beers.

YEAST ●

HOPS ● ●

beer & fish pairings

Fish with lager can be a sound pairing strategy if your fish is light and prepared simply, but it's a little limiting. The best beer to choose will depend on a variety of factors, such as the species of fish, how it's prepared, as well as whether it's oily or light. Given all these variables, in a lot of cases, an ale will work nicely, too—and sometimes better.

1

SUSHI/SASHIMI &
Avery White Rascal

For sushi and sashimi, I would recommend a wheat beer, since it has a malty backbone that will stand up to spicy wasabi, but it's also subtle enough that it won't overwhelm the delicate varied flavors of the sushi rolls themselves. You won't be disappointed with White Rascal from the Avery Brewing Company in Colorado.
This works too: German Hefeweizen

2

FRIED FISH AND CHIPS &
Bink Blond Hoppy Golden Ale

A straightforward dish like this is best served with a straightforward beer that is dry and bubbly enough to cut through the palate-coating batter. Try a Belgian Pale Ale, like Bink Blond Hoppy Golden Ale from Belgium's Brouwerij Kerkom Brewery.
This works too: English Pale Ale

3

SMOKED SALMON &
Ridgeway Bitter

Smoked fish dishes have a deep, dark flavor, so you'll want to lean away from lighter lagers and toward an English Bitter that's both malty and hoppy. Try serving your smoked salmon with a glass of Ridgeway Bitter from England's Ridgeway Brewing Company.
This works too: Smoked Porter

4 GRILLED SARDINES &
Singha Lager

Sardines are tiny, oily fish that pack a lot of flavor. Here, you may want to contrast the intense flavor of your dish with a lighter lager. Try this one from Thailand's Singha Brewery.

This works too: Scotch Ale

5 SOLE WITH LEMON BUTTER &
Russian River Damnation

Sole is a relatively light fish, but serve it with a rich butter sauce and you'll need a beer with more muscle. Look to a Belgian-style Strong Golden Ale, such as Russian River Damnation from the Russian River Brewing Company.

This works too: Irish Red Ale

6 GRILLED TUNA &
Troeg's Troegenator Doublebock

Assuming this dish is lightly seasoned and unadorned with heavy cream or butter sauce, you will want to pair it with a robust malty lager. Lean toward beers with a reddish hue, since they were probably brewed with some version of Crystal malt, which imparts a nutty sweetness and a bit more body. A good example would be Troeg's Troegenator Doublebock from Pennsylvania.

This works too: Saison

---

specific beers
objective characteristics

The chart below lists each suggested beer's objective characteristics, as described by the number of dots used. Five dots indicate a very strong characteristic, while one dot means that the property is less prominent.

1. Avery White Rascal
Pairs well with sushi/sashimi.

Color	●
Sweet	●●●
Body	●●●
Yeast	●●●●
Hops	●

2. Bink Blond Hoppy Golden Ale
Pairs well with fried fish and chips.

Color	●●
Sweet	●●
Body	●●
Yeast	●
Hops	●●●

3. Ridgeway Bitter
Pairs well with smoked salmon.

Color	●●
Sweet	●●
Body	●
Yeast	●
Hops	●●

4. Singha Lager
Pairs well with grilled sardines.

Color	●
Sweet	●
Body	●
Yeast	●
Hops	●

5. Russian River Damnation
Pairs well with sole with lemon butter.

Color	●●
Sweet	●●
Body	●●●
Yeast	●●●
Hops	●●●

6. Troeg's Troegenator Doublebock
Pairs well with grilled tuna.

Color	●●
Sweet	●●●
Body	●●●
Yeast	●●
Hops	●

which **drink** wins

Marnie and Sam will each state their case for wine or beer, but there has to be a winner for each pairing. Conduct your own beer, wine, and food tasting, and choose which drink wins on the score card at right.

You know how a squeeze of lemon can brighten almost any fish dish? Well, wine's tartness produces similar results. A cool, **TANGY GLASS OF WHITE** or sparkling wine makes a tasty, relaxing "sauce-on-the-side" for almost any fish recipe.

While a lemon can work wonders, it is, like the wine you mention, rather **one-dimensional**. Fish can be as different as night and day, ale and lager. The amazing diversity within these two families of beer has the breadth to "hook" any fish in the deep blue sea.

The flavor rainbow in wine is **much broader** than that of beer. And I guess you'd rather avoid other issues, like wine's ability to deliver refreshment and flavor long after each sip.

Wine's flavor may linger after each sip—kind of **like a bruise** that just won't fade. Lasting side effects aren't always desirable! And while some white wines may be okay with certain fish dishes, tannic reds give all fish dishes a serious beating.

Sam

I'll agree that there are a lot of big reds that don't flatter fish, but that's only because they are so **perfectly designed** for meat. There are plenty of soft, silky reds that are brilliant with fattier fish, like salmon and tuna.

Two of the best-selling items at my restaurant are fish dishes—and with both of them, almost everybody **drinks beer**. Wines are available, too, but hardly anyone orders them.

You and the brew-boys must have been **skipping chemistry** class in high school. Most fish swim in salt water, and many fish dishes are given a salty preparation as well. To balance salt, we need acids, which all but a handful of beers lack. Wine, on the other hand, is admirably equipped to balance salty food, thanks to naturally high levels of tartness in fresh fruit. In fact, not only do salty foods taste best with tangy beverages like wine, but wine often tastes better with salty foods than on its own.

Interesting, Marnie. So what you're saying is that wine sometimes needs food to make it **taste "right"**? I've never had that problem with a beer. And when the dish in question is fish, there are plenty of beer styles to do the trick.

Marnie

you choose
which wins

After you've tasted each dish with every wine and beer, use this score card to keep track of which combinations you prefer.

	Wine	**Beer**
Sushi/sashimi	☐	☐
Fried fish and chips	☐	☐
Smoked salmon	☐	☐
Grilled sardines	☐	☐
Sole with lemon butter	☐	☐
Grilled tuna	☐	☐

wine,

beer & poultry

There's a lot more to poultry than just chicken. From tiny quail to giant geese, these birds can cover a lot of ground. Mild poultry, birds like chicken and turkey, are the blank slates of the food world. They are admirably delicious alone, or can step into virtually any recipe with ease. Denser duck and game birds provide far more flavor depth, anchoring meatier poultry dishes. And, of course, this family also encompasses foie gras, a delectable specialty of incomparable richness.

wine
& poultry

Poultry holds an enviable middle-ground among proteins—more substantial than seafood, but less so than red meat. By combining some of the strengths of both, poultry is highly flexible—a perfect foil for just about any sauce. Since wine is so food-friendly, it's a natural partner for poultry dishes of all kinds.

The chicken or the sauce?
While there are exceptions, of course, pairing with most birds follows the "white meat with white wine" rule. And among poultry, chicken reigns supreme as one of the world's most versatile and popular foods. Widely available and easy to prepare, it is a protein staple in many cultures. Chicken is as delicious when prepared simply as it is when made with complex recipes, so in pairing wines with

> ## "Alone or simply prepared, chicken lends itself to richly textured whites, like Chardonnay."

chicken, we must first determine which comes first in flavor intensity—the chicken or the sauce?

Subtle chicken recipes, like roasted chicken, let the tender meat flavors and rich, crisp skin take center stage. Such dishes pair beautifully with white wines and sparkling wines, particularly those where barrel fermentation or aging on the wine's yeasty lees add toasty, bready richness of flavor and texture, like Chardonnay and Champagne. As we move into

more intensely flavored preparations, our choice of wine partner for chicken must take its cues from the strongest flavor on the plate, and this is most often the sauce. So, spicy curried chicken will have different pairing needs than either sweet, nutty chicken Marsala or tangy, citrus-scented chicken piccata.

Talking turkey
Turkey rivals chicken in the delicate flavor of its meat, but is lower in fat content—a dieter's delight. In turkey recipes, sauces and seasonings tend to take the lead more often to balance its drier flesh, as with the traditional American cranberry sauce. Pairing wine with turkey follows similar patterns to chicken overall, although lighter-bodied wines work best with low-fat preparations, especially where turkey replaces stonger meats in burgers or sausages.

Richer poultry

On the other end of the poultry spectrum, sheer decadence makes duck more splurge than staple. As rich and flavorful as most meats, duck can handle opulent red wines, though its paler flesh favors the understatement of paler varieties like Pinot Noir. When topped with sweet, fruity glazes, duck is especially yummy with sweet, fruity wines, too. Small game birds, like quail and squab with their dense, tasty, dark meat, follow a similar pattern overall.

Richest of all are pâtés such as foie gras — the butter of the meat world. Like the richest cheeses, foie gras is brilliant when served with wines whose texture rivals its own. Thick, viscous dessert wines are especially apt when foie gras is given sweet-tart accompaniments.

Matching flavors

Flavor matching in wine has something in common with color matching in fashion: white wines tend to favor white meats, while red wines are often better suited to darker meats. Poultry favors the middle range of wine styles overall, like rich whites and light reds. But, of course, sauces and preparations can trump the protein if they are stronger in flavor, and if they dominate the taste of the dish.

Chicken is the workhorse of the poultry world, able to step into virtually any recipe with ease. Alone or simply prepared, chicken lends itself to richly textured whites, like Chardonnay and Pinot Gris. As seasoning levels increase, however, we adapt in kind, most often pairing like with like, sweet with sweet and sour with sour, as with most food pairings. Turkey rewards a similar strategy, although wine choices with lower alcohol may better flatter its low-fat meat.

Intensely does it

As flavor intensity rises with duck and game birds, we choose more intense wines. Red wine is often an ideal choice for darker fleshed poultry, though paler styles, such as Pinot Noir and Grenache, generally pair better than inky opaque wines, like Cabernet Sauvignon or Syrah/Shiraz. Some traditional recipes such as duck á l'orange or honey-basted squab slather on sweet sauces. These dishes pair best with wines that aren't fully dry.

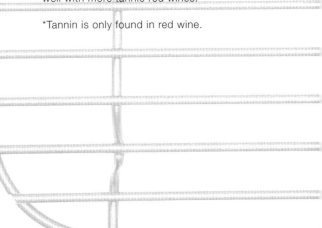

rules of thumb
wine for poultry

The dots on this chart represent some simplified rules on the characteristics to look out for when pairing wine with poultry. There can be exceptions to the rules and, where applicable, these are mentioned in the text below each entry. On a scale of one to five the dots below represent the suggested intensity of a wine's objective characteristics. Five dots indicate a very strong characteristic, while one dot means that the property is less prominent.

BODY ● ● ●
Exception: Rich poultry dishes can pair well with stronger wines.

SWEET ● ● ●
Exception: Sweet sauces can pair well with sweeter wines.

ACID ● ● ●

FRUIT ● ●

OAK ● ● ●

*TANNIN ● ●
Exception: Fattier poultry dishes can pair well with more tannic red wines.

*Tannin is only found in red wine.

wine &
poultry pairings

Poultry hugs the middle range of intensity among proteins, and it pairs beautifully with mid-intensity wines—richly textured whites and delicate reds. As with other food groups, though, we put greater pairing emphasis on the sauce or preparation if it takes the leading flavor role in the dish. In general, pairing "like with like" is the best bet.

1 | ROTISSERIE CHICKEN &
Rosemount Estate Show Reserve Chardonnay
My favorite wine partner for roasted chicken is traditional Australian Chardonnay. It echoes the flavors of the chicken with toasty oak flavor and tropical fruit aromas, like buttered pineapple cake and grilled mango. As rich as a white wine can get, this luscious example from Rosemount Estate is sure to please.
This works too: Washington Chardonnay

2 | ROASTED HOLIDAY TURKEY &
Georges Duboeuf Brouilly
Served with sweet-tart cranberry sauce, the traditional holiday turkey poses a pairing quandary. My favorite answer is Beaujolais from one of the region's premium villages, like this Brouilly from leading producer Georges Duboeuf. Soft and fruit-forward, this low-tannin red delivers lip-smacking spiced raspberry flavors without red wine's typical astringent bite.
This works too: Alsace Pinot Gris

FRIED CHICKEN & | 3
Freixenet Cordon Negro Cava
Sparkling wine is the perfect partner for fried chicken. Spanish Cava, a modestly priced sparkler inspired by luxe French Champagne is especially good. Frothy and friendly, Cavas like Cordon Negro from Freixenet provide a perfect counterpoint for the toasty crunch of fried foods. With its delicate apple-pear flavors and cleansing bubbles, Cava is awesome with fried chicken.
This works too: Chilean Chardonnay

4 | DUCK CONFIT &
Faiveley Mercurey

This tender, succulent dish is an ideal match for pale red wines that provide ample flavor and acidity, like the earthy Pinot Noirs of France's Burgundy region. This accessible wine from respected producer Faiveley is tart and mid-weight with aromas of sour cherries and autumn leaves, a perfect counterpoint for duck confit.

This works too: Italian Rosso di Montalcino

5 | FOIE GRAS/COUNTRY PÂTÉ &
Chateau de Montfort Vouvray

Foie gras is traditionally accompanied by sweet-tart fruit sauces or compotes. Wines like this Vouvray from respected Loire estate Chateau de Montfort, provide similar pairing assets—toothsome sweetness and vibrant sharpness. Their fresh fruit qualities highlight and balance the decadent depth of foie gras.

This works too: German Riesling Spätlese

6 | GRILLED QUAIL &
Rancho Zabaco SHV Select Zinfandel

Big, juicy reds like this dense and robust Zinfandel from California's Ranch Zabaco are great with these dark-fleshed fowl. Packed with dense, dark fruit flavors, like dried fig and blueberry pie, plush Zinfandels are soft in astringency and flirt with overt sweetness, all pluses with the smoky-sweet taste of grilled quail.

This works too: Australian Grenache

specific wines
objective characteristics

This chart lists each suggested wine's objective characteristics, as described by the number of dots used. Five dots indicate a very strong characteristic, while one dot means that the property is less prominent. Zero dots indicate that the characteristic is not present.

1. Rosemount Show Reserve Chardonnay
Pairs well with rotisserie chicken.

Body	● ● ● ●
Sweet	● ●
Acid	● ● ●
Fruit	● ● ● ● ●
Oak	● ● ● ● ●

2. Georges Duboeuf Brouilly
Pairs well with roasted holiday turkey.

Body	● ● ●
Sweet	●
Acid	● ● ●
Fruit	● ● ● ●
Oak	●
Tannin	●

3. Freixenet Cordon Negro Cava
Pairs well with fried chicken.

Body	● ● ●
Sweet	● ●
Acid	● ● ● ●
Fruit	● ●
Oak	

4. Faiveley Mercurey
Pairs well with duck confit.

Body	● ● ●
Sweet	
Acid	● ● ● ●
Fruit	● ● ●
Oak	● ●
Tannin	● ●

5. Chateau de Montfort Vouvray
Pairs well with foie gras/country pâté.

Body	● ●
Sweet	● ● ● ●
Acid	● ● ● ●
Fruit	● ● ●
Oak	

6. Rancho Zabaco SHV Select Zinfandel
Pairs well with grilled quail.

Body	● ● ● ● ●
Sweet	● ●
Acid	● ● ●
Fruit	● ● ● ● ●
Oak	● ● ● ●
Tannin	● ● ●

beer
& poultry

Poultry runs the gamut in terms of flavor, fat content, and texture, so it's not surprising that different types of poultry have different pairing requirements. Luckily, there are lots of great beers to choose from, no matter what type of poultry you happen to be serving.

Poultry: the Tabula Rasa

Poultry is one of America's most popular meats, and it is the classic blank canvas in terms of beverage pairing potential. Its flavor is generally more neutral than that of fish or beef, and the tender, porous meat is a perfect base for absorbing the variety of flavors that come from spice rubs, marinades, sauces, and cooking techniques.

Identify the main flavors

As you approach your poultry pairings, disregard all axioms and focus on the brightest component in the character of the dish. What flavors and aromas jump out at you? If it is a

above and beyond the neutral flavors of the meat itself. But, in general with these types of lighter, leaner poultry, it's best to veer toward the ales and dark lagers, and steer clear of hoppy, acidic beers. Milder malty beers are rich and lush enough to lift and accentuate the subtle flavors of the bird, whereas beers with intense spices and flavors will almost certainly overwhelm a simple chicken or turkey dish.

Fattier poultry

Spicy or acidic beers and highly hopped, astringent varieties can make lighter poultry such as chicken and light meat turkey

> ## "Poultry is one of America's most popular meats, and it is the classic blank canvas in terms of beverage pairing potential."

simple chicken sauté, it might be the subtle, nutty character of the meat itself, or if it's sweet and sour chicken, you're more likely to focus on the sweet, vinegary sauce. Pair your beverage choice with these flavors.

Light meat poultry

With light, low-fat poultry, such as chicken and light meat turkey, the odds are pretty good that you will get your pairing cues from something

taste dry and cardboardy. However, these drinks, when paired with fattier fowl such as duck, goose, or dark turkey meat can be

magnificent. This is because the hoppiness of IPAs, Farmhouse Ales, and lagers, and the acidic bite of dry Lambics serve to cut through the greasiness of the bird, making for a more balanced pairing combination. So, armed with this knowledge, if you happen to be assigned the task of selecting the celebratory alcohol for the holiday goose, you know what to do.

Gamey birds

While less common than chicken, duck, and turkey, game birds, such as pheasant and quail, can make for a memorable meal. They aren't as fatty as goose and duck, and tend to have a sweeter, more robust flavor. With these stronger-tasting meats, look to a Strong Ale for a good match, but you should also seek out a roasty brown ale, which will work, too.

Saucy birds

Sauces and seasonings can be the deciding factor in food and beer pairing, and nowhere is this more true than with poultry. As I mentioned before, most poultry has a very subtle taste, and, therefore, most recipes rely heavily on seasoning to rev up the flavor. If your poultry dish derives most of its flavor from a sauce or seasoning, you should first determine whether that sauce is sweet, savory, or spicy. This will guide you toward the optimum beer partner.

Poultry prepared with a sweet sauce, such as barbeque chicken, sweet and sour duck, and chicken salad accented with raisins or other fruits, will work best when supported by spicy or acidic beers, such as IPAs and Lambics.

For poultry made with dry rubs and spicy sauces, such as tandoori chicken and Cajun-style chicken, look for a beer that will reign in the dish's heat and pungent flavors. Malty, sweet beers, such as Marzens and Oktoberfests will do this nicely.

rules of thumb
beer for poultry

The dots on this chart represent some simplified rules on the characteristics to look out for when pairing beer with poultry. There can be exceptions to the rules and, where applicable, these are mentioned in the text below each entry. On a scale of one to five the dots below represent the suggested intensity of a beer's objective characteristics. Five dots indicate a very strong characteristic, while one dot means that the property is less prominent.

COLOR ● ● ●
Exception: Simply prepared poultry can pair well with paler beers.

SWEET ● ● ●

BODY ● ●
Exception: Richer poultry dishes can pair well with stronger beers.

YEAST ●
Exception: Flavorful poultry dishes can pair well with yeastier beers.

HOPS ● ●

beer &
poultry pairings

From goose to game to chicken, poultry comes in all flavors and textures. In addition to that, it's an incredibly adaptable food that can withstand seasonings and sauces of all kinds, which makes it a worldwide hit. It also has the added benefit of pairing fantastically well with beer.

1 ROTISSERIE CHICKEN & Escura Eisenbahn

Rotisserie chicken needs a rich, dark lager like a Schwarzbier to showcase its flavors. The roasty malts used in brewing Escura Eisenbahn infuse it with notes of chocolate that play to the dish's many assets.
This works too: Trappist Ale

2 ROASTED HOLIDAY TURKEY & De Dolle Extra Export Stout

A slow-roasted turkey will have more intense, gamey flavors than chicken. Impress your relatives by pulling out the big guns—something from your beer cellar. (Most beers over 8 percent abv will improve in subtlety and complexity after a year in a wine—oops, I mean beer cellar.) Try pulling out a few bottles of Extra Export Stout—an inky, warming ale from De Dolle Brewery.
This works too: Brown Porter

3 FRIED CHICKEN & Alpine Pure Hoppiness

Chicken, a lean meat, is imbued with rich, buttery goodness when it's fried. And, since fried chicken is an American classic, it makes good sense to pair it with an American IPA. As you might expect, Pure Hoppiness (from the Alpine Beer Company), has enough hop character to cut through this dish's greasiness.
This works too: Imperial Pilsner

166

4

DUCK CONFIT &
Jenlain Blonde
Duck is pretty high in fat, so it needs a beer that's hoppy enough to balance out this heaviness. And, it's only fitting to pair a French culinary classic like duck confit with another French classic: Jenlain Blonde, a noteworthy Bière de Garde.
This works too: Bohemian Pilsner

5

FOIE GRAS/
COUNTRY PÂTÉ &
Kulmbacher EKU 28
Pâté and foie gras are such rich foods that they are best enjoyed spread thinly over bread, much like butter. A beer with ample palate-cleansing carbonation is in order here, so try a German Eisbock Lager, such as Kulmbacher EKU 28.
This works too: Belgian Tripel

6

GRILLED QUAIL &
Adnams Broadside Ale
A gamey bird like quail will pair best with an English Strong Ale. Adnams Broadside Ale has an earthy, malty quality that will meld perfectly with the rich, earthy flavors of the grilled quail.
This works too: American Amber Ale

specific beers
objective characteristics

The chart below lists each suggested beer's objective characteristics, as described by the number of dots used. Five dots indicate a very strong characteristic, while one dot means that the property is less prominent.

1. Escura Eisenbahn
Pairs well with rotisserie chicken.

Color	● ● ●
Sweet	● ● ●
Body	● ●
Yeast	●
Hops	

2. De Dolle Extra Export Stout
Pairs well with roasted holiday turkey.

Color	● ● ● ●
Sweet	● ● ●
Body	● ● ●
Yeast	● ●
Hops	● ●

3. Alpine Pure Hoppiness
Pairs well with fried chicken.

Color	● ●
Sweet	● ●
Body	● ● ●
Yeast	●
Hops	● ● ● ●

4. Jenlain Blonde
Pairs well with duck confit.

Color	● ●
Sweet	● ● ●
Body	● ● ●
Yeast	● ● ●
Hops	● ●

5. Kulmbacher EKU 28
Pairs well with foie gras or country pâté.

Color	● ●
Sweet	● ● ●
Body	● ●
Yeast	●
Hops	●

6. Adnams Broadside Ale
Pairs well with grilled quail.

Color	● ● ●
Sweet	● ● ●
Body	● ● ●
Yeast	●
Hops	● ●

which **drink** wins

Marnie and Sam will each state their case for wine or beer, but there has to be a winner for each pairing. Conduct your own beer, wine, and food tasting, and choose which drink wins on the score card at right.

On its own, poultry can be kind of bland, which is probably why, in its simplest form, it works so well with wine. But amp up the sauces or seasonings, and poultry dishes become **WORTHY OF PAIRING** with a beer.

I can't believe a brew-geek like you is using words like "bland" to malign wine—**pot, meet kettle**. The majority of beer tastes like water gone bad. Besides, wine goes better with poultry because wine goes better with food, period.

Full-flavored specialty craft beers are **hardly bland**, and they work magic with the best poultry dishes. Craft beers (not wine) represent the fastest growth in the adult beverage market.

Spin the numbers all you like, Sam, but wine is always in demand. At least part of the reason wine sales are on fire is that it's a natural food partner that goes with everything. People just drink beer **for the buzz.**

Sam

168

Marnie

That buzz you mention is the sound of beer overtaking wine as the go-to beverage for food pairing. With poultry, a mouth-watering beer lubricates your palate for the next scrumptious bite, while wine just **dries it out**.

I'm hearing a lot of talk, but I'd like to see some substance. Just show me the beer that can reach the **TRANSCENDENT HEIGHTS** of duck confit with red Burgundy.

I'll give you two: a caramelly Maibock or a French Farmhouse Ale! The rules for pairing beer and poultry are very simple. Can you show me a simple wine pairing paradigm—or are you chicken?

Wine pairing does require a little more thought, but only because the results are so much more **complex and delicious**. What you call simple, I call simplistic. By your logic, Rembrandt would fall far short of paint-by-numbers.

you choose
which wins

After you've tasted each dish with every wine and beer, use this score card to keep track of which combinations you prefer.

	Wine	**Beer**
Rotisserie chicken	☐	☐
Roasted holiday turkey	☐	☐
Fried chicken	☐	☐
Duck confit	☐	☐
Foie gras/ country pâté	☐	☐
Grilled quail	☐	☐

wine, beer

& meat

Meats like beef, lamb, and pork rank among the most intense of proteins, delivering heaping helpings of taste and texture. The depth of flavor found in these meats allow them to easily stand alone as a satisfying entrée, and when served with sauces, meats can handle stronger seasoning better than any other type of food. Whether it's cured or smoked, seared or grilled, meat provides an opportunity to bring intense and flavorful beverages to the table.

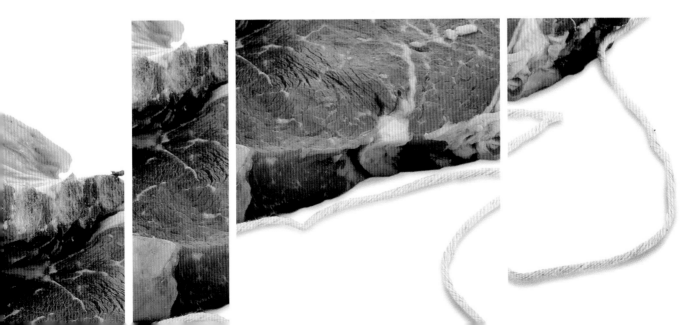

wine & meat

Just by looking at meats, our natural pairing instincts lead us to red wine, and for good reason. A near perfect match in flavor and heft, red with red won't let you down. The majority of beers, which are light and fizzy, pale in comparison. Stop by any steakhouse and see for yourself what people drink with fine cuts of beef.

Tannic magic

In addition to the natural flavor and color synergies of red wine and red meats, food chemistry also works in this pairing's favor. Red wines acquire a component called tannin, since they must "stew" on their skins to pick up color and flavor during fermentation. Tannin triggers a palpable "drying" effect in the mouth by blocking normal salivation. In the case of highly tannic wines, like Cabernet Sauvignon or Barolo, an arid "cottonmouth" feeling can linger and intensify.

Red wine's tannic "drying" effect on the palate can be a challenge when pairing wines with foods that are low in fat. But, when combined with rich or oily foods, tannins can be a boon. Their mild astringency counteracts the "greasiness" on the palate, sopping up the excess oils and fats like a bread crust mopping up drippings.

As the saying goes...

So, as it turns out, the old adage of "white wine with fish, red wine with meat" has had it right all along—mostly. Both the concentration of deep, dark flavors and the tannic qualities of red wines are tremendous assets in partnering with the dense heft of hearty meats. As with any rule, though, there are always exceptions. For example, some pale meats, like pork and veal, can partner well with flavorful white wines. This is especially true when the meat has been cured, as with prosciutto or sausages. Even darker meats, like beef, can work better with tangy white if they're served raw and lightly dressed, as with steak tartare or carpaccio.

Like with like

The flavors found in meats resonate best with wines that echo their saturation of color, from the palest veal and limpid Pinot Noir to the darkest venison and inky Petite Sirah. Matching colors and matching flavors often go hand in hand. While the pale flavors of lemon or Champagne vinegar may suit seafood, meats turn our thoughts toward barbeque sauce or balsamic vinegar. Since wine is but another "sauce on the side", it stands to reason that the meatier, spicier flavors found in big red wines are at home with hearty steaks and roasts.

Seasoning matters

When seasonings are understated, choose wines with modest alcohol contents, like medium-bodied European reds. Bolder spicing or dense reduction sauces will reward stronger wines with riper and more concentrated

> **❝ As it turns out, the old adage of 'white wine with fish, red wine with meat' had it right all along—mostly. ❞**

flavors, like fruit-forward new world reds from the Americas or the Southern Hemisphere. In addition to the seasoning used in a recipe, extra fat content in a meat dish, from sources such as melted butter or a stock-based demi-glaze, will also boost its overall intensity and capacity for handling intense red wine flavors.

What about sweet dishes?

If a meat dish is topped with a sweet or fruity sauce, such as barbeque sauce or honey glaze, look to wines that burst with ripe fruit aromas and aren't aggressively dry. Warm regions and modern winemaking tend to produce such red wines, whose sweet jammy fruit aromas can balance sweet preparations.

Cool zones and traditional winemaking, such as that practiced in the classic regions of France and Italy, are far better suited to the salty, savory, and herbal ends of the flavor spectrum. When sugary sauces are paired with old-fashioned French Bordeaux or Italian Brunello, they can leave the wine tasting brittle and twiggy.

rules of thumb
wine for meat

The dots on this chart represent some simplified rules on the characteristics to look out for when pairing wine with meat. There can be exceptions to the rules and, where applicable, these are mentioned in the text below each entry. On a scale of one to five the dots below represent the suggested intensity of a wine's objective characteristics. Five dots indicate a very strong characteristic, while one dot means that the property is less prominent.

BODY ● ● ● ●
Exception: Low-fat preparations can pair well with lighter wines.

SWEET ●
Exception: Sweet glazes and sauces can pair well with sweeter wines.

ACID ● ●
Exception: Acidic sauces can pair well with wines that are more tart.

FRUIT ● ● ● ●

OAK ● ● ● ●

*TANNIN ● ● ● ●

*Tannin is only found in red wine.

wine & meat pairings

While the palest meats may occasionally wander into white wine territory, meat dishes generally favor red wines and rosés. Red meats are flavorful and high in fat compared to other food groups. This richness softens the astringent tannic edge found in nearly all red wines that can make them seem harsh or leathery alone.

1 | SIRLOIN STEAK &
Joseph Phelps Cabernet Sauvignon

One whiff of steak on the grill and we crave a big red wine. Nothing can compete with a complex, full-bodied red wine like Napa Valley Cabernet Sauvignon. Packed with layers of black fruit and smoky oak flavors, like cassis liqueur and vanilla, this inky red from legendary Joseph Phelps is velvety soft enough to drink young, yet muscular enough to man-handle a juicy steak.
This works too: Italian Aglianico

2 | PORK CHOPS &
Josmeyer Le Kottabe Riesling

Most pork chop recipes pair best with sharp white wines. Many consider Riesling a light-weight, but Alsace in northern France makes a dry version that has the heft to cut through savory meats. Unusually dry, richly textured Rieslings, like this one from Josmeyer, feature piercing aromatics and acidity that make the mouth water.
This works too: California Pinot Noir

POT ROAST & | 3
Pio Cesare Barolo

Earthy and dense, classic Italian Barolo is my favorite partner for pot roast. Deceptively pale, Barolos, like this one from Pio Cesare, can seem harsh alone: aggressively acidic, alcoholic, and tannic. But, one bite of rich braised meat will tame this tiger and leave it purring like a kitten, unfurling flavors of wild berries and dried flowers.
This works too: Washington State Merlot

4 | BARBEQUE RIBS &
Montecillo Rioja Crianza

This dish is a natural partner for red Spanish Rioja, like this vibrant Crianza from trusted Montecillo. Medium-bodied Rioja is as lithe as a dancer, expressive with aromas of cherries and exotic spices, but not overly alcoholic. Plus, Rioja's overtly oaky flavors marry beautifully with smoked foods like barbeque ribs.

This works too: Australian Shiraz

5 | LAMB CHOPS &
Chateau Phélan-Ségur St. Estèphe

Lamb chops work magically with red wines from Bordeaux's famed "left bank". These wild berry and cedar-scented wines are broodingly dark, but exude sophistication and elegance. Chateaux like Phélan-Ségur make wine the traditional way, solidly structured with savory food in mind.

This works too: Chilean Carmenère

6 | GLAZED HAM &
Sanford Pinot Noir

For sweet and salty glazed ham, I turn to soft, silky reds like this Pinot Noir from Sanford in Santa Barbara. Bright fruit meets a wisp of smoky oak in a package that is as refreshing as it is rich, redolent of raspberries and cloves. Pinot Noir's delicate flavors satisfy without overwhelming, perfectly suited for gracing glazed ham.

This works too: Alsace Pinot Gris

specific wines
objective characteristics

This chart lists each suggested wine's objective characteristics, as described by the number of dots used. Five dots indicate a very strong characteristic, while one dot means that the property is less prominent. Zero dots indicate that the characteristic is not present.

1. Joseph Phelps Cabernet Sauvignon
Pairs well with sirloin steak.

Body	●●●●
Sweet	●
Acid	●●●
Fruit	●●●●●
Oak	●●●●
Tannin	●●●●

2. Josmeyer Le Kottabe Riesling
Pairs well with pork chops.

Body	●●●
Sweet	●
Acid	●●●●●
Fruit	●●●
Oak	

3. Pio Cesare Barolo
Pairs well with pot roast.

Body	●●●●●
Sweet	
Acid	●●●●
Fruit	●●●
Oak	●●●
Tannin	●●●●●

4. Montecillo Rioja Crianza
Pairs well with barbeque ribs.

Body	●●●
Sweet	●
Acid	●●●●
Fruit	●●●●
Oak	●●●●
Tannin	●●●

5. Chateau Phélan-Ségur St. Estèphe
Pairs well with lamb chops.

Body	●●●●
Sweet	
Acid	●●●
Fruit	●●●●
Oak	●●●
Tannin	●●●

6. Sanford Pinot Noir
Pairs well with glazed ham.

Body	●●●
Sweet	●
Acid	●●●●
Fruit	●●●
Oak	●●●
Tannin	●●

beer
& meat

Most people assume that red wines pair best with meat. And, while Marnie will point out exceptions to the rule, the association between the two is still a strong one. Luckily, beer drinkers tend to take a more broad-minded approach to food pairing—and this is a good thing because there are nearly as many great lagers as ales for pairing with meat.

Fit for a king

When archaeologists excavated a tomb thought to house the legendary King Midas, they discovered bowls of petrified lamb stew and drinking cauldrons laced with residue. Upon analysis, they learned that the cauldrons contained a concoction consisting of barley, honey, white-muscat grapes, and saffron. That's right, folks—they found beer, an exalted beverage for an exalted leader. King Midas was honored on his burial day with a grand send-off, complete with an ample supply of this heady brew and a meat stew to give him sustenance for his journey from this world to the next.

Then as now, a meat dish paired with beer is the height of good taste. In fact, one might say that beer is like a liquid time capsule, capable of transporting us back in time and connecting us, as beer drinkers, with the birth of civilization. And even if you don't necessarily agree with that sentiment, you have to admit that beer does pair majestically with meat.

Gamey and fatty meats

When pairing beer with meat, the first thing to consider is the flavor and texture of the meat itself. Some meats, such as lamb and buffalo, are inherently more pungent and gamey than others. Since the strong flavors of these meats can overpower a light lager, a stronger beer is in order. A spicy ale or a robust fruit ale will pair well with these foods, since these beer styles are higher in alcohol, and have the full body and complexity to match the intensity of the meat. Milder, fattier meat dishes, such as roast beef and steak, tend to partner beautifully with a well-hopped Pale Ale or Strong Belgian Ale. This is because hops give beer an astringency that can cut through fattiness in foods.

Lighter meats

Some meats, such as pork and veal, are actually quite light when compared with a burly cut of beef. Pork and veal therefore have more in common with chicken than they do with a big ol' cut of porterhouse. Their flavors are delicately nuanced and, if paired with a strong beer, these types of meat are likely to be overwhelmed by the beer's intensity.

So, for light meats like these I recommend a classic, malty Brown Ale or a Continental Lager. While richer in body and more complex than the traditional light lagers, these styles

are mellow and approachable. They're less hoppy and lower in alcohol than the styles of beer that work best with the heavier, fattier, and more pungent meats.

The secret's in the sauce

As with any food and drink pairing, it's always important to acknowledge the most prominent flavor of the dish. It may be the meat itself, but it could equally well be the sauce the meat dish is prepared with, especially if it's a very heavy one, or if it incorporates a lot of spices and seasonings. For example, a dish served with a cream sauce will undoubtedly be heavy—even if the meat itself is a light one, such as pork. Since thick, rich sauces tend to coat the palate, you'll need a well-carbonated beer whose ample effervescence will slice through all that heavy cream.

Incidentally, it's here, in the sauce and spice department, that wine falls short of beer. Cream sauces can stifle most wines. And spicy preparations are also a real challenge for wine, since its high alcohol content actually exacerbates the heat of the dish. Fortunately, there are no such limitations with beer. Malty beers of a more traditional alcohol content (4–6 percent abv) are the perfect foils for fiery meat sauces. The sweetness of malt reduces heat perception, and the lower alcohol content muffles spice intensity. Marzens, Dark Lagers, and English Brown Ales are all well-suited to heavily spiced meats, while German Doppelbocks and Belgian Saisons go well with cream-based meat dishes.

Method in the madness

In addition to spices, sauces, and the type of meat in question, the cooking method itself must also be factored into the beer-pairing equation. If a dish is boiled or baked, these methods will contribute very little to the final flavor of the meat. But sautéing tends to give meat a sweetish flavor, while grilling gives it a roasty, caramelized character. Ales that are both sweet and malty (rather than hoppy) will pair nicely with grilled and sautéed meats. These ales work so well, in fact, that they can also make great marinades for certain cuts of meat that will be prepared on the grill or skillet.

rules of thumb
beer for meat

The dots on this chart represent some simplified rules on the characteristics to look out for when pairing beer with meat. There can be exceptions to the rules and, where applicable, these are mentioned in the text below each entry. On a scale of one to five the dots below represent the suggested intensity of a beer's objective characteristics. Five dots indicate a very strong characteristic, while one dot means that the property is less prominent.

COLOR ● ● ● ●

SWEET ● ● ● ●
Exception: Savory meat dishes can pair well with drier beers.

BODY ● ● ●

YEAST ● ● ●

HOPS ● ● ●
Exception: Highly seasoned meat dishes can pair well with hoppier beers.

beer & meat pairings

The world of beer offers many perfect pairing opportunities for all kinds of meat dishes. For meat recipes that involve rich sauces, beer has the dual secret weapons of carbonation and hops, which both serve to cut through grease, fat, and cream. Whether it's lager or ale, beer is simply tailor-made for meat.

1
SIRLOIN STEAK &
Chimay Première
Sirloin steak—the ultimate simple, succulent restaurant classic is traditionally matched with dry tannic red wines in less-enlightened corners of the world. But it would be better paired with a complex, fruity brown ale. Pair a classic with a classic: Chimay Première (also known as Chimay Red)—the Bordeaux-bashing spicy favorite from Belgium.
This works too: Belgian Dubbel

2
PORK CHOPS &
Schneider Aventinus
Pork is a light meat that has a subtle flavor. To avoid overpowering this dish, try a German Weizenbock, which is a wheat beer brewed in the Bock style. A great example would be Schneider Aventinus from G. Schneider & Sohn Brewery in Germany.
This works too: Wee Heavy

3
POT ROAST &
Unibroue Maudite
Smoky, roasted meat dishes quickly throw wine on the defensive, but dark beers step right up to the challenge. In this case, good partners exist on both the ale and lager sides of the aisle. But here, I would recommend a Belgian-style Strong Dark Ale. One of my favorites is Maudite, a beer from Canada's Unibroue.
This works too: Dortmunder Lager

4

BARBEQUE RIBS &
Hop Back Entire Stout

Barbeque ribs are both sweet and smoky, but this one tends to throw a bit more spice into the mix. Look to a sweeter beer with lower alcohol levels to reign in the spiciness. At 4.5 percent abv, Entire Stout from the Hop Back Brewery is moderately low in alcohol, and it's rich, roasty, and malty enough to extinguish the spicy fire of any barbeque.

This works too: Australian Lager

5

LAMB CHOPS &
Hair of the Dog Fred

Wines can't hang with the mint jelly that often accompanies these chops. But gamey meats with tangy relishes are quickly tamed by full-flavored, stronger beers. An American Barleywine with lots of hop character, like Oregon's Hair of the Dog Fred, will pair nicely with this dish and its zingy accompaniments.

This works too: English Brown Ale

6

GLAZED HAM &
Theakston Old Peculier Ale

Glazed ham is both sweet and salty, so it needs a smooth, mellow beer partner. Theakston Old Peculier, a world-famous English Old Ale, is earthy, fruity, and malty enough to make the flavors in this dish shine.

This works too: Marzen

specific beers
objective characteristics

The chart below lists each suggested beer's objective characteristics, as described by the number of dots used. Five dots indicate a very strong characteristic, while one dot means that the property is less prominent.

1. Chimay Première
Pairs well with sirloin steak.

Color	● ● ●
Sweet	● ● ●
Body	● ●
Yeast	● ● ●
Hops	● ●

2. Schneider Aventinus
Pairs well with pork chops.

Color	● ●
Sweet	● ● ● ●
Body	● ● ●
Yeast	● ● ●
Hops	● ●

3. Unibroue Maudite
Pairs well with pot roast.

Color	● ● ●
Sweet	● ● ●
Body	● ● ●
Yeast	● ●
Hops	● ●

4. Hop Back Entire Stout
Pairs well with barbeque ribs.

Color	● ● ● ●
Sweet	● ● ● ● ●
Body	● ● ●
Yeast	● ● ●
Hops	●

5. Hair of the Dog Fred
Pairs well with lamb chops.

Color	● ● ●
Sweet	● ● ● ●
Body	● ● ●
Yeast	● ●
Hops	● ● ●

6. Theakston Old Peculier Ale
Pairs well with glazed ham.

Color	● ● ●
Sweet	● ● ●
Body	● ● ●
Yeast	● ●
Hops	● ●

which **drink** wins

Marnie and Sam will each state their case for wine or beer, but there has to be a winner for each pairing. Conduct your own beer, wine, and food tasting, and choose which drink wins on the score card at right.

There is only one way to go with a sizzling steak or rack of lamb: rich red wines. They deliver enough **flavor concentration** to stand up to meats, and manage to be refreshing. That's why red wine is king in every steakhouse in the world.

True—red meat pairs best with a red-hued beverage. Problem is, you've bet on **THE WRONG ONE**. Mahogany-toned beers like Belgian Dubbels, Flemish Reds, and even certain fruit varieties cut through palate-pounding fat and into the meat of the matter better than your glorified grape juice.

My **beef with beer** is that it sits heavily on the palate and in the belly. Wine's asset is its miraculous balance of powerful flavor and delicate refreshment. Unlike beer, a little sip of wine goes a long way!

Big, bold beers truly **do pair best** with gut-busting dishes like meat loaf or prime rib. But the more delicate dishes like lamb chops or steak tartare will also find perfect partners in beer—albeit lighter, more delicate styles, such as apricot ales or Hefeweizens.

Marnie

Sam

Not quite. Wine and meat **BALANCE ONE ANOTHER** in a way that beer just can't match. Red wine's tannin acts to sop up the greasiness of fatty meats, while meat softens the tannic edge that wine can have when served alone.

Can't winemakers make wine that tastes good **on its own**? Oh wait—wine is made by weather, not people. Thankfully, beer is made by the people, for the people, so brewers can add more hops to cut the richness of meat dishes down to size.

The best flavors in the world are natural, not dreamed up in Dr. Frankenstein's laboratory! Wine is superior to beer because it is exactly the way **nature intended**.

Is that "whine" spelled with an "h", Marnie? If man wasn't meant to improve upon nature, we'd still be hunting meat with a spear. **Civilization was born** out of agriculture, and the first crops weren't grapes, but grains—you know, the stuff found in beer!

you choose
which wins

After you've tasted each dish with every wine and beer, use this score card to keep track of which combinations you prefer.

	Wine	**Beer**
Sirloin steak	☐	☐
Pork chops	☐	☐
Pot roast	☐	☐
Barbeque ribs	☐	☐
Lamb chops	☐	☐
Glazed ham	☐	☐

wine, beer

& fruit desserts

From pale melons to dark figs, from tart berries to creamy bananas, fruit is a pleasure to behold and to savor. Like a gracious gift from the sun and the earth, perfectly ripe fruits in their colorful wrappings are a sweet revelation. Poignantly balanced flavors make fruit a natural choice to take the starring role in sweet desserts. Whether baked in a pie or frozen in a sorbet, fresh fruits need little adornment or seasoning to taste delicious, but can be complemented by a wide range of flavorful beverages.

wine
& fruit desserts

Dessert wines are the ultimate choice to complement fruit desserts. After all, these wines are, themselves, desserts. Dessert wines are broadly defined as those with an obvious presence of sweetness. Ripe grapes are such delightful treats that every wine region on earth makes wines that mimic their sweet-tart balance.

The world of dessert wines

While all dessert wines are sweet, they range widely in sugar content, from medium-sweet, like apple juice, to super-sweet, like maple syrup. Since winemaking transforms naturally occurring sugar into alcohol, making dessert wine involves tweaking the standard practice. It's most common to manipulate the ratio of water to sugar in the grapes or juice before fermentation begins, but simply halting fermentation prematurely can also do the trick.

Late harvest wines

Wines made in the late harvest style, where grapes are left to hang longer on the vine than for dry wines, are especially good for pairing with fruit desserts. The grapes continue to ripen, getting sweeter and developing more flavor. They also begin to shrivel, driving up concentration further by shedding water. Dubbed "late harvest" for the delay in picking, the wines made from such ultra-ripe fruit are honeyed and rich. These wines are expensive to make, so few are modestly priced.

An elite category of late harvest wines are those whose shriveling stage is expedited by the fungus *Botrytis cinerea*, also called "noble rot". By weakening grape skins, botrytis speeds evaporation, concentrating sugar and flavor before fresh-tasting grape acids drop. The fungus also adds its own haunting flavor, reminiscent of wildflower honey and saffron. Originally pioneered in the Tokaji region of

Hungary, botrytis wines soon spread to other countries. The most famous dessert wines of France and Germany, like Sauternes and Auslese, are luscious botrytised styles, which are now themselves imitated in any region cool enough to do it well.

In cold climates, like Germany and Canada, an extreme variation on the late harvest theme produces the rare, prized "ice wine". Left on the vine into mid-winter, raisinated grapes freeze solid, trapping most of the remaining water in solid crystal form. Squeezed quickly at freezing temperatures, their nectar is staggeringly sweet and flavorful, producing epic wines in teeny tiny quantities.

Asti wines

Another style friendly to fruit desserts is made by far less costly means, by interrupting yeasts before they convert all sugar to alcohol. This process preserves the freshness of flavor present in the grapes. The light, sparkling wines of Asti, in northwestern Italy, taste as sappy as biting into a juicy peach. Made by stopping fermentation midstream, Asti's unique taste is like a snapshot documenting the transition of white grape juice into wine.

Mirroring tricks

Our senses cannot process two sources of similar sensation at once. Sweet food and sweet wine do not taste more sweet together—they will both taste less sweet. Sam may complain that some dessert wines seem syrupy. But this is simply because wine is designed as a food partner.

Sweetness in food leaves wines tasting more sour and less sweet than they do alone, rarely a flattering effect with dry wines. Fruit desserts, whether they are made with apples or lemons, raisins or raspberries, are usually both sweet and tart, and so need wine partners that share both qualities. The more sugary the dessert, the more sweetness is needed in the wine to achieve harmony. On the flipside, the more tart the dessert, the more acidity is required. Therefore, the most favorable wine pairings with fruit desserts tend to be those whose flavor balance most closely mirrors that of the fruit in the dish.

Pairing patterns

Most fruit desserts retain the sweet-tart qualities of their main ingredient. Within the dessert wine universe, vibrant sweet-tart styles are a specialty of cool climates, since excessive heat breaks down fresh fruit acids. Stylistically, these are largely white and sparkling dessert wines. Most fall in the late harvest family of dessert wines, but some may be made by interrupting fermentation before it is complete.

As with most pairings, color matching helps to fine-tune pairings as well. With darker-skinned fruit desserts, like berries and cherries, pink and red wines will sync up nicely flavor-wise. But few red dessert wines are cool climate styles, and the strongest, like Port, can overwhelm the delicate flavors of fresh fruit. However, when fruit is dried, stewed, or brandied, warm climate dessert wines and fortified wines start to fit the bill.

rules of thumb
wine for fruit desserts

The dots on this chart represent some simplified rules on the characteristics to look out for when pairing wine with fruit desserts. There can be exceptions to the rules and, where applicable, these are mentioned in the text below each entry. On a scale of one to five the dots below represent the suggested intensity of a wine's objective characteristics. Five dots indicate a very strong characteristic, while one dot means that the property is less prominent.

BODY ●●●
Exception: Fresh fruits and sorbets can pair well with lighter wines.

SWEET ●●●●

ACID ●●●●
Exception: Cooked fruit desserts can pair well with wines that are less tart.

FRUIT ●●●●

OAK ●
Exception: Caramelized fruit desserts can pair well with oakier wines.

*TANNIN ●
Exception: Rich dark fruit desserts can pair well with more tannic red wines.

*Tannin is only found in red wine.

wine &
fruit dessert pairings

Fruit desserts are especially good with dessert wines. In general, tart and fresh-tasting fruit desserts pair best with wines that mirror these qualities, like sweet wines from cool climates. Fruit desserts made with dried or stewed fruit will work better with wines from warmer climates, where raisiny caramelized flavors dominate.

1 | LEMON TART &
Joh. Jos. Prüm Wehlener Sonnenuhr Riesling Auslese
Only wines of exceptional balance can manage desserts as sweet-tart as lemon tarts. The fine Rieslings of Germany's Mosel valley are tops in my book for purity of fruit expression. Auslese is a late harvest style that retains thrilling acidity and freshness; though nuanced with botrytis, it is not syrupy. This iconic example from Joh. Jos. Prüm is laden with aromas of green apples, apricots, and jasmine.
This works too: French Champagne Demi-Sec

2 | STRAWBERRY SHORTCAKE &
Inniskillin Cabernet Franc Ice Wine
Pink dessert wines, where brief skin contact with red grapes gives just a kiss of color, are ideal choices for flattering the flavor of strawberries. Using Cabernet Franc for ice wine is a brilliant innovation from Niagara's pioneering Inniskillin, adding a piquant wild berry dimension to its honeyed aromatic profile. Thick with flavor and sweetness, this Canadian wine is a truly rare and joyful experience.
This works too: Italian Brachetto

APPLE COBBLER & | 3
Royal Tokaji 5 Puttonyos Aszú
Hungarian Tokaji Aszú—the original botrytised wine—is both fresh and complex, and is an ideal partner for a tangy-sweet apple cobbler. This Tokaji's sweetness is helpfully ranked, with "5 puttonyos", just shy of the top of the line. This ambrosial wine displays the style's full glory, like a glass of sunshine—or candied nectarines and mandarins, drizzled with saffron-honey.
This works too: California Botrytis Dessert WIne

4 | BLUEBERRY PIE &
Pacific Rim Vin de Glacière Riesling

While red may be more traditional with desserts this dark, I like a contrasting wine such as this vibrant, citrusy Washington State Riesling. Its startlingly fresh green-appley flavor comes thanks to a high-tech variation on ice wine techniques, where flash freezing replaces months of shriveling on the vine.

This works too: Portuguese Ruby Porto

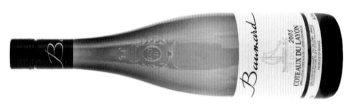

5 | BANANA SPLIT &
Baumard Carte d'Or Coteaux du Layon

For this frozen treat, I look to opulent late harvest wines whose dried fruit flavors have a faint caramel quality. Coteaux du Layon, from France's Loire Valley, is made from extremely ripe Chenin Blanc grapes. This one from Domaine des Baumard tastes like an exotic liqueur made from baked apples and honeycomb.

This works too: Australian Muscat

6 | GRAND MARNIER MOUSSE &
Cascinetta Vietti Moscato d'Asti

Moscato d'Asti is a wine that is just as delicate and frothy as this dessert. This unusual style of dessert wine from northern Italy is made by stopping fermentation midway between white grape juice and dry wine. This one from Vietti is like a mildly alcoholic white peach soda flavored with honeysuckle blossoms.

This works too: New York Late Harvest Riesling

---

specific wines
objective characteristics

This chart lists each suggested wine's objective characteristics, as described by the number of dots used. Five dots indicate a very strong characteristic, while one dot means that the property is less prominent. Zero dots indicate that the characteristic is not present.

1. Joh. Jos. Prüm Wehlener Sonnenuhr Riesling Auslese
Pairs well with a lemon tart.

Body	●●●
Sweet	●●●●
Acid	●●●●
Fruit	●●●●●
Oak	

2. Inniskillin Cabernet Franc Ice Wine
Pairs well with strawberry shortcake.

Body	●●●●●
Sweet	●●●●
Acid	●●●
Fruit	●●●●
Oak	
Tannin	●

3. Royal Tokaji 5 Puttonyos Aszú
Pairs well with apple cobbler.

Body	●●●●
Sweet	●●●●
Acid	●●●●
Fruit	●●●●●
Oak	

4. Pacific Rim Vin de Glacière Riesling
Pairs well with blueberry pie.

Body	●●●●
Sweet	●●●
Acid	●●●
Fruit	●●●
Oak	

5. Baumard Carte d'Or Coteaux du Layon
Pairs well with a banana split.

Body	●●●●
Sweet	●●●●
Acid	●●●
Fruit	●●●
Oak	

6. Cascinetta Vietti Moscato d'Asti
Pairs well with Grand Marnier mousse.

Body	●
Sweet	●●●
Acid	●●●●
Fruit	●●●●●
Oak	

beer
& fruit desserts

Desserts that feature fruit tend to be more complex than those that don't. They have rich, creamy, sweet flavors, as well as tart, vibrant, and acidic fruit components. Beer is complex enough to tackle both of these elements. From spritzy wheat beers to substantial Porters, beer with a fruit dessert is a natural pairing.

A blissful marriage

You just don't see people putting fruit in their wine. Well, okay, there is sangria, but that's really more of a cocktail than a straightforward marriage of fruit and wine. In the world of beer, however, you see the wonderful, symbiotic relationship between fruit and beer all the time, the world over. For example, the Germans will often serve a glass of Hefeweizen with a slice of lemon, while over in the United States, it's pretty common to see Blue Moon White Beer served with a slice of orange. In the summer at Dogfish Head we make a tart, refreshing Berliner Weisse with fermented peaches— and guess what? It's even better served with a chunk of grapefruit or a wedge of fresh peach. Certain beers and fruit just happen to go together perfectly, and most fruit desserts will find their ideal partner in the world of beer, not wine.

Tangy, light fruit desserts

While there are plenty of beers that are brewed using fruit as an ingredient, you may be surprised to learn that these beers are not always the best partner for a fruit-based dessert. Wheat beers, however, tend to have an acidity that squares up to tangy fruit. This makes them very well-suited to desserts made with fresh, vibrant fruits.

But that's not to say that fruit beers never pair well with these sorts of desserts. They're simply not always the best choice. Along with traditional wheat beers, fruit beers can work well with very light, delicate desserts, such as a simple fruit salad. Wheat beers and fruit beers that range from 3–6 percent abv will be your best bets for these lighter desserts. But for desserts such as lemon tarts, which have a tangy fresh fruit flavor as well as a creamy, sugary texture, you should choose a wheat or fruit beer that is slightly stronger and higher in alcohol.

Heavy, intense fruit desserts

More intensely fruity desserts, or desserts that feature pastries, custards, or other sweet sauces will typically require bigger, bolder beers in order to keep pace with the dish's strong, complex flavors. Look for something in the 7–18 percent abv range for these bolder desserts. Barleywines and Scandanavian and

"At Dogfish Head we make a tart, refreshing Berliner Weisse with fermented peaches. It's even better served with a chunk of grapefruit."

Slavic Strong Porters often feature a lot of deep pit-fruit flavors, and therefore they work well with rich, thick fruit desserts. Brown Ales tend to have a biscuity, bready, caramel character that can lend itself nicely to pairing with cakey and baked fruit desserts. But remember, in all these instances, the beer you select should be a bit stronger than average.

"You just don't see people putting fruit in their wine. Well, okay, there is sangria..."

rules of thumb
beer for fruit desserts

The dots on this chart represent some simplified rules on the characteristics to look out for when pairing beer with fruit desserts. There can be exceptions to the rules and, where applicable, these are mentioned in the text below each entry. On a scale of one to five the dots below represent the suggested intensity of a beer's objective characteristics. Five dots indicate a very strong characteristic, while one dot means that the property is less prominent.

COLOR ● ● ●
Exception: Dark fruit desserts can pair well with darker beers.

SWEET ● ●
Exception: Low-sugar desserts can pair well with drier beers.

BODY ● ● ● ●
Exception: Rich desserts can pair well with stronger beers.

YEAST ● ●

HOPS ● ●

beer & fruit dessert pairings

Fruit desserts are wonderful treats that run the gamut from tart, tangy, and light to lush, creamy, and rich. Some desserts have a baked bready or cakey component, while others are served fresh and "naked". These are all important things to keep in mind when choosing the right beer to serve with your fruit dessert.

1

LEMON TART &
Portsmouth Wheat Wine

The natural acidity of lemon complements the acidity of a wheat beer, but the sugary, creamy texture of this dessert means you'll need a strong one. I'd recommend Wheat Wine from the Portsmouth Brewing Company.
This works too: Imperial IPA

2

STRAWBERRY SHORTCAKE &
Great Divide Yeti Imperial Stout

There's a lot going on in this dessert—a confluence of glorious flavors that come from the berries, the cream, and the cake. Go big and bold with your beer choice with Great Divide Brewery's Yeti Imperial Stout. The beer's dark, roasty character stands up to the creamy cake components of the dessert.
This works too: Bourbon Stout

3

APPLE COBBLER &
Ølfabrikken Porter

This dessert features a syrupy sweet, bready component, and the fruit is baked rather than fresh, which brings out a savory flavor in the apples. A dark Porter will shine in contrast. I would recommend the Ølfabrikken Porter from the eponymous brewery in Denmark.
This works too: Scotch Ale

The food debate Beer & fruit dessert pairings

190

4

BLUEBERRY PIE &
Nøgne Ø Imperial Brown Ale

This dense, meaty pie requires a strong, caramelly beer with a lot of body, but not a lot of bitterness. I would check out the Imperial Brown Ale from Nøgne Ø brewery in Norway.
This works too: Doppelbock

5

BANANA SPLIT &
Erdinger Dunkel

A great complementary beer for this light but complex dish is a German Dark Wheat Beer, such as Erdinger Dunkel. It has decent acidity, and aromas of clove and banana.
This works too: Christmas Beer

6

GRAND MARNIER MOUSSE &
La Choulette Framboise

Light mousse gets potent when it's made with Grand Marnier. You'll need a beer that is flavorful, but one that won't overwhelm the nuances of the dish. Seek out a French Farmhouse Ale like La Choulette Framboise.
This works too: Wood-aged Sour Beer

specific beers
objective characteristics

The chart below lists each suggested beer's objective characteristics, as described by the number of dots used. Five dots indicate a very strong characteristic, while one dot means that the property is less prominent.

1. Portsmouth Wheat Wine
Pairs well with a lemon tart.

Color	●●●
Sweet	●●●
Body	●●●●●
Yeast	●●
Hops	●●●

2. Great Divide Yeti Imperial Stout
Pairs well with strawberry shortcake.

Color	●●●●●
Sweet	●●●
Body	●●●●
Yeast	●
Hops	●●

3. Ølfabrikken Porter
Pairs well with apple cobbler.

Color	●●●●
Sweet	●●●
Body	●●●
Yeast	●
Hops	●

4. Nøgne Ø Imperial Brown Ale
Pairs well with blueberry pie.

Color	●●●
Sweet	●●●●
Body	●●
Yeast	●●
Hops	●●

5. Erdinger Dunkel
Pairs well with a banana split.

Color	●●●
Sweet	●●
Body	●●
Yeast	●●●
Hops	●●

6. La Choulette Framboise
Pairs well with Grand Marnier mousse.

Color	●●
Sweet	●●●
Body	●●
Yeast	●●●
Hops	●

which **drink** wins

Marnie and Sam will each state their case for wine or beer, but there has to be a winner for each pairing. Conduct your own beer, wine, and food tasting, and choose which drink wins on the score card below.

Try a glass of Hefeweizen with a wedge of lemon and you'll see: fruit with beer can produce **sublime** results. Now imagine a wine equivalent: a glass of Merlot with a sprig of barley. Not gonna happen, because wine lacks that crossover appeal.

So gallant of you, Sam, to make a girl's argument for her, but what could barley possibly add to a near perfect glass of Merlot? Fruit desserts are **INNATELY SUITED** to pairing with fruit-based dessert wines, whose sweet-tart flavors go hand-in-hand.

Sweet wine + sweet dessert = sweet-tooth overload! Syrupy dessert wines are too cloying to partner well with fruit desserts, but a light, spritzy wheat beer with a lemon tart is pure **pairing bliss**.

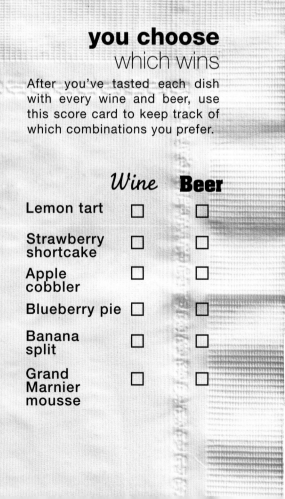

you choose
which wins

After you've tasted each dish with every wine and beer, use this score card to keep track of which combinations you prefer.

	Wine	**Beer**
Lemon tart	☐	☐
Strawberry shortcake	☐	☐
Apple cobbler	☐	☐
Blueberry pie	☐	☐
Banana split	☐	☐
Grand Marnier mousse	☐	☐

If you'd ever tried Port with cherry pie you'd know that sweet foods and sweet wines actually make each other taste less sweet! Rather than making sweet wine seem cloying, the reverse is true: the multi-faceted flavors of dessert wines are **easier to appreciate** when partnered with fruit desserts.

Not sure why you have to drag wine's big brother, Port, into the debate...unless it's because wine is **too wimpy** to fight its own battles. You don't see me calling in beer's burly cousin, whiskey!

I hate to break it to you, Sam, but Port is a wine, and **proof positive** that wine isn't wimpy. Face it, fruit desserts are happiest matched with fruit beverages every time.

I beg to differ. A meaty fruit cake or juicy pie needs an **assertive**, dark, roasty beer like a Brown Ale or Porter.

Yeah—what pie wouldn't taste awesome next to Porter? But not for reasons you should be proud of! You beer guys keep trying to convince us that burnt barley malt tastes great. Keep your Porter, I'll take my **luscious dessert wine**, thank you very much.

Marnie

Sam

193

Beyond the realm of fruit desserts lies a promised land full of custard, caramel, and chocolate. Some experiences we can create at home, like the toe-curling pleasures of a simple bowl of ice cream or the soothing comfort of a smooth butterscotch pudding. Others are special occasion treats best left to professional pastry chefs, like the refined grace of an almond cake or the molten decadence of chocolate soufflé. Everything from nuts to coffee, cocoa to toffee falls into this delightful category of desserts.

wine, beer

& other desserts

wine
& other desserts

Many would argue that dessert is the best part of dinner. And dessert wines of all kinds, sparkling or fortified, white or red, can be just as delightful with desserts as dry wines are with the main course. Yet, there's no question that dessert wines are unusual and provoke uncommonly strong responses.

Love it or loathe it

Desserts are natural partners for sweet dessert wines. Some people fall head over heels for these rare wines; for them, it's love at first sip. The first experience of fine dessert wine is one of child-like joy, like stumbling on a jewel-toned world of liquid candy made for adults only. The idea that such flavors can be all-natural, acquired through patience and diligence in the vineyard and the winery, can come as a revelation. To be sure, Port and Sauternes are hardly everyday wines, but for some, they are a treasured treat, the epitome of self-indulgence.

Others, however, take one sip and react in the exact opposite way. Finding dessert wines overly sugary on first impression, they reject them as cloying or syrupy. There's nothing wrong with deciding you don't like something, but first impressions can be misleading, especially with wine.

Unlike beer, wines are made specifically to partner with foods in a flattering way, to provide complementary flavors. Since everything you put in your mouth will change the way the next thing tastes, many wines taste slightly "askew" alone. For dessert wines, the two qualities that can turn some people off at first are extreme sweetness and "thick" texture. However, both become less prominent when "balanced" by the sweetness and richness found in desserts.

Sweet + sweet = less sweet?

In pairing wines with desserts such as chocolate and caramel, custard and cake, we generally choose sweet wines not to make the dessert experience even sweeter, but because sugary food makes wine taste less sweet and more sour. A dry Cabernet Sauvignon can be a great flavor combination with bittersweet chocolate, for example. But, add sugar to make a brownie, and the same wine will taste unpleasantly dry and acidic, like orange juice after toothpaste.

Balancing the equation

So, the sweeter the dessert, the sweeter a wine must be to find a mutually flattering pairing. For our chocolate brownie, a better choice might be a Port, another dark, full-bodied red wine, but one that is far sweeter than dry Cabernet Sauvignon. On first impression, the Port may seem syrupy and overly alcoholic, but the sweetness and rich texture found in each bite of brownie will change all that. It will tone down the wine's sweetness and strength, revealing a pretty core of dark fruit flavors perfectly suited to our chocolate dessert.

That's sweet

The sweetest dessert wines, like Cream Sherry and Ice Wine, work best where the dessert's sugar content is highest, as with ice cream or desserts dominated by caramel, or maple or brown sugar. Milder sweetness, like that found in Port and late harvest botrytis wines, is better suited to the standard range of desserts, like most cakes, puddings, and tarts. Some dessert wines are lower in overall sweetness, like Vin Santo from dried grapes, and Moscato from fresh grapes. These are ideal for desserts that are comparatively low in sugar, like biscotti and traditional flan.

Pairing cribsheet

As to other pairing considerations, the same "like with like" guidelines apply. So, rich and "sticky" dessert wines, like fortified Port and Sherry, or Ice Wine low in water content, are best suited when desserts are high in fats and oils. Lighter dessert wine styles are better suited to lower fat recipes, like biscotti or simple fruit dishes.

Color and flavor are connected. While it isn't the only option, deep, dark dessert wines, like Port, are well suited to dark desserts, like chocolate or spice cake.

Toasty dessert wines, like oxidative Sherry and Madeira, and those made from dried grapes, like Vin Santo, are best suited when desserts are nutty, caramelized, or flavored with dried fruit. Tangy dessert wines, like Rieslings, Madeira, Moscato, and Tokaji, are best suited to desserts that have a sweet-tart flavor, such as cheesecake, pie, or sorbet.

rules of thumb
wine for other desserts

The dots on this chart represent some simplified rules on the characteristics to look out for when pairing wine with dessert. There can be exceptions to the rules and, where applicable, these are mentioned in the text below each entry. On a scale of one to five the dots below represent the suggested intensity of a wine's objective characteristics. Five dots indicate a very strong characteristic, while one dot means that the property is less prominent.

BODY ● ● ● ● ●
Exception: Low-fat desserts can pair well with lighter wines.

SWEET ● ● ● ● ●
Exception: Low-sugar desserts can pair well with drier wines.

ACID ● ● ●

FRUIT ● ● ● ● ●

OAK ● ● ●

*TANNIN ● ● ● ●
Exception: Low-fat desserts can pair well with less tannic wines.

*Tannin is only found in red wine.

wine & other dessert pairings

The easiest way to find the perfect dessert wine is to partner like with like. Since sugar in food provokes such an extreme change in our perception of wine, leaving wine tasting less sweet and more sour, it is most important to choose a wine that is similar in sweetness level to the dessert. Also, look for similar flavors, colors, and textures in both the wine and dessert.

1 VANILLA ICE CREAM &
Harveys Bristol Cream Sherry

While most desserts respond best to pairing like with like, simple vanilla ice cream is something of a "blank slate". Therefore, it rewards contrasting wine pairings, almost like a topping or sauce. Thick Cream Sherry is nutty and raisiny, like the essence of a heady Christmas fruit cake. The intensity of Harveys Bristol Cream is lightened by rich vanilla ice cream, whether it's on the side or poured on top.
This works too: Australian Tawny Port

2 CHOCOLATE CAKE &
Dow's Late Bottled Vintage Porto

Dark chocolate desserts have a depth of flavor unrivalled among sweets. Pairing partners need powerful flavors, like those found in red, fortified Port. The most intense of wines, Port is inky red wine spiked mid-fermentation with raw brandy. This Late Bottled Vintage from Dow's is vibrantly youthful. It packs brandied cherry flavor into every luscious sip, layered with a fiery spice.
This works too: Port-style Zinfandel

CRÈME BRÛLÉE & 3
Chateau Lafaurie-Peyraguey Sauternes

Crème brûlée served with French Sauternes, a late harvest botrytis wine from Bordeaux, is a match made in heaven. This one, from Chateau Lafaurie-Peyraguey, is an epic dessert wine. Its flavors evoke dried apricots, vanilla chai, and saffron-honey in a viscous, golden elixir.
This works too: South African Botrytis Chenin Blanc

198

4 | CHEESECAKE &
Banfi Rosa Regale Brachetto d'Acqui

For cheesecake, a "fresh grape" dessert wine, like the Rosa Regale Brachetto from Banfi is sure to please. This sparkling red from northern Italy is a sibling of the Piedmont region's famous Moscato d'Asti. Made by interrupting fermentation, it's low in alcohol, yet bursts with fresh aromas of wild strawberries and roses.

This works too: Hungarian Tokaji Aszú

5 | CHOCOLATE CHIP COOKIES &
Taylor-Fladgate 10 Year Old Tawny Porto

My favorite indulgence with chocolate chip cookies is a Tawny Port, like this one from Taylor-Fladgate. A paler, nuttier style of Porto, tawnies are aged in casks. Their vibrant red color fades to auburn over time, and their youthful berry flavors become toasty and cognac-y, acquiring a nutty, raisiny, caramelized quality.

This works too: Portuguese Bual Madeira

6 | PECAN PIE &
Jaboulet Muscat de Beaumes-de-Venise

Unctuous, heady Muscats from the South of France, like Paul Jaboulet's blonde bombshell from the town of Beaumes-de-Venise, are a perfect partner for pecan pie. Peachy Muscat grapes are given treatment similar to Port, and the resulting wine is almost perfumey with extraordinary sweetness and rich texture.

This works too: Spanish Pedro Ximenez Sherry

specific wines
objective characteristics

This chart lists each suggested wine's objective characteristics, as described by the number of dots used. Five dots indicate a very strong characteristic, while one dot means that the property is less prominent. Zero dots indicate that the characteristic is not present.

1. Harveys Bristol Cream Sherry
Pairs well with vanilla ice cream.

Body	•••••
Sweet	•••••
Acid	•••
Fruit	••••
Oak	

2. Dow's Late Bottled Vintage Porto
Pairs well with chocolate cake.

Body	•••••
Sweet	•••••
Acid	•••
Fruit	•••••
Oak	••
Tannin	••

3. Chateau Lafaurie-Peyraguey Sauternes
Pairs well with crème brûlée.

Body	••••
Sweet	••••
Acid	••••
Fruit	•••• •
Oak	••••

4. Banfi Rosa Regale Brachetto d'Acqui
Pairs well with cheesecake.

Body	•••
Sweet	•••••
Acid	•••••
Fruit	••••
Oak	
Tannin	•

5. Taylor-Fladgate 10 Year Old Tawny Porto
Pairs well with chocolate chip cookies.

Body	•••••
Sweet	•••••
Acid	•••
Fruit	••••
Oak	••••
Tannin	••

6. Jaboulet Muscat de Beaumes-de-Venise
Pairs well with pecan pie.

Body	••••
Sweet	••••
Acid	••
Fruit	•••••
Oak	

beer
& other desserts

When Marnie and I host our beer versus wine food-pairing dinners it's always a close race right to the finish, and neither beer nor wine usually wins by more than one course. But beer almost always wins the dessert course, especially when the dessert in question is chocolatey, caramelly, or nutty.

Liquid assets
Some dessert wines are wonderful beverages and, when pressed, most people will admit that many taste great as a dessert unto themselves. But, for a true wine to work in harmony with a dessert it has to be at least as sweet as the dessert, or it is going to taste flabby and sour. This is not necessarily true for pairing beer with dessert, and because of this there are a lot more pairing options available to beer drinkers.

Endless possibilities
With desserts based on rich, heavy flavors, such as chocolate, vanilla, caramel, and nuts, beer offers a spectacular range of pairing options. In fact, the beer world offers so many great pairing partners for these desserts that it can be a little overwhelming. To simplify things, there are two main tacks you can take—the complementary path and the contrasting one.

Compare and contrast
When putting together a complementary pairing, you're essentially matching like with like. So, for example, a sweet Milk Stout will work wonders with a chocolate parfait. This is because both the beer and the dessert are moderately sweet and have a middling heaviness. On the flipside, you can just as easily take the path of contrasting flavors, where you select a beer whose flavor and heaviness is diametrically opposed to that of

the dessert. To see the miraculous powers of this tactic in action, try coupling a very sweet pecan pie with a tart and acidic Belgian Lambic beer. I promise that you won't be disappointed!

Brewer knows best
Dark, heavily roasted barley is beer's secret weapon when it comes to pairing with sweet foods, and there is no equivalant in the wine world for barley. Because the brewer can

"There is probably no pairing more perfect than a ROASTY STOUT AND DARK CHOCOLATE."

change the volume and types of dark grains for infinite variation, more bitterness, more roastiness, and more chocolate nuance within the beer itself, there is just more opportunity for perfecting the marriage between bitter and sweet than there is with wine. In winemaking, it's pretty much up to the land and Mother Nature to make a memorable vintage. With beer, it's up to the brewer, who has a vast array of grains, malts, hops, yeast, and specialty fruits and spices at his or her creative beck and call. The flexibility of the beer is only matched by the durability of bold, complex flavors that can stand up to the most intense, sweet desserts.

Some pairing guidelines

Generally speaking, when pairing dessert with a beverage you'll want to pair intense, rich beers with intense, rich desserts, and light fluffy desserts with light, well-carbonated beers. Cakes and bread-based desserts will often work well with more yeasty, unfiltered beers. But if the dessert has a lot of frosting, icing, or chocolate, then you'll need something dark or strong. And sometimes, for the most intense death-by-chocolate desserts, you'll want a beer that is both strong and dark.

Double happiness

There is probably no dessert pairing more simply perfect and decadent than a roasty Stout and dark chocolate. At Dogfish Head we've been bringing a big bowl of locally made dark chocolates to serve with our Chicory Stout at beer festivals since 1996. Not many people were talking about pairing beer with food back then, especially dark beer and dessert. But this combination always draws a crowd and creates a lot of true believers.

The fact is, the creamy character of chocolate sauces, custards, and ice creams are just better-calibrated to the body, carbonation level, and grainy flavors of darker, stronger beers than they are to wines. And it all comes down to beer's secret weapon again—dark, roasty barley, used in intricate combinations that leave a certain one-dimensional grape-based beverage in the dust—er, *terroir*.

rules of thumb
beer for other desserts

The dots on this chart represent some simplified rules on the characteristics to look out for when pairing beer with dessert. There can be exceptions to the rules and, where applicable, these are mentioned in the text below each entry. On a scale of one to five the dots below represent the suggested intensity of a beer's objective characteristics. Five dots indicate a very strong characteristic, while one dot means that the property is less prominent.

COLOR ● ● ● ●

SWEET ● ● ●

BODY ● ● ●
Exception: Low-fat desserts can pair well with lighter-bodied beers.

YEAST ● ●

HOPS ●

beer & other dessert pairings

For the perfect alcoholic beverage for a nutty, chocolatey, caramelly dessert, look no further than the world of beer. Thanks to the amazingly versatile properties of roasted barley, beer has enough range to outgun wine at the dessert table every time. From cookies to ice cream, rich confections just pair better with beer.

VANILLA ICE CREAM & Maui CoCoNut Porter

1

Vanilla is often used as an adjective to mean boring, but if you take a super-premium ice cream, made with real vanilla beans, then you have the perfect canvas to paint with a full-flavored beer. A black, malty Porter will exceed your expectations. Try the Maui Brewing Company's CoCoNut Porter, which is spiked with toasty coconut flavors.
This works too: Belgian Lambic

CHOCOLATE CAKE & Dogfish Head World Wide Stout

2

For death-by-chocolate desserts you won't find a better partner than a strong, dark Stout. Intensely rich, chocolatey cakes will need an equally big, boozy beer such as Dogfish Head's World Wide Stout. And, at 18 percent abv, this may be the world's strongest dark beer. With a roasty flavor and notes of raisins and tobacco, this Stout ages well, so try a three- or four-year-old vintage to complement your dessert.
This works too: English Barleywine

CRÈME BRÛLÉE & New Glarus Wisconsin Belgian Red

3

This classic dessert should be re-named Crème-BREW-lée for how magically it pairs with certain beers, especially American fruit beers. The tart sour cherry flavors in New Glarus Wisconsin Belgian Red highlight the crème brûlée's creamy, caramelized flavors.
This works too: Bière de Garde

202

4 CHEESECAKE &
Spezial Rauchbier

Cheesecake can be heavy, but its flavors are delicate. A beer that's too sweet or too strong will overwhelm this dessert in a New York minute. Instead, seek out a subtle smoked beer, such as a Spezial Rauchbier.
This works too: Smoked Porter

5 CHOCOLATE CHIP COOKIES &
Eisenbahn Lust

Pair dark chocolate chip cookies with a glass of Brazil's Eisenbahn Lust Bière de Champagne. This sweet, strong, fruity ale has an incredible complexity and age-ability.
This works too: Milk Stout

6 PECAN PIE &
Nørrebro La Granja Espresso Stout

Assuming you are serving your pie naked and not à la mode, you are going to want a big beer that has enough malt presence to complement this pie's intensely sweet nut and sugar filling. As a satisfying alternative to the standard cup of coffee with dessert, try La Granja Espresso Stout from Denmark's Nørrebro Bryghus.
This works too: English Barleywine

specific beers
objective characteristics

The chart below lists each suggested beer's objective characteristics, as described by the number of dots used. Five dots indicate a very strong characteristic, while one dot means that the property is less prominent.

1. Maui CoCoNut Porter
Pairs well with vanilla ice cream.

Color	●●●●
Sweet	●●●
Body	●●●
Yeast	●
Hops	●

2. Dogfish Head World Wide Stout
Pairs well with chocolate cake.

Color	●●●●
Sweet	●●●●●
Body	●●●●●●
Yeast	●●●
Hops	●●

3. New Glarus Wisconsin Belgian Red
Pairs well with crème brûlée.

Color	●●●
Sweet	●●●
Body	●●
Yeast	●●●
Hops	●

4. Spezial Rauchbier
Pairs well with cheesecake.

Color	●●●
Sweet	●●●
Body	●●
Yeast	●●
Hops	●●

5. Eisenbahn Lust
Pairs well with chocolate chip cookies.

Color	●●
Sweet	●●●●
Body	●●●
Yeast	●●●
Hops	●●

6. Nørrebro La Granja Espresso Stout
Pairs well with pecan pie.

Color	●●●●
Sweet	●●
Body	●●●
Yeast	●●
Hops	●●

which **drink** wins

Marnie and Sam will each state their case for wine or beer, but there has to be a winner for each pairing. Conduct your own beer, wine, and food tasting, and choose which drink wins on the score card at right.

Creative winemakers have dreamt up techniques for coaxing out ambrosial flavors worthy of serving with any dessert. So, from caramel to chocolate and vanilla to almond, the **stunning range** of dessert wine styles provide exponential pairing options.

Maybe dessert wine works for nuts—but by nuts, I mean the people who enjoy dessert wine. But chocolate? Please! There could be no more **quintessential pairing** than chocolate and a dark, roasty Stout.

I'll admit that dark beer and chocolate doesn't taste as awful as it sounds. But it's a long way from "not awful" to **unfreakingbelievable** —people's response to pairing chocolate with wines like Brachetto, Madeira, or Port.

This "unfreakingbelievable" condition you speak of: can it be treated with antibiotics? If not, those who experience it could be healed and satisfied by the **MAJESTIC PAIRING** of a malty Barleywine and crème brûlée or a smoked beer coupled with a classic New York cheesecake.

Sam

Just like a guy—content to **merely satisfy**. Wines paired with desserts don't just meet expectations, but exceed them, leaving the palate quivering with excitement.

Come on—beer and dessert pairings not only live up to diners' expectations—they blow them all away! In our pairing dinners, isn't it true that **BEER BEATS WINE** on the dessert course most of the time? Care to explain this, Marnie?

Maybe that's because the world class beers you bring out-gun the modest dessert wines I can afford. Actually, those were probably just **pity votes** for you.

you choose
which wins

After you've tasted each dish with every wine and beer, use this score card to keep track of which combinations you prefer.

	Wine	**Beer**
Vanilla ice cream	☐	☐
Chocolate cake	☐	☐
Crème brûlée	☐	☐
Cheesecake	☐	☐
Chocolate chip cookies	☐	☐
Pecan pie	☐	☐

It's a bummer that the world's best dessert wines are prohibitively expensive. Thankfully, you don't have to be a tweed-wearing multi-millionaire to afford the best dessert pairing beers in the world. **Another feather** in beer's cap, for sure.

Marnie

the great debate
at home

the **beer** versus *wine* party

You don't have to buy a ticket to a beer versus wine tasting dinner in order to experience the thrill of the game. You can host one in your own home. This section offers 12 delicious recipes, complete with wine and beer pairing recommendations for each. You can also wing it, and try out your own dishes and pairings.

Good times, the democratic way
What could be more fun than hosting your own beer versus wine party at home? Tackling this thorny debate American-style, by voting, is bound to turn any gathering into a rollicking good time—equal parts dinner party and sporting event. Just take great beer, fine wine, and terrific food—all the party essentials—and add a dollop of good-natured competition. Before you know it, you'll have your own gastronomic "reality show" going.

It takes all kinds
In any group of friends, family, or colleagues, you'll find a healthy mix of guys and gals whose tastes in beverages run the gamut. Some will have firm preferences: beer fans or wine lovers who firmly favor their beverage of choice. Others will be equal opportunity drinkers, willing to partake of both beer and wine with relish. But all of them will enjoy the "taste-off", and most will be surprised at how well both beverages perform as food partners. Die-hard beer geeks and budding wine snobs alike will find common ground.

It's always more interesting to try two different beverages with a dish than one, even if it's two beers or two wines. When we only taste one pairing, our conclusions are pretty much limited to whether we like it or not. But when we try two side by side, we can compare strengths and weaknesses. We can decide which one we prefer and why we prefer it. For those of us curious to explore the wonderful world of food pairings, the more beverage options on the table at once, the more we can learn. The challenge is that when we dine alone or in small groups, it's wasteful to open more beverages than will be consumed. This really limits our tasting opportunities. But, if you get a few couples together or invite the extended family around, you're in business.

> ## " Tackling this thorny debate by voting is bound to turn any gathering into a good time. "

Take the challenge
Hosting your own beer versus wine party is, admittedly, a touch complicated. You'll need to do some careful planning on who to invite, what foods to prepare, which beverages to serve, and how to organize the voting process. But, the rewards are well worth the effort. Your gathering will be memorable, and anything but boring. The range of delicious options and the spirited party game atmosphere will be sure to delight your guests. And, best of all, competitive beer versus wine dining is an all-season sport, so you can challenge your friends to host a re-match any time of year.

Start small(ish)
So you want to throw your own beer versus wine dinner at home, but where do you start? Your first objective is to keep it simple and start small. While we typically host large five-course dinners, we have been doing this for a long time, and have a lot of help from chefs and organizers. For your first dinner, try starting with a simple three-course meal. Remember that beyond having fun and hanging out with friends, the goal of the dinner should be to educate and entertain with great beer, wine, and food.

Begin planning your dinner a few weeks in advance. The first step is figuring out who you want to invite. Try to invite a crowd where everyone already knows each other, so that conversation will revolve around the pairings, rather than introductions and "getting to know you" chitchat. Aim to keep the total number of diners somewhere around six. Any less than this and the night could unravel into a few one-on-one conversations; any more than that and the general party atmosphere could get overwhelming and difficult to direct.

Communication is key
The next step is to get everyone you are inviting into an e-mail loop so you can easily get a final head count well in advance of the dinner. Your initial invitation should cover the basics of the beer versus wine dinner. As the host you should plan on buying all of the

alcohol needed to pair with all courses and plan to cook the main course, at the very least. To have more control you may want to cook every course yourself but it's sometimes more fun, communal, and manageable if you ask each of the diners on the e-mail loop to bring one dish of their choice—an appetizer, side dish, or dessert. Try not to tell them what to make, since they will feel more comfortable preparing dishes that they know how to make well. But do ask them what they are making, so that you can pair it with the most appropriate beer and wine.

Keep it simple
Shy away from elaborate, fussy food since you may end up spending more time worrying about the dish than enjoying yourself. If you don't have enough glassware, it's a good idea to ask the guests to bring a set of red wine glasses or brandy snifters with them. None of these wonderful beverages should be served in plastic! While you could argue all day about which glassware styles are best for which beverages, you can't go wrong with red wine glasses or brandy snifters for all beers and wines, as their balloon-shape captures and directs the subtle aromas and flavors toward your senses really well.

A logical progression
Aim for your pairings to work toward the crescendo of dessert. Serve your good beers and wines early, and your great beers and wines late. Start with lighter beverages and dishes early, and move toward the more intense and heavy stuff in the later courses. Beer styles such as Barleywines, Imperial IPAs, and Belgian Strong Ales that are over 9 percent alcohol are as deserving of their place in your wine cellar as the finest Bordeaux since they will improve and gain complexity and subtlety with age.

Decant your more full-bodied wines an hour or so before they are served and be conscious of the temperatures of your white wines and beers throughout the dinner. In general, pull them from the fridge about half an hour before they are served to bring the temperature up a bit and maximize the flavor and aroma profiles of the beverage. Try to seek out the chance to introduce friends to some of your personal, off-the-beaten-path favorites.

The little details

Create all the voting ballots (*see sample, right*) that you're going to need (one per person, per course, plus extras) well ahead of time. Make

> ❝ **You can serve as many courses as you like, but make sure the number is an odd one to avoid a stalemate.** ❞

sure there is ample drinking water and simple rustic bread or crackers on hand throughout the evening. These essentials will serve a dual purpose throughout the night: to cleanse the palate between tastings, and to keep your guests from falling down drunk!

Sit-down dinners tend to be more manageable and conducive to drink-related conversations than buffets. You can serve as many courses as you like, but make sure the number of courses you serve is an odd one to avoid a stalemate. And remember that each diner will be having two drinks with each course; welcome your guests with a full glass of wine or beer, but provide smaller "tasting" portions throughout the rest of the evening.

A word to the wise

Each pairing portion of wine and beer should be about 3 fluid ounces (90ml), so bear this in mind as you shop for your drinks. It's a good idea to buy more than you need, but resist the urge to fill your guests' glasses up to the brim. It's also preferable (and more hospitable) to pour the drinks yourself, rather than having your guests self-serve. If you don't, you may end up with a house full of inebriated guests who no longer care about discussing the pairings.

sample ballot

with this dish, I think the

beer   *wine*

☐   ☐

is the best food partner.

how to vote
& other ideas

Here are some simple steps on how to pull off your own beer versus wine party. And, if you're still game, but are looking for a few shortcuts, check out the ideas on the opposite page.

1. PREPARE BLANK BALLOTS

Small paper ballots are easy to make ahead of time, and ideal for anonymous voting by checking or circling "beer" or "wine". Whether printed electronically or by hand, you'll be able to get at least a dozen ballots per standard letter-size page. Slice these pages down into ballot slips before your guests arrive. You'll need one ballot per course for each participating guest, as well as enough pens or pencils for everyone.

2. COMMUNICATE THE RULES

The premise of the event needs to be conveyed clearly from the outset. Depending on the formality of the event, a host can either announce the rules of the game verbally, or print up simple instructions to be passed out with the blank ballots. (*For sample instructions, see opposite, top.*)

3. SET UP THE VOTING STATION

Just about anything can be used to collect ballots: an ice bucket, a gift bag, a vase, or even a child's piggy bank. Or, make your own "ballot box" by cutting a drop slot in the top half of a shoe box, dressed up for the job with colorful wrapping paper. Or, simply use an empty tissue box. Just remember, you'll need to be able to reach the ballots easily to count up the results for each course. (*For sample ballot, see p211.*)

4. SCHEDULE A VOTING TIMELINE

For seated dinners, guests should be asked to vote after each course and before the next is served. Announcing the winner and loser for each course adds to the excitement and fuels discussion. If the format is self-serve, consider creating multiple voting stations, each stocked with one food item, accompanying beer and wine and its own ballot box. Or, for less structured parties, the host can announce each upcoming vote. Let guests know they'll have a set period of time to sample a specific pairing and cast their votes before the "polls close" (no less than a half hour per vote).

sample instructions

more **beer** versus *wine* ideas

When dining out with a large group, try conducting a "taste off" with a shared dish. Ask the server for recommendations, and for extra glasses. Each glass of wine will yield 2–3 tasting portions, and each bottle of beer will yield 3–4.

Beer versus wine parties can require a lot of planning. One way to make it easier is to ask your friends to each bring a dish, as well as a bottle of wine and a six-pack of beer they like to drink with it.

Not sure which beverages to choose? Many wines and beers now give suggestions of the type of foods they are designed to complement right on the back label. If not, try looking up the product online, where wineries and breweries typically provide far more information on each of their products.

fig compote
& red onion confit

The best way to enjoy a delicious chunk of cheese, other than pairing it with a delightful wine or beer (*see opposite*), is to serve it with a flavorful accompaniment. These simple, but mind-blowing twin condiments for a cheese platter come courtesy of Chef Sondra Bernstein of the girl and the fig restaurant in Sonoma, California.

Yields: **6 servings**
Ease of preparation: **Simple**

INGREDIENTS

For the fig compote:
4 tbsp minced shallots or onion
¼ cup olive oil
2 cups dried figs, diced
¼ cup mustard seed
½ cup sugar
1 cup balsamic vinegar (or substitute red wine vinegar)
2 tbsp whole-grain mustard (or substitute standard mustard)
Salt and freshly ground black pepper

For the red onion confit:
1 tbsp olive oil
3 medium-sized red onions, thinly sliced
1 small red beet, peeled and diced into large, rough chunks
½ cup red wine
1 sprig fresh thyme (or substitute ½ tsp dried thyme)
1½ tbsp honey
Salt and freshly ground black pepper

Fig compote

1 Sauté the shallots or onion in the olive oil in a medium-sized saucepan over medium heat until soft and translucent. Then add the figs, mustard seed, sugar, vinegar, and mustard.

2 Reduce the heat and simmer uncovered until the figs are soft and the compote has thickened to the consistency of fruit preserves. Then add salt and pepper to taste. Remove from heat and let cool. Yields about 3 cups.

Red onion confit

1 Warm the oil in a large sauté pan over medium heat. Cook the onions and beet chunks until the onions are soft and translucent. Add the red wine and thyme sprig, and cook the mixture over medium heat until the liquid has reduced completely.

2 Remove from heat. Then remove and discard thyme sprig and beet chunks. Stir honey into the onions, and add salt and pepper to taste. Yields approximately 2 cups.

3 Serve both condiments with a selection of sharp, flavorful cheeses, such as Parmigiano Reggiano, Manchego, and aged Cheddar, and chunks of toasted focaccia bread.

Cantillon Kriek Lambic

"Kriek" is the Flemish word for sour cherry and this beer has them by the boat-load. This beer from Cantillon is aged in oak barrels for many months, and cherry stones give it notes of almond and vanilla, too. The resulting complex and sour flavors pair well with the figs, red onions, and cheese in this dish.

Chehalem Reserve Pinot Gris

Sweet and tart accompaniments for cheeses tend to work best with clean, fresh whites, like this luscious beauty from Chehalem in Oregon. This wine is honeyed and texturally rich, made more in the model of zaftig French Pinot Gris from Alsace than rail-thin Italian Pinot Grigio.

vegetable
samosas

Impress your friends by cooking up these piquant vegetarian samosas and serving them with a great beverage (*see opposite*) to complement the nuanced spices. This fragrant recipe has been supplied by Chef Bradley Moore of Xacutti restaurant in Toronto, Ontario. These are so delicious you might want to make an extra batch to enjoy later!

Yields: **6 servings**
Ease of preparation: **Moderate**

INGREDIENTS
2½ cups frozen peas, thawed
1½ tsp fresh puréed ginger
1 small green chili pepper,
  deseeded and minced (2 for extra spicy)
2 tbsp clarified butter (or substitute
  melted butter)
1 tsp cumin seeds (or substitute
  ground cumin)
¾ cup canned corn kernels, drained
  (or substitute frozen corn, thawed)
1 tsp salt
1 tsp garam masala (or see spice
  substitution below)
½ tsp sugar
1 x 1-pound (500g) package frozen filo dough
1½ tbsp fresh chopped cilantro
  (or substitute fresh parsley)

* If you can't find garam masala in the grocery store, you can substitute this spice blend: 4 parts each cumin and paprika, 2 parts each cinnamon and cayenne pepper, and crumbled bay leaves, and 1 part ground cloves

1 To make the filling, mix peas, ginger, and chilies in a food processor or blender, until it becomes a smooth, fine paste. Heat the butter in a medium-sized saucepan on medium heat and add the cumin seeds. Reduce heat to low when they start to crackle (or as the ground cumin releases its aroma), and then add the pea mixture.

2 Stir until almost all the moisture has evaporated from the mixture. Add the corn and cook for another 2–3 minutes. Stir in the salt and garam masala*. Adjust seasoning to taste, and cook for another 3 minutes. Stir in sugar and remove from heat. Let the mix cool completely then stir in the cilantro.

3 For the pastry, thaw frozen filo dough overnight in the refrigerator. Gently remove 1 sheet of defrosted filo dough at a time. Using kitchen shears, carefully cut each leaf into lengthwise strips approximately 4 inches (10cm) wide, to make 18 strips.

4 Place 2–3 tablespoons of pea mixture 2 inches (5 cm) above the base of each strip. Bring the bottom right-hand corner of the strip up and across the filling to line up with the left-hand edge of the strip. Continue to fold up the strip into a triangle form, like folding a flag, until the end of the strip is reached. Moisten the last edge of pastry with oil and press to seal.

5 To cook the samosas, heat ½ cup oil in a large non-stick sauté pan over medium heat, until hot, but not smoking. Place samosas gently into oil with a slotted spoon for half a minute on each side, or just long enough for the pastry to turn golden brown.

6 Remove samosas from the pan, and drain briefly on paper towels. Arrange them on a cookie sheet or broiler pan, and broil for 10 minutes, or until heated through the center, in a pre-heated 350°F (180°C) oven.

Serve with a spicy chutney on the side.

Bonterra Viognier

While these tasty vegetable fritters pack a little heat, they are more "highly seasoned" than "fiery hot", and they're full of sweet, delicious corn and peas. Fragrant with floral and peachy aromatics, Bonterra's plump, juicy California Viognier is as complex as the garam masala and will drape the fresh veggies with buttery goodness.

Short's Anniversary Ale

Short's Anniversary Ale is a triple-brewed, triple-hopped, triple-boiled Imperial IPA, so the hops shine through front and center. Since a tremendous amount of vegetation went into producing this beer it only makes sense to pair it with a tremendous amount of vegetation from the kitchen.

bacon & egg
cheeseburgers

For the ultimate in hearty sandwiches, you just can't beat a bacon cheeseburger topped with a fried egg, sunny side up. This decadent creation comes courtesy of Chef David Ansill of the eponymous Ansill restaurant in Philadelphia. To truly do this burger justice, you have to pair it with a drink that's up to the challenge, so check out our recommendations on the opposite page.

Yields: **6 servings**
Ease of preparation: **Moderate**

INGREDIENTS
4½ lbs (2¼kg) ground beef, not too lean, shaped into 6 patties
Salt and freshly ground black pepper
1 lb (500g) smoked bacon, thickly sliced
6 large slices American or mild Cheddar cheese
6 large Kaiser rolls (or substitute large hamburger buns, brioche buns, or potato rolls)
2 tbsp butter
6 eggs
1 red onion, sliced
2 tomatoes, sliced

1 Pre-heat the broiler and arrange the patties on a self-draining broiler pan or a flat pan. Sprinkle patties liberally with salt and pepper, and set aside.

2 While patties come to room temperature, fry bacon in a non-stick pan to desired degree of crispiness. Remove bacon from pan and place on a paper towel-lined plate. Reserve the bacon fat from the pan and set aside the bacon slices.

3 Drizzle the patties with two-thirds of the reserved bacon fat, and broil until the tops brown. Then flip the patties and continue to broil until desired "doneness" is reached (about 15 minutes for medium-rare). Top each burger with a slice of cheese and place under the broiler for 2 minutes. Once patties are cooked and the cheese has melted, remove from broiler. Placed sliced rolls in the oven on a separate pan to warm for about 1 minute.

4 Return bacon pan to stove-top on medium heat, adding butter to remaining bacon fat. Fry eggs sunny side up, or to desired doneness.

5 To assemble, layer each bun bottom with onion, tomato, bacon, and burger patties. Top each burger with a fried egg, hot from the pan, and the toasted bun top.

Penfolds Thomas Hyland Shiraz

This burger is a big boy, and needs a bold red playmate. This deep, dark Shiraz from Penfolds is a perfect choice for this finger-licking fiesta of proteins. Its blackberry pie flavors are custom-built for beef, while the aromatic black pepper and smoke accents will sync up nicely with the breakfasty fried eggs and bacon.

Dogfish Head Indian Brown Ale

Grease is the word, so you'll need a strong, well-carbonated, dark, hoppy beer to cut through the heaviness of the dish. Dark brown and 7 percent abv, Dogfish Head Indian Brown Ale has the body to stand up to this burger's explosive flavors, and enough alcohol and carbonation to cut through the grease.

grilled chicken
& scallion pizza

Pizza is always a hit, but this grilled chicken and vegetable topped recipe, from Chef Marcel Lavalée of Dogfish Head Brewings & Eats in Rehoboth Beach, Delaware, is phenomenal. If you're feeling pressed for time, simply use store-bought pizza crusts, pre-heat the grill on low, and skip steps 2–5. You'll have homemade pizza in no time flat—and more time to source our beer and wine suggestions (*see opposite*).

Yields: **6 servings**
Ease of preparation:
  with homemade crusts: **Advanced**
  with store-bought crusts: **Simple**

INGREDIENTS
For homemade pizza crust:
1 cup Pale Ale
1 packet yeast (1 tbsp)
2½ cups bread flour (high-gluten)
2 tsp sugar
1 tsp salt
4 tsp canola oil

*Or substitute 2 x 8-inch/20-cm
  store-bought pizza crusts)

For the topping:
1 cup store-bought pizza sauce
½ cup caramelized onions
  (pan-fried with butter)
½ cup roasted red pepper strips
2 cups diced grilled chicken breast
½ cup sliced scallions
2 cups shredded mozzarella

1 Pre-heat outdoor grill on medium-high heat and lower the lid.

2 To make the homemade pizza crusts, heat the beer gently in a saucepan on low heat until lukewarm, then transfer to a mixing bowl. Whisk in yeast, and then slowly add the flour and sugar, mixing in well with a wooden spoon (or use a mixer with the "dough hook" attachment on the low-speed setting).

3 Once flour and sugar are mixed in thoroughly, add the salt, followed by the oil. When the dough is smooth, cover the bowl tightly with plastic wrap.

4 Place the dough in a warm location (such as on a windowsill or on top of an oven or refrigerator) to allow dough to rise or "proof". When it has doubled in size, approximately 45 minutes, remove dough from its container and divide into 2 equal parts with a spatula

5 On a floured surface, slowly and gently roll out each portion into a round pizza crust shape, approximately 8 inches (20cm) in diameter. Place both floured rounds on the hot grill briefly, just long enough to define their shape and mark each side with "grill lines". Remove crusts from grill, reduce the heat to low, and lower the grill lid to retain heat.

6 Top each crust with half of the pizza sauce, spreading evenly, followed by half of each of the other toppings, except the cheese. To finish, top each pizza with half of the mozzarella cheese. Return the pizzas to the grill, on low heat with lid lowered, until the cheese melts and the crust bottoms are golden brown. If the bottoms are getting scorched, place a layer of aluminum foil under each pizza crust. (Alternatively, pizzas may be finished in a 375°F/190°C oven.)

Paulaner Hefe-Weizen

The yeasty dough of this lighter dish will work well with a yeasty wheat beer. The classic Paulaner Hefe-Weizen is just the thing. The spicy, clove-centric notes of the beer complement the pizza toppings and the carbonation breaks through the greasiness of the cheese.

Montecillo Rioja Crianza

Mid-weight European reds are a sure-fire hit with pizza's melted cheese and tomato-y tang. This Spanish Rioja by Montecillo, with its sandalwood aromas, is extremely well-suited to pizzas cooked on an outdoor grill. Rioja's sensuous combination of satiny texture, spice box smells, and wild berry flavors is particularly apt for this chicken and scallion pie.

angel hair
pasta Bolognese

This recipe comes courtesy of Chef Marcel Lavalée of Dogfish Head Brewings & Eats. It's a modern twist on classic spaghetti Bolognese, replacing spaghetti with delicate angel hair pasta. The sauce can be made in advance and frozen, so before the guests arrive all you'll have to do is defrost the sauce, cook up the pasta, and head for the wine (or beer) cellar.

Yields: **6 servings**
Ease of preparation: **Moderate**

INGREDIENTS
2 lbs (1kg) of angel hair pasta

For the sauce (to be made in advance):
2 lbs (1kg) ground beef
¼ cup butter
1 medium carrot, finely diced
1 large white onion, finely diced
2 celery stalks, finely diced
6 cloves garlic, minced
8 large tomatoes, diced
2 cups tomato juice
¼ cup sugar
¼ cup chopped fresh basil, thyme, or
  oregano, or 3 crumbled bay leaves
Salt and pepper to taste
Grated Parmesan cheese (optional)

1 In a large saucepan, brown the ground beef over a medium heat. When beef is thoroughly browned, discard the fat and set aside.

2 Using the same pan, melt the butter over a high heat. Add carrot, onion, and celery, and sauté. When vegetables are soft, add garlic, and sauté for 2–3 minutes.

3 Turn the heat down to medium, add the tomatoes, and let stew for about 45 minutes or until tomatoes start to break down. Stir frequently.

4 Reduce the heat to low and add the tomato juice, sugar, and herbs and cook slowly for about 6 hours, stirring periodically. Add reserved meat back into pot and add salt and pepper to taste.

5 Cook the pasta just before serving. In a large stock pot, bring water to a full boil. Add the angel hair pasta, and stir gently to prevent noodles from sticking together. Drain noodles when they reach the "al dente" stage, about 3 minutes.

6 Place pasta portions in 6 wide bowls and pour sauce over pasta. Top with grated Parmesan cheese, if desired, and serve immediately.

Secco-Bertani Valpolicella Ripasso

A happy northern Italian marriage, meaty Bolognese pasta and supple, plummy Valpolicella have a lot in common. Both are substantial and satisfying without feeling heavy. Especially well suited are "Ripasso" style Valpolicellas, like this oft-imitated icon from Bertani. Fermented twice, Ripassos gain extra flavor from the addition of raisiny Amarone skins.

Newcastle Brown Ale

This dish has sweet notes from the beef, acidic notes from the sauce, and bready notes from the pasta itself. Newcastle Brown Ale has all these elements. It's drier than its russet color would suggest, but the Crystal malt imparts a subtle sweetness. Newcastle's house yeast gives this beer spicy bready notes, too.

spicy Gulf
shrimp

This spicy, flavorful shrimp recipe rivals anything you can find in the bayous of Louisiana, and comes courtesy of Chef Allyson Thurber from the restaurant Lobster in Los Angeles, California. In order to do this dish justice, make sure you use the freshest whole shrimp you can find. And, of course, pairing it with an appropriately stellar wine or beer (*see opposite*) won't hurt either!

Yields: **6 servings**
Ease of preparation: **Moderate**

INGREDIENTS
36 large whole shrimp,
  shells and head-on

For the shrimp stock:
1 tbsp corn oil
½ yellow onion, chopped
1 tbsp chopped garlic
½–1 jalapeno pepper, deseeded
36 shrimp shells
1 tomato, quartered
1 cup white wine
2 cups water
5 whole black peppercorns
1 bay leaf

For the shrimp:
1½ tbsp Cajun Spice blend
1 tsp salt
3 tbsp corn oil
1 tbsp fresh chopped garlic
1 cup shrimp stock (*see recipe, above*)
1½ tbsp Tabasco sauce
1 tsp fresh ground black pepper
5 tbsp unsalted butter
6 fresh cilantro sprigs (or substitute
  parsley sprigs)

1 Peel the tail portion of the shrimp, leaving head attached. Refrigerate shrimp, and reserve shells for stock.

2 For the stock, heat oil in a 3-quart (3-liter) saucepan. Add chopped onion, garlic, and jalapeno, and sauté on medium heat until onion is soft, about 5 minutes.

3 Add shrimp shells and tomato and sauté for 2 minutes on medium heat. Add wine to the pan and stir to loosen and dissolve browned juices and residue. Add all other ingredients and simmer for 30 minutes. Strain the mixture through a sieve and reserve liquid.

4 To prepare the shrimp, season peeled shrimp with a mixture of half of the Cajun spices and all of the salt.

5 Heat oil on high heat in a large sauté pan, and then add garlic to hot oil. Add shrimp to pan, so that they lay flat on the pan's bottom. Turn shrimp after about 1 minute, and brown on both sides. Remove shrimp and return pan to heat.

6 Add stock to pan and stir to loosen and dissolve browned spices and shrimp residue. Add remaining Cajun spices and let stock reduce by half on low heat. Add Tabasco and black pepper, reduce heat to low, and add butter. Shake pan until all butter is melted to finish the sauce.

7 Serve 6 shrimp per person, over rice, spooning "sauce" over shrimp. Garnish with fresh sprigs of cilantro.

Domaine Longval Tavel Rosé

Multi-faceted Cajun flavors laced with spicy heat leave me torn between white and red, so I turn to vivid rosés to save the day. Think pink is wimpy? Think again. Tavel from France's Rhône Valley explodes with tart raspberry flavors that belie a meaty depth. Perfect for this complex dish, Longval is a bone-dry revelation for those suspicious of sugary "blush".

Moortgat Duvel

Spicy dishes love malty beers—the residual sweetness of the barley malt keeps the heat in check. However, the bright citrusy notes of the shrimp are best coupled with lighter-style beers. Duvel offers the perfect middle ground—light-gold in color but nearly 9 percent abv.

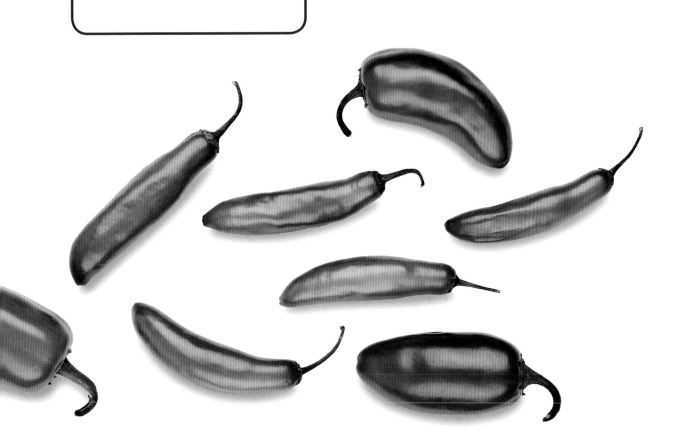

steamed mussels
with red sauce

This delectable shellfish dish, created by Chef David Ansill of the restaurant Ansill in Philadelphia, has all the right stuff. Plump, juicy mussels, shallots, garlic, tomatoes, and herbs make this recipe a wonderful, warming treat that is especially good during the cooler months of the year. Bring out the best in this dish with a beer or wine that plays to its strengths (*see opposite*).

Yields: **6 servings**
Ease of preparation: **Simple**

INGREDIENTS
6 quarts (6 liters) fresh live mussels in
 the shell (or substitute frozen
 "whole shell" mussels)

For the red sauce:
2 tbsp unsalted butter
6 shallots, thinly sliced (or substitute
 1 medium-sized onion)
6 cloves garlic, minced
1½ cups dry white wine
1 quart (1 liter) canned tomato purée
½ cup chopped fresh parsley, rinsed and
 stems removed
1 tsp red pepper flakes
Salt

1 Rinse live mussels well. If any live mussel shells are not tightly closed, tap the shell and discard any that do not close within one minute. If using frozen mussels, thaw overnight in the refrigerator.

2 Remove any beards, or byssus threads (bundles of brown fibers found between the two shells), by pulling them out with a quick tug or cutting them with scissors. (Frozen whole shell mussels will have already been cleaned and blanched.)

3 In a large pot, melt the butter and sauté the shallots until soft and translucent. Add garlic, wine, tomato purée, and mussels. Cook covered on medium heat, stirring occasionally for 10–15 minutes or until all mussel shells have opened. (To avoid overcooking, steam live mussels only until the shells open wide and the meats loosen from their shells.)

4 Using a slotted spoon, scoop the mussels into 6 wide shallow serving bowls.

5 Add the parsley and red pepper flakes to the tomato-mussel liquid and bring to a boil. Season with salt to taste. Pour tomato sauce over mussels and serve.

Banfi Centine Toscana Rosso

Red wine with seafood? When flavor intensity is high, as with mussels in savory tomato sauce, absolutely. However, light-hearted, youthful reds are our best bet, like this tangy Sangiovese blend from Tuscany. Banfi is known for their modern approach, as with this cherry-scented "Centine", a plumper, juicier variation on the traditional Chianti style.

Birra Moretti La Rossa

You would expect an Italian beer to work well with a pot of mussels slathered with red sauce, but this reddish brown lager (as opposed to the lighter flagship Moretti Lager) has a more pronounced caramel character and heightened flavor profile. It starts sweet and ends dry, which makes it ideal for pairing with acidic foods like tomato sauce.

merluza
salsa verde (cod with green sauce)

This recipe, from Chef Dominick Cerrone of the French Culinary Institute in New York, is prepared with robust ingredients such as potatoes. Its richness comes from the cod, but the mildly acidic salsa verde gives it another layer of flavor complexity. Bear these elements in mind when picking out a good wine or beer to pair with it—or, simply check out our suggestions (*see opposite*).

Yields: **6 servings**
Ease of preparation: **Advanced**

INGREDIENTS
1 cup fresh or frozen green peas
1 cup fresh or frozen green beans, chopped
2 cups red potato, diced and skin on
1½ cups fish stock (or substitute equal parts clam juice and water)
3 cloves garlic, green germ removed, finely minced
¾ cup chopped fresh parsley
Pinch of cayenne pepper
Salt and freshly ground pepper
6 x 6-oz (175-g) portions fresh filleted cod or haddock, preferably skin on (or substitute other white fish such as orange roughy or snapper)
1 cup all-purpose flour
4 tbsp olive oil
Fresh lemon juice, a few drops
6 parsley sprigs to garnish

1 In two small saucepans, bring salted water to a boil. Cook the peas and beans together in one pan and the potatoes in the other, until all are just tender. Drain both and set aside separately.

2 In a mixing bowl, loosely combine fish stock, minced garlic, and half the chopped parsley. Stir in a pinch each of cayenne pepper and salt, and set aside.

3 Season both sides of the fillets with salt and pepper. Place the skin side of each fillet in the flour. Heat 1 tablespoon of oil in a large deep frying pan on medium heat. Place the fish fillets into the pan, skin side down, and sauté until skin is golden, but fish is not fully cooked. Remove fillets to a side plate. Rinse the pan and return to heat.

4 Add the 6 fillets to the pan, skin side up. Pour in the reserved stock mixture into the pan, so that it surrounds the fish. Add the potatoes to the liquid around the fish, and bring the contents of the pan to a simmer. Reduce to low heat and cover for approximately 5 minutes, or until flesh splits when pressed lightly. Remove the fish and potatoes, cover them and keep warm.

5 Add the remaining parsley and olive oil to the pan liquid and stir. Add a few drops of lemon juice and salt and pepper to taste. Add reserved vegetables and any juices from the fish plate to the sauce to reheat briefly. Arrange the fillets and potatoes in the center of 6 warmed plates. Once vegetables are reheated, top the fish with equal portions of the sauce mixture and garnish with sprigs of parsley.

228

Russian River Damnation

You'll need a strong, well-spiced beer to keep up with this complex dish. Damnation works well because it has spicy, tropical fruit notes in the aroma that align nicely with the grassy notes of the salsa verde. But it also has a clean, malty finish and enough alcohol to cut through the oil of the fish.

Chateau Villa Bel-Air Graves Blanc

Green flavors dominate leafy sauces such as salsa verde, while searing the fish imparts a toasty taste. Barrel-fermented white Bordeaux, like this classy Graves from the legendary Cazes family, will faintly echo both qualities. A blend of two grapes that feature herbal aromas, Semillon and Sauvignon Blanc, this wine's flavors of green plums and honeydew are delicately seasoned with vanilla.

roasted chicken
with herbs

Roasted chicken is an elegant and unfussy dish. This recipe, from Chef Marcel Lavalée of Dogfish Head Brewings & Eats, ups the ante with lots of fresh, green, herbal flavors. Serve with boiled new potatoes on white china and you've got a simple, but special, go-to meal. Of course, don't forget to include an impressive beer and wine, too (*see opposite*).

Yield: **6 servings**
Ease of preparation: **Simple**

INGREDIENTS
¼ cup unsalted butter (room temperature)
3–6 cloves garlic, peeled and chopped
½ cup chopped fresh basil
2 fresh rosemary sprigs, chopped
1 whole chicken (6–8 lbs/3–4kg)
Salt and pepper

1 Pre-heat oven to 350°F (180°C). In a medium-sized mixing bowl soften up the butter, and then blend in the garlic, basil, and rosemary. Set aside.

2 Rinse the chicken and wash your hands thoroughly. Using your fingers, gently find the separation between skin and breasts, and carefully lift the skin to access the breast meat. Do not tear or fully detach the skin.

3 With your fingers, spread the butter mixture under the skin, covering all accessible meat surfaces. Replace skin and dust the chicken with salt and pepper.

4 Bake the chicken for 20 minutes per pound (plus an additional 20 minutes), basting periodically, or until an internal temperature of the breast reaches 160°F (70°C), and the thigh reaches 170°F (75°C). Allow chicken to cool for about 10 minutes before carving and serving.

Rosemount Estate Show Reserve Chardonnay

Roasted chicken is one of life's simple pleasures. With its crisp golden-brown skin, it pairs beautifully with golden-hued Chardonnay from sunny regions. Toasty and rich, this outstanding Australian example from Rosemount Estate is loaded with flavor, like a grilled pineapple topped with butter-pecan ice cream.

Escura Eisenbahn

Roasted chicken may be the ultimate bedfellow for dark lagers. This one from Escura has a roasty, round, dry character that enhances the flavors of the dish. The lager's bitter notes come more from the roasted and chocolate barley than from the hops, which complements the silky, soft flavors of roasted chicken.

classic beef
tenderloin

You would be hard-pressed to find a more stunning beef tenderloin recipe than this one, courtesy of Chef Alain Sailhac of the French Culinary Institute. It may be an ambitious dish, but rest assured, the results are definitely worth the effort. To complement its rich flavor, serve the tenderloin with a big red wine or a hearty ale, such as the ones we recommend on the opposite page.

Yields: **6 servings**
Ease of preparation: **Advanced**

INGREDIENTS
9 Belgian endives, washed and cut in
  half lengthwise
2½ tsp unsalted butter
2½ tsp canola or vegetable oil
Salt and fresh ground black pepper
3 shallots, minced (or substitute
  ½ medium-sized onion, minced)
¾ cup dry white wine
1½ cups veal stock (or substitute equal
  measure of beef broth plus 2 tbsp butter)
6 x 4-oz (125-g) beef tenderloins,
  trimmed of excess fat
3 cups sliced button mushrooms
2 cloves garlic, minced
3 tbsp chopped parsley

1 Core the endives by trimming ¼ inch (5mm) from the bottoms and cutting out the small core with a paring knife. In a large non-stick sauté pan warm 1½ teaspoons butter and 1½ teaspoons oil over medium-low heat. Add the endives in a single layer. Sprinkle with salt and freshly ground black pepper. Cover the pan and cook for 15 minutes.

2 Turn the endives and continue to cook for 10 more minutes. Using a slotted spoon, remove the endives from the pan, cover, and keep warm. Return the sauté pan to medium heat, and add the shallots and remaining butter. Sauté for 4 minutes, or until the shallots are soft and translucent.

3 Add the wine and bring to a boil, stirring to loosen any endive residue. Boil for 5 minutes uncovered, or until wine is reduced by half. Add the stock and boil for 5 minutes, or until the liquid is reduced by a third. Remove from heat and cover to keep warm.

4 Season the beef tenderloins with salt and freshly ground black pepper. Lightly brush a medium-sized non-stick sauté pan with the remaining oil. Place over medium heat until very hot, but not smoking. Add the tenderloins, and cook for 3 minutes. Turn tenderloins and cook for 3 minutes for medium-rare. Remove tenderloins to a plate, and cover to keep warm.

5 Return the tenderloin pan to medium heat, add the sliced mushrooms, and season with salt and freshly ground black pepper. Stir to loosen pan residues and sauté for 5 minutes, or until mushrooms have released all their moisture. Add the garlic, and sauté for 30 seconds. Toss in parsley, and remove from heat.

6 To serve, place a tenderloin in the center of each of 6 warm dinner plates. Arrange equal portions of endive around each tenderloin, spoon over the sauce, and top each portion with the sautéed mushrooms.

Chimay Première

The granddaddy of Trappist ales, Chimay Première, is an ideal partner for beef. It has the body and alcohol to stand up to the juicy, caramelly elements of the sautéed meat, but a spicy-yeasty component that suggests cloves and nutmeg on the palate. A classic pairing, for sure.

Joseph Phelps Cabernet Sauvignon

Red meat just cries out for red wine, and nothing else will do a steak justice. Strapping young Napa Valley Cabernets, like this classic from Joseph Phelps, can seem overwhelming alone, thick with cedar and dark chocolate flavors. But, one bite of tenderloin reveals its exuberant core of woodland berries and releases its tannic grip on the palate.

summer fruit &
Grand Marnier mousse

A refreshing fruit dessert like this one, from Chef Dominick Cerrone of the French Culinary Institute, is an unbeatable sweet treat after any meal. Pair it with a winning drink, like the ones recommended on the next page, and your guests will be clamoring for more. It's easiest to use an electric mixer to get the mousse to the right consistency, but you can achieve the same result by hand.

Yields: **6 servings**
Ease of preparation: **Advanced**

INGREDIENTS

For the fruit:
1 cup each: fresh sliced strawberries, fresh raspberries, fresh blueberries, diced or balled cantaloupe or honeydew melon, diced fresh peaches, and diced fresh plums (equal amounts of other bite-sized summer fruits may be substituted)
2 tbsp finely chopped fresh mint
1 tsp orange-flower water
  (or subtitute Grand Marnier liqueur)

For the mousse:
3 cups heavy cream
1 cup sugar
⅔ cup water
Small branch fresh rosemary
  (or substitute another fresh herb, such as tarragon or thyme)
5 egg yolks
Pinch of salt
½ cup Grand Marnier liqueur

To garnish:
Candied orange peel, cut into thin strips
Mint sprig to garnish (optional)

1 Combine all the fruit with the mint and orange-flower water, and toss gently in large bowl (should fill bowl halfway or less). Cover and set aside at room temperature. In a mixing bowl, whip the heavy cream until it shows soft peaks. Cover and refrigerate until needed.

2 Place the sugar, water, and rosemary in a small saucepan and bring to a boil. Simmer for 1 minute. Remove and discard the rosemary sprig, and remove from heat. Place the egg yolks and salt in a large electric mixer bowl and whisk them gently, gradually increasing the speed to medium

3 Return rosemary syrup to a boil to thicken. When the syrup has thickened enough to spin a thread, or to form a soft ball when drizzled into a glass of water, reduce the mixer speed and immediately begin to pour the hot syrup very slowly over the fluffed yolk mixture. Once all the syrup is added, increase the speed slowly to medium again. Continue to whip the mixture until it is cool to the touch, then remove the bowl from the mixer.

4 Add the Grand Marnier liqueur to the chilled whipped cream and re-whip slightly to regain a "soft peak" consistency. Fold the whipped cream gently into the cooled egg yolk mixture. Pour this "mousse" into a chilled bowl, and set over ice. Cover and refrigerate.

5 Spoon the mousse over the fruit mixture immediately before serving. Spread the mousse gently until it covers the fruit in an even layer. Garnish with thin strips of candied orange peel and a mint sprig, if desired.

Cascinetta Vietti Moscato d'Asti

Made by interrupting fermentation, Moscato d'Asti is as hedonistic as wines get. Light and frothy, bursting with juicy apricot and sweet honeysuckle flavors, it makes a perfect partner for this airy mousse and fresh fruit. This gem from the icon Barolo house of Vietti will evoke rapture from your inner child, and proves that "serious" winemakers needn't take wine too seriously.

La Choulette Frambroise

This sweet, creamy mousse could be cloying if paired with a similarly sweet beer. Opt for a drier fruit beer like La Choulette Framboise. It has a dry and spicy Bière de Garde base and raspberries give it additional complexity. The berries' sugars are fermented out, so the beer isn't overly sweet.

chocolate pecan
upside-down cake

Why does upside-down cake always have to be made with pineapple? This delicious nutty cake is courtesy of Chef Gale Gand of Tru restaurant in Chicago. And you don't have to use pecans—hazelnuts, walnuts, or whatever nuts you like best will work just as well! Serve this decadent dessert with an inspired Port or Stout, and you won't have any leftovers.

Yields: **10 servings**
Ease of preparation: **Moderate**

INGREDIENTS

For caramel "topping":
6 tbsp unsalted butter, melted, plus extra for buttering the cake pan
¾ cup light brown sugar, packed
¼ cup honey
1¼ cups whole shelled pecans, lightly toasted

For the cake:
1¼ cups cake flour
½ cup cocoa powder (preferably Dutch-process)
1 tsp baking soda
½ tsp salt
8 tbsp (1 stick) unsalted butter (room temperature)
1½ cups sugar
3 eggs
1 cup buttermilk
1 tsp pure vanilla extract

1 Pre-heat oven to 350ºF (180ºC). Thickly butter the sides of a 10-inch (25-cm) round cake pan. Pour the melted butter into the cake pan and swirl to coat the bottom and then sprinkle in the brown sugar. Evenly drizzle the honey and sprinkle the pecans over the bottom to form the cake's "topping".

2 To make the cake batter, sift the flour, cocoa powder, baking soda, and salt together three times, in order to make the cake extra light. Set aside

3 Cream the butter in a mixer (using a whisk attachment, if possible) until smooth and fluffy, then add the sugar and mix. Add the eggs one at a time, mixing after adding each one. Beat until fluffy and light

4 With the mixer on low speed, add a third of the dry ingredients. Then add half of the buttermilk and mix. Add another third of the dry ingredients and mix. Add the remaining buttermilk and vanilla extract and mix. Add the remaining dry ingredients and mix until smooth.

5 Pour the batter into the pan. Bake in the pre-heated oven for approximately 25–35 minutes, or until set in the center and springy. Let cool a little, and then run a serrated knife around the edge of the pan. Turn it out, upside down, onto a serving platter.

6 Let stand, inverted, for about 5 minutes, so the caramel can soak into the cake a bit. Before the caramel sets fully, score the topping with a knife where it will be sliced. Serve while still warm.

Dogfish Head World Wide Stout

For this chocolatey dessert, you'll want a dark beer that has lots of body, alcohol, and roasty character. Dogfish Head's World Wide Stout, one of world's strongest dark beers, is up to the task. At 18 percent abv, it approaches Port-like proportions, and the high ratio of dark barley malt in the recipe keeps it dry and roasty enough to off-set the sweet, fatty weight of the chocolate.

Dow's Late Bottled Vintage Porto

Darkly delicious and bittersweet, Port and chocolate are natural companions. Dripping with brandied cherry flavors, Port is unusually alcoholic and unctuous, a sweet Portuguese red wine fortified with distilled grape spirit. As sinfully decadent as this cake, Dow's Late Bottled Vintage Porto is packed with sweet jammy fruit and fiery spice aromas.

Marnie says:
maybe beer's all right

Going into this project I had a bit of a wine-centric attitude. I couldn't imagine that beer could deliver the complexity and food-pairing strengths I'm so fond of in wine. So much of my beer experience had been with insipid bargain brands that I had passed judgment on the category as a whole. So, I've been thinking...

Maybe all beer's not so bad

Okay, so I may have gotten a touch snippy when Sam insisted beers could measure up to wine. After all, beer has always been the beverage people settled for when they couldn't make, acquire, or afford wine. I thought it was safe to assume wine was inherently superior. But, in the course of our beer versus wine dinners I've learned a thing or two. First, that there is a huge range of beer styles out there: strong beers, sour beers, wheat beers, fruit beers, spiced beers, smoked beers—specialty brews of all stripes. Second, Sam's choices demonstrated that skilled brewers using quality ingredients make all the difference.

On common ground

So, I had a revelation. Don't ask me why it hadn't occurred to me before, but I was truly surprised to see how much common ground wine and beer share. Both are naturally fermented alcoholic beverages that retain the nutrition of their raw materials. Both harness the miraculous action of yeast to add layers of delightful flavor complexity. Both are capable of being terrific food partners, amplifying the pleasure we take in eating. And both come in a rainbow of flavors and styles that can flatter the breadth of the world's cuisines.

The imposters

But both wine and beer can be mass-produced, sacrificing quality in favor of quantity. What I hadn't realized before was that because cheap beer is so much more popular than cheap wine, I had dismissed beer based on that alone. But, that's like deciding all cheese sucks after a bite of processed cheese. Where beer differs from wine is in the extraordinary dominance that one narrow style has in the marketplace: mass-produced light lager. If the entire planet equated wine with dire, watery Pinot Grigio, the wine industry would have a serious image problem, too.

Luckily for craft brewers like Sam, the beer landscape is changing fast. High-quality beers pioneered centuries ago are surging in popularity and innovative craft breweries are raising the bar every year, offering styles as diverse and food-friendly as wines. Where beer choices were once limited to a dozen brands of "vanilla", today's beer market reflects every flavor under the sun.

The verdict

I still prefer wine, to be honest. While beer may have potential, I think wine has an unshakeable head start in the pursuit of quality. In the splurge category, wine blows even the world's finest beers away. But it isn't quite fair to assess the quality of something without also factoring in its price.

In reality, few people can afford to drink top-tier wines every day. When price per serving is considered, I'll admit there are some beers that can hold their own with wine when it comes to food pairing. There may even be a handful of occasions where I might choose to drink beer over wine—just don't tell anyone I said that.

" There may even be a handful of occasions where **I MIGHT CHOOSE TO DRINK BEER INSTEAD OF WINE**—just don't tell anyone I said that.**"**

Sam says:
maybe wine's okay

At Dogfish Head, I've spent years championing beer's rightful place at the dinner table. Luckily, as society gains a deeper appreciation for life's finer things—reprioritizing quality over quantity—we have better beer and wine options available to us. And, at the end of the day, beer and wine aren't that different after all.

Making up is hard to do

Marnie and I have worked together for many years and I'd be lying if I said I haven't learned an awful lot from her throughout this period. While beer still suffers from a dumbed-down image, Marnie has taught me that wine has its own stereotypes to fight. The most obvious being the belief that you need to spend over twenty bucks for a good bottle of wine. Throughout the course of writing this book and in presentations we've done together I've been lucky to try many great, affordable, accessible wines. I didn't always like them better than the beers they were up against, but I didn't dislike them, either.

A seismic shift

Watching high-quality, mid-priced wines gain traction gives me hope for the path we are now on in the beer world. Let's not forget that only a generation ago American wine was a disparaged commodity. Images of jug wine and fortified-hobo-rotgut come immediately to mind. So, as a brewer trying to raise the profile of my beverage I take my hat off to winemakers like Robert Mondavi who have helped to usher in an age of universal respect for American wines.

There is now a whole generation of brewers throughout the world who are beginning to succeed in a similar initiative. The difference is that the bias we brewers experience is international rather than national. So, brewers the world over are fighting shoulder-to-shoulder to improve the image and appreciation of beer: great beer, gourmet beer, food-friendly beer.

Another thing that I have learned from Marnie is that, as with the beer world, there are essentially two parallel wine industries: mass-produced industrial wines, and small scale, artisanal, flavor-forward wines. There are occasions when mass-produced wines and beers might pair well with a food, but most of the breathtakingly euphoric combinations are realized when pairing with the small-scale, artisanal producers.

Closing argument

I hope that Marnie and I have offered convincing arguments on why certain foods work best when paired with certain types of beer and wine. But, of course, you should follow your own pairing muse within our general advice. Marnie and I may squabble and joust, maybe a touch of that is posturing and grandstanding to help us make our points, but we really are proud of our respective drinks. That said, ultimately, we share an overlapping desire to help beer lovers become more comfortable with pairing good wine with food and vice versa for wine lovers. I know I've learned my lesson: I'm writing this final section while enjoying a glass of Amity Gandy Pinot Noir from Oregon with my steak frites. But fear not, my loyal beer brethren: for dessert I intend to have my pears and vanilla ice cream with a snifter of 90 minute IPA.

"I'M ENJOYING A GLASS OF PINOT NOIR with my steak frites. But for dessert I intend to have my pears and vanilla ice cream with a snifter of 90 minute IPA.**"**

wine glossary

Acidity/acid—a taste sensation of sourness, like lemon or vinegar, perceived most vividly along the sides of the tongue.

Appellation—a regulated label statement of a wine's region of origin; in Europe appellation laws govern grape varieties and minimum quality standards in addition to regional provenance.

Aroma—an olfactory sensation, or smell. When wine is in the mouth, aromas rise from the throat to the olfactory center, where they are perceived as "flavors".

Astringent—a harsh, drying tactile sensation, as from the tannins found in red wines.

Balance—the harmony of a wine's major sensory characteristics.

Body—the tactile sensation of weight or thickness on the palate, which increases with wine's alcohol content or viscosity.

Complexity—a descriptor for wines projecting multi-faceted aromas or flavors.

Dessert wine—a sweet wine customarily served with dessert, or after a meal.

Dry/dryness—a wine's lack of perceptible sweetness; the absence of a taste sensation of sugar on the tip of the tongue.

Fermentation—the conversion of sugar into alcohol and carbon dioxide by the action of micro-organisms called yeasts; the main process of winemaking.

Finish—aftertaste of wine that lingers in the mouth after it is swallowed. Both the character and the length of the finish are considered in evaluating wine. The longer a pleasant finish lasts, the better the wine's quality.

Fortified wine—a wine whose alcohol content has been boosted with distilled spirit.

Fruit—an umbrella term for aromas and flavors that come from grapes and their fermentation; includes most olfactory sensations found in wine other than those imparted by the use of new oak.

Fruity/fruit-forward—descriptors for wines with strong aromas or flavors reminiscent of any fruit (not just grapes).

Green—herbal aroma qualities reminiscent of under-ripe fruit or vegetables.

Late harvest—a wine style where grapes were picked at a later date and a higher level of ripeness than for the normal harvest; generally for dessert wines.

Lees—the sediment of spent yeasts that remains after fermentation.

Nose—another term for the olfactory sensations of a wine.

Oak/oaky—olfactory sensations of aroma or flavor imparted by fermenting or aging wine in new oak barrels. Like those of cognac and bourbon, oak characteristics in wine can smell like vanilla, caramel, nuts, or dessert spices, in addition to wood.

Olfactory—of the sense of smell. Other than the five tastes the tongue can perceive (sweet, sour, salt, bitter and umami), all flavor sensations are perceived by the olfactory center behind the nose.

Residual sugar—unfermented grape sugar in a finished wine.

Rich—term used to describe body and texture in wine; may also describe concentrated flavor, high alcohol, sweetness, low acid, or a combination of these.

Sweet/sweetness—a taste sensation perceived at the tip of the tongue in wines where not all grape sugar has been converted to alcohol; often described in terms of its absence, called "dryness".

Tannin—an astringent compound found in grape skins and stems, only prominent in red wines; perceived as a lingering drying tactile sensation in the mouth.

Variety/varietal—a grape variety within the vine species *Vitis vinifera*, or system of wine labelling emphasizing dominant grape variety.

Vintage—year in which the grapes were grown and harvested, usually printed on a wine's label.

Vitis vinifera—the European grape species which encompasses all high-quality wine grape varieties, such as Chardonnay, Merlot, Shiraz, etc.

beer glossary

Aging—allowing a strong beer (usually over 10 percent abv) to gain added complexity and depth by storing it in a cool, dark place, such as a wine cellar.

Alcohol by volume (abv)—alcohol content calculated by the space it occupies.

Body—the tactile sensation of weight or thickness on the palate, which increases with beer's alcohol content or viscosity.

Bottle-conditioned—Re-fermentation of residual sugars in each bottle to give beer natural carbonation.

Bottom-fermentation—process by which lagers are made. Since lager yeasts sink, they ferment sugars from the bottom of the batch of beer.

Carbon dioxide—natural by-product of fermentation that gives beer refreshing carbonation. This gas is commonly added to make beer more bubbly.

Color—coloration of the beer, important because it varies along with flavor. As malt roasting imparts darker color to malt, toasty, roasty aromas and flavors emerge as well.

Complexity—the depth and distinctive flavor characteristics of a beer; the extent to which a particular beer engages all of your five senses.

Craft beers—beers produced in small batches, using high-quality ingredients; usually made by independently run breweries.

Dry-hopping—the process of incorporating additional volumes of hops post-fermentation and late in the brewing process. This gives the beer an enhanced aromatic complexity and heightened perceived bitterness.

Extreme beers—beers brewed with an enhanced volume of traditional ingredients like hops and barley, or beers brewed with non-traditional ingredients (eg, coffee).

Fermentation—the conversion of sugar into alcohol and carbon dioxide by the action of micro-organisms called yeasts; the main process of brewing.

Hop flowers/hops—cone-shaped "flower" of the hop plant, a robust perrennial relation of cannabis. Hops are one of beer's main ingredients; essential for preserving beer's freshness, hops also impart spicy aromas and quenching bitterness. See "Hoppy" for sensory qualities.

Hoppy—sensations imparted by hops in beer, which include floral, grassy, spicy, and herbal olfactory aromas and flavors, as well as the distinctive bitterness perceived by the tastebuds.

Malt—malted grain, often shorthand for malted barley, one of beer's main ingredients. Malting is a process of grain germination, or sprouting, interrupted by roasting. Malting develops enzymes that will convert starch into fermentable sugar, an essential pre-requisite for brewing beer. See "Malty" for sensory qualities.

Malty—sensations imparted by malt in beer, which increase in intensity with higher proportions of malt used. These include grainy, toasty, nutty, and caramelized aromas and flavors, as well as sweetness.

Mouthfeel—the tactile sensations of beer (eg, body and carbonation).

Palate—technically the roof of the mouth, but commonly used to describe the mouth's apparatus for sensing taste, olfactory, and tactile sensations as a whole.

pH—scale used for measuring acidity; acidic beers taste tangy, sharp, or tart.

Specialty grain—the more distinct, usually darker malted barley varieties beyond the lighter base malts that maintain the highest volume of fermentable sugar in a beer.

Spontaneous fermentation—allowing air-borne micro-flora and yeast to ferment beer, as popularized through the Belgian Lambic brewing tradition; also known as wild fermentation.

Top-fermentation—process by which ales are made. Since ale yeasts float, they ferment sugars from the top of the batch of beer.

Yeast—micro-organisms that eat sugar and convert it into alcohol and carbon dioxide, a process called fermentation.

wine & beer
resources

**FOR MORE INFORMATION ON
SAM CALAGIONE & DOGFISH HEAD:**

DOGFISH HEAD CRAFT BREWERY
6 Cannery Village Center
Milton, DE 19968
Phone: (302) 684-1000
Phone: 1-888-8Dogfish Head
Website: www.dogfish.com

DOGFISH HEAD BREWINGS & EATS
320 Rehoboth Avenue
Rehoboth Beach, DE 19971
Phone: (302) 226-2739

**DOGFISH HEAD ALEHOUSE
(GAITHERSBURG, MD)**
800 West Diamond Avenue
Gaithersburg, MD 20878
Phone: (301) 963-4847

**DOGFISH HEAD ALEHOUSE
(FALLS CHURCH, VA)**
6363 Leesburg Pike
Seven Corners Shopping Center
Falls Church, VA 22044
Phone: (703) 534-3342

**FOR MORE INFORMATION ON
MARNIE OLD & OLD WINES**:

OLD WINES LLC
710 Chestnut Street
Philadelphia, PA 19106
Phone: (215) 351-9985
Website: www.marnieold.com

THE FRENCH CULINARY INSTITUTE (FCI)
462 Broadway
New York, NY 10013
Toll free: (888) FCI-CHEF
Website: www.frenchculinary.com
Offers wine classes for all levels of study.

**USEFUL BEER ADDRESSES
& WEBSITES:**

BREWERS ASSOCIATION
736 Pearl Street
Boulder, CO 80302
Phone: (303) 447-0816
Fax: (303) 447-2825
Website: www.beertown.org
For information on American brewers and the
Great American Beer Festival.

BEER ADVOCATE MAGAZINE
Website: beeradvocate.com
Monthly magazine dedicated to beer.

WWW.RATEBEER.COM
E-community that offers ratings and in-depth
information on a wide range of beers.

WWW.REALBEER.COM
Beer website that discusses a variety of
topics, including new developments in the
beer world.

CRATE & BARREL
Website: www.crateandbarrel.com
Offers a range of different beer glasses.

**USEFUL WINE ADDRESSES
& WEBSITES:**

WWW.LOCALWINEEVENTS.COM
Searchable international listing site for wine
dinners, seminars and tastings.

WWW.ASTORCENTERNYC.COM
Deluxe wine events and wine class venue in
Manhattan's NoHo.

WWW.WINE.COM
Online shopping for wine and wine-related
products.

WWW.WINE.CA
Online wine shopping in Canada.

WWW.WINES.COM
Online resource for learning more about wine
and wine tasting.

WWW.VINO.COM
Information on a variety of wine-related topics, including local tastings.

RIEDEL CRYSTAL
Website: www.riedel.com
Produces a huge range of wine glasses.

FEATURED BREWERIES & WEBSITES:

ADNAMS
Website: www.adnams.co.uk/

ALLAGASH BREWING COMPANY
Website: www.allagash.com

ALPINE BEER COMPANY
Website: www.alpinebeerco.com

ANDERSON VALLEY BREWING COMPANY
Website: www.avbc.com

AVERY BREWING COMPANY
Website: www.averybrewing.com

BAVIK-DE BRABANDERE
Website: www.bavik.be

BIRRA MORETTI
Website: www.birramoretti.it

BOON RAWD BREWERY
Website: www.boonrawd.co.th

BRASSERIE DUYCK
Website: www.duyck.com/

BRASSERIE LA CHOULETTE
Website: www.lachoulette.com

BRAUEREI SCHLOSS EGGENBERG
Website: www.schloss-eggenberg.at

BRAUEREI SPEZIAL
Website: www.brauerei-spezial.de/

BROOKLYN BREWERY
Website: www.brooklynbrewery.com

BROUWERIJ DE RANKE
Website: www.deranke.be

BROUWERIJ DER TRAPPISTEN VAN WESTMALLE
Website: www.trappistwestmalle.be

BROUWERIJ KERKOM
Website: www.brouwerijkerkom.be

BROUWERIJ LINDEMANS
Website: www.lindemans.be

BROUWERIJ RODENBACH
Website: www.rodenbach.be

CANTILLON
Website: www.cantillon.be

CERVEJARIA SUDBRACK
Website: www.eisenbahn.com.br/

CHIMAY
Website: www.chimay.be/

CONISTON BREWING COMPANY
Website: www.conistonbrewery.com/

COOPERS BREWERY
Website: www.coopers.com.au

DE DOLLE BROUWERS
Website: www.dedollebrouwers.be/

DOGFISH HEAD BREWERY
Website: www.dogfish.com

DORTMUNDER ACTIEN BRAUEREI
Website: www.dab.de

ELLEZELLOISE
Website: www.brasserie-ellezelloise.be

ERDINGER WEISSBRÄU
Website: www.erdinger.de/

FULL SAIL BREWING COMPANY
Website: www.fullsailbrewing.com

GREAT DIVIDE BREWING COMPANY
Website: www.greatdivide.com/

GREAT LAKES BREWING COMPANY
Website: www.greatlakesbrewing.com

GRUPO MODELO
Website: www.gmodelo.com

HAIR OF THE DOG BREWING COMPANY
Website: www.hairofthedog.com

HARPOON BREWERY
Website: www.harpoonbrewery.com

BREWERIES, CONTINUED

HEINEKEN NEDERLAND
Website: www.heineken.com/

HEPWORTH
Website: www.thebeerstation.co.uk

HOP BACK
Website: www.hopback.co.uk/

JEVER
Website: www.jever.de/

KULMBACHER BRAUEREI
Website: www.kulmbacher.de/

MAGOR/INBEV
Website: www.interbrew.co.uk/locations.shtm

MAUI BREWING COMPANY
Website: www.mauibrewingco.com

NEW GLARUS BREWING COMPANY
Website: www.newglarusbrewing.com/

NØGNE Ø
Website: www.nogne-o.no

NØRREBRO BRYGHUS
Website: www.noerrebrobryghus.dk

PAULANER BRAUEREI
Website: www.paulaner.com

PENNSYLVANIA BREWING COMPANY
Website: www.pennbrew.com

PORTSMOUTH BREWERY
Website: www.portsmouthbrewery.com/

O'HANLONS
Website: www.ohanlons.co.uk

ØLFABRIKKEN BREWERY
Website: www.olfabrikken.dk

RUSSIAN RIVER BREWING
Website: www.russianriverbrewing.com

SCOTTISH & NEWCASTLE PLC
Website: www.scottish-newcastle.com

SHORTS BREWING COMPANY
Website: www.shortsbrewing.com/

STOUDTS BREWING COMPANY
Website: www.stoudtsbeer.com

THEAKSTON
Website: www.theakstons.co.uk/

TRÖEGS BREWING COMPANY
Website: www.troegs.com/

UNIBROUE
Website: www.unibroue.com/

VICTORY BREWING COMPANY
Website: www.victorybeer.com

WARSTEINER BRAUEREI
Website: www.warsteiner.de

WEISSBIERBRAUEREI G. SCHNEIDER & SOHN
Website: www.schneider-weisse.de/

WINERIES & DISTRIBUTORS

BANFI VINTNERS
Website: www.banfivintners.com
(Wines featured: Maschio Brut Prosecco; Concha y Toro Casillero del Diablo Merlot; Banfi Centine Toscana Rosso; Banfi Rosa Regale Brachetto d'Acqui)

BERINGER
Website: www.beringer.com
(Wine featured: Beringer Merlot)

BODEGA NORTON WINERY
Website: www.norton.com.ar
(Wine featured: Bodega Norton Malbec)

BONTERRA VINYARDS
Website: www.bonterra.com
(Wine featured: Bonterra Viognier)

CASA LAPOSTOLLE
Website: www.casalapostolle.com
(Wine featured: Casa Lapostolle Chardonnay)

CAVE SPRING CELLARS
Website: www.cavespringcellars.com
(Wine featured: Cave Spring Riesling)

CHAMPAGNE PERRIER-JOUËT
Website: www.perrier-jouet.com
(Wine featured: Perrier-Jouët Grand Brut Champagne)

CHEHALEM WINES
Website: www.chehalemwines.com
(Wine featured: Chehalem Reserve Pinot Gris)

DIAGEO (CHATEAU & ESTATES)
Website: www.diageowines.com
(Wines featured: Domaine Longval Tavel Rhône Rosé; Trimbach Reserve Pinot Gris; Domaine Matrot Meursault; Chateau de Montfort Vouvray Demi-Sec; Chateau Phélan Ségur St. Estèphe; Chateau Lafaurie-Peraguey Sauternes)

DR. LOOSEN ESTATE
Website: www.drloosen.com
(Wine featured: Dr. Loosen Dr. L Riesling)

EX CELLARS WINE AGENCIES
Website: www.excellars.com
(Wine featured: Baumard Carte d'Or Coteaux du Layon)

FREDERICK WILDMAN AND SONS, LTD.
Website: www.frederickwildman.com
(Wines featured: Pascal Jolivet Chateau Du Nozay Sancerre; Jaboulet Muscat de Beaumes-de-Venise)

FREIXENET
Website: www.freixenetusa.com
(Wine featured: Freixenet Cordon Negro Cava)

GEORGES DUBOEUF
Website: www.duboeuf.com
(Wine featured: Georges Duboeuf Brouilly Cru Beaujolais)

GEYSER PEAK WINERY
Website: www.geyserpeakwinery.com
(Wine featured: Geyser Peak Chardonnay)

HARVEYS USA
Website: www.harveys-usa.com
(Wine featured: Harveys Bristol Cream Sherry)

HOGUE CELLARS
Website: www.hoguecellars.com
(Wine featured: Hogue Genesis Cabernet Sauvignon)

ICON ESTATES
Website: iconestateswine.com
(Wine featured: Kim Crawford Sauvignon Blanc)

INNISKILLIN
Website: www.inniskillin.com
(Wine featured: Inniskillin Cabernet Franc Ice Wine)

JACOB'S CREEK AUSTRALIAN WINE
Website: www.jacobscreek.com
(Wine featured: Jacob's Creek Reserve Riesling)

JOSEPH PHELPS VINEYARDS
Website: www.jpvwines.com
(Wine featured: Joseph Phelps Cabernet Sauvignon)

KEN FORRESTER VINEYARDS
Website: www.kenforresterwines.com
(Wine featured: Ken Forrester Chenin Blanc)

KOBRAND WINES
Website: www.kobrandwine.com
(Wines featured: Domaine Carneros Sparkling Wine; Taylor-Fladgate 10 year old Tawny Porto)

LAUBER IMPORTS
Website: www.lauberimports.com
(Wines featured: Joh Jos Prüm Riesling Auslese; Pacific Rim Vin de Glacière Riesling; Cascinetta Vietti Moscato d'Asti)

MARCHESI ANTINORI SRL
Website: www.antinori.it
(Wine featured: Antinori "Pèppoli" Chianti Classico)

MCWILLIAM'S WINES
Website: www.mcwilliams.com.au
(Wine featured: McWilliam's Cabernet Sauvignon)

MUMM NAPA
Website: mummnapa.com
(Wine featured: Mumm Napa Blanc de Noirs Sparkling Rosé)

NEIL ELLIS WINES
Website: www.neilellis.com
(Wine featured: Neil Ellis Sincerely Sauvignon Blanc)

PALM BAY INTERNATIONAL
Website: www.palmbay.com
(Wines featured: Anselmi San Vincenzo; Secco-Bertani Valpolicella Classico; Chateau Villa Bel-Air Graves Blanc)

PENFOLDS
Website: www.penfolds.com
(Wine featured: Penfolds Thomas Hyland Shiraz)

WINERIES & DISTRIBUTORS, CONTINUED

PREMIUM PORT WINES, INC.
Website: www.premiumport.com
(Wines featured: Blandy's 10 year old Malmsey Madeira; Dow's Late Bottled Vintage Porto)

RANCHO ZABACO WINERY
Website: www.ranchozabaco.com
(Wine featured: Rancho Zabaco SHV Zinfandel)

ROSEMOUNT ESTATE AUSTRALIA
Website: www.rosemountestate.com.au
(Wine featured: Rosemount Estate Show Reserve Chardonnay)

SCHLOSS GOBELSBURG
Website: www.gobelsburg.com
(Wine featured: Schloss Gobelsburg Gobelsburger Grüner Veltliner)

STERLING VINEYARDS
Website: www.sterlingvineyards.com
(Wine featured: Sterling "Vintner's Collection" Sauvignon Blanc)

TERLATO WINES INTERNATIONAL
Website: www.terlatowines.com
(Wines featured: M. Chapoutier "Belleruche" Côtes-du-Rhône; Sokol Blosser Pinot Noir; Josmeyer Le Kottabe Riesling; Sanford Pinot Noir)

TIO PEPE
Website: www.tiopepe.co.uk
(Wine featured: Tio Pepe Fino Sherry)

WILSON DANIELS LTD.
Website: www.wilsondaniels.com
(Wines featured: Faiveley Mercurey Red Burgundy; Royal Tokaji 5 Puttonyos Aszú)

WINEBOW, INC.
Website: www.winebow.com
(Wines featured: Zenato Amarone; Tiefenbrunner Pinot Grigio)

WINESELLERS LTD.
Website: www.winesellersltd.com
(Wines featured: Hermanos Lurton Rueda Blanco; Araucano Cabernet Sauvignon)

W.J. DEUTSCH & SONS, LTD.
Website: www.wjdeutsch.com
(Wine featured: Montecillo Rioja Crianza)

BEER RETAILERS

AMERICAN BEER DISTRIBUTORS
256 Court Street
Brooklyn, NY 11231
Phone: (718) 875-0226
Website: www.americanbeerbuzz.com

BIERKRAFT
191 5th Avenue
Brooklyn, NY 11217
Phone: (718) 230-7600
Website: www.bierkraft.com

BOTTLEWORKS
1710 N 45th Street (Suite 3)
Seattle, WA 98103
Phone: (206) 633-2437
Website: www.bottleworks.com

BREWERY CREEK COLD BEER AND WINE STORE
23045 Main Street
Vancouver, BC, V5T 3G6, Canada
Phone: (604) 872-3373

CHARLES STREET LIQUORS
143 Charles Street
Boston, MA 02114
Phone: (617) 523-5051
Website: www.csliquors.com

LCBO QUEEN'S QUAY
2 Cooper Street
Toronto, ON, M5E 1A4, Canada
Phone: (416) 864-6777
Website: www.lcbo.com

LIQUID SOLUTIONS
275 Beavercreek Road #C149
Oregon City, OR 97045
Phone: (866) 286-9722
Website: www.liquidsolutions.biz

LIQUOR MART
1750 15th Street
Boulder, CO 80302
Phone: (303) 449-3374
Website: www.liquormart.com

**THE STRATH ALE, WINE,
AND SPIRIT MERCHANTS**
919 Douglas Street
Victoria, BC, V8W 2C2, Canada
Phone: (250) 370-9463
Website: www.strathliquor.com

WINE RETAILERS

ADEL'S WINE CELLAR
1400 Cole Street
San Francisco, CA 94117
Phone: (415) 731-6319
Website: www.adelswine.com

ASTOR WINES & SPIRITS
399 Lafayette Street
New York, NY 10003
Phone: (212) 674-7500
Fax: (201) 703-1355
Website: www.astoruncorked.com

BEEKMAN LIQUORS
500 Lexington Avenue
New York, NY 10017
Phone: (212) 759-5857
Fax: (212) 753-4534
Website: www.beekmanliquors.com

BEST CELLARS
Website: www.bestcellars.com

BIN 36
Website: www.bin36.com/index.php

LE DÛ WINES
Website: www.leduwines.com

KENSINGTON WINE MARKET
1257 Kensington Road NW
Calgary, AB, T2N 3P8, Canada
Phone: (403) 283-8000
Fax: (403) 283-4283

Website: www.kensingtonwinemarket.com

THE LOCAL VINE
2520 Second Avenue
Seattle, WA 98121
Phone: (206) 441-6000
Fax: (206) 441-6001
Website: www.thelocalvine.com

MARQUIS WINE CELLAR
1034 Davie Street
Vancouver, BC, V6E 1M3, Canada
Phone: (604) 684-0445
Fax: (604) 684 2471
Website: www.marquis-wines.com

MOORE BROTHERS
Website:
www.wineaccess.com/splash/moorebrothers

NAPA VALLEY WINERY EXCHANGE
415 Taylor Street
San Francisco, CA 94102
Phone: 800-653-9463
Website: www.nvwe.com

PINO
(for accessories only)
227 Market Street
Philadelphia, PA 19106
Phone: (215) 627-9463
Website: www.pinoboutique.com

TRILOGY WINE MERCHANTS
730 Yonge Street, Suite 212
Toronto, ON, M4Y 2B7, Canada
Phone: (416) 968-0758
Fax: (416) 968-9394
Email: info@trilogywinemerchants.com

VINO 100
Website: www.vino100.com

VINOPOLIS WINE SHOP
1025 SW Washington Street
Portland, OR 97205
Phone: (503) 223-6002
Fax: (503) 248-2247
Website: www.vinopoliswineshop.com

WINE GALLERY
516 Commonwealth Avenue
Boston, MA 02215
Phone: (617) 266-9300
Fax: (617) 266-9330
Website: www.wine-gallery.com

INDEX

Index

acknowledgments

Marnie's acknowledgments:

As with any big project, this book could not have gotten off the drawing board without a lot of help. Above all, I'd like to thank all my students for all they've taught me, particularly about what's important about wine and what isn't. A heartfelt expression of gratitude is also due to the wine companies who have faithfully sponsored my classes and provided samples for this book, particularly Banfi Vintners, Gallo Family Vineyards, and Charmer-Sunbelt. And, of course, I must thank DK Publishing for immediately grasping what Sam and I were trying to do and why it was important. Extra-special appreciation is due to editor Shannon Beatty and designer Tia Romano for helping to make this book better than we ever dreamed.

I need to express personal and specific thanks, however, to friends and family who have supported me in making this happen: to my mom for poring over texts, to my dad for clear-headed critiques, to Melissa and Lauren for picking up my slack, to James for boundless hospitality, and to Jeff and Clare for sound counsel. Which brings me to two huge debts of gratitude. Sam, thanks for being such a sport. Ewan, there are no words...

Sam's acknowledgments:

I'd like to begin by thanking my co-author Marnie Old; what a long, strange, and rewarding trip it has been. I always enjoy working with you even though we don't always agree! I'd be lost without the support and encouragement of my family—Mariah, Sammy, and Grier Calagione. Special thanks to Shannon, Tia, and everyone at DK for your tireless championing, directing, and refining of this project. Especially Shannon, who kept me focused as I was pulled in a million directions during the writing of this book. Thanks to Daniel Shelton for being a very good [and very opinionated:-)] second set of eyes. Thanks to the hundred-ish amazing co-workers I am lucky to work with every day at Dogfish Head—I love you guys! Most importantly, thanks to the adventurous and evangelical beer lovers and brewers out there who are battling alongside me every day, proving that there is so much more to the beer world than light lager. We shall overcome!

DK Publishing acknowledgments:

The publisher would like to thank all the wineries and breweries who kindly donated their products for photography. Thanks also to Mark, Kathy, Garret, and Brett Lieb, and the staff at Lieb Family Cellars, LLC for opening their vineyard to us. And thank you to Steve Carlino for his assistance and patience throughout the process.

DK would also like to thank Amy Stinson at Riedel USA (www.riedel.com) for the kind loan of wine glasses for photography; Tamami Mihara for hair and makeup on the shoot; Tim Solomon, our "Master of Cheese", for picking out photogenic cheese; Elizabeth Lyons, Dana Carlisle, and Frederick Mazzeo at Dogfish Head for helping to source beers and beer glasses; John Vallecillo and José Leon, for arranging space for photography. And special thanks to Nanette Cardon for compiling the index, and Nicole Turney and Simon Harley for their editorial assistance.

Picture credits:

The publisher would like to thank Domaine Matrot and Geyser Peak Winery for their kind permission to reproduce their wine labels on page 33, and Michelle Baxter for photographs on pages 30 and 31.
All other images © DK Publishing.